ENGINEERING DESIGN
FOR
ELECTRICAL
ENGINEERS

ENGINEERING DESIGN FOR ELECTRICAL ENGINEERS

Alan D. Wilcox

Micro Resources Company,
Lewisburg, PA

with
Lawrence P. Huelsman, *University of Arizona*
Stanley V. Marshall, *University of Missouri, Rolla*
Charles L. Phillips, *Auburn University*
Muhammad H. Rashid, *Purdue University, Calumet*
Martin S. Roden, *California State University, Los Angeles*

PRENTICE HALL, ENGLEWOOD CLIFFS, NJ   07632

Library of Congress Cataloging-in-Publication Data

WILCOX, ALAN D.
   Engineering design for electrical engineers / Alan D. Wilcox with
LAWRENCE P. HUELSMAN . . . [ET AL.].
     p. cm.

   Includes bibliographies and index.
   ISBN 0-13-278136-0
   1. Electric engineering. 2. Engineering design. I. Huelsman,
Lawrence P. II. Title.
TK153.W55 1990
621.3—dc19   89-3730
                                      CIP

Editorial/production supervision and interior design: *Debbie Young*
Cover design: *20/20 Services, Inc.*
Manufacturing buyer: *Mary Noonan*

© 1990 by Prentice-Hall, Inc.
A Division of Simon & Schuster
Englewood Cliffs, New Jersey 07632

Printed in the United States of America

10 9 8 7 6 5 4 3

ISBN 0-13-278136-0

PRENTICE-HALL INTERNATIONAL (UI) LIMITED, *London*
PRENTICE-HALL OF AUSTRALIA PTY. LIMITED, *Sydney*
PRENTICE-HALL CANADA INC., *Toronto*
PRENTICE-HALL HISPANOAMERICANA, S.A., *Mexico*
PRENTICE-HALL OF INDIA PRIVATE LIMITED, *New Delhi*
PRENTICE-HALL OF JAPAN, INC., *Tokyo*
SIMON & SCHUSTER ASIA PTE. LTD., *Singapore*
EDITORA PRENTICE-HALL DO BRASIL, LTDA., *Rio de Janeiro*

One rarely has the opportunity to witness the very first spark of interest,
the trials and hard work, and finally the culmination:
the graduation of an electrical engineer.
Fully expecting that his real education is just beginning,
this book is dedicated to a new engineer I've watched develop over many years:

Kenneth L. Crocker.

CONTENTS

2   PROJECT IMPLEMENTATION   14

3   DESIGN GUIDELINES AND IMPLEMENTATION   30

4   PROJECT COMMUNICATION   46

Part II   Practice

ABOUT THE AUTHOR AND CONTRIBUTORS

ALAN D. WILCOX

Alan D. Wilcox is the founder and president of Micro Resources Company, a manufacturer of 68000-based computer boards and systems. He is presently involved in new-product development and embedded-systems engineering.

Before starting Micro Resources in 1988, Dr. Wilcox was an Associate Professor of Electrical Engineering at Bucknell University where he taught courses in computer programming, digital logic, and computer system design. Earlier, he worked in Virginia with E-Systems as a Principal Engineer doing advanced development of digital speech-enhancement hardware.

Alan Wilcox received his Ph.D in electrical engineering in 1976, his MEE in 1974, and his MBA in 1972, all from the University of Virginia; he received his BEE from Rensselaer Polytechnic Institute in 1965. He is a licensed Professional Engineer and has been involved with computers since the mid-60's. His current technical interests are microprocessor architecture, troubleshooting, and digital control systems. He is a member of the IEEE, ACM, ASEE, and Eta Kappa Nu.

In addition to *Engineering Design for Electrical Engineers,* Dr. Wilcox is the author of two other Prentice Hall books. The first is *68000 Microcomputer Systems: Designing and Troubleshooting;* it presents the principles and techniques necessary to specify, design, and build a complete 68000 system. The other book is *Engineering Design: Project Guidelines;* it provides an approach to digital design projects.

The author can be contacted at Micro Resources Company, 60 South 8th Street, Lewisburg, PA 17837. Telephone (717) 523-0777, (717) 524-7390 (recorder).

LAWRENCE P. HUELSMAN

Lawrence P. Huelsman is a professor of electrical and computer engineering at the University of Arizona, where he teaches courses in circuit analysis and synthesis, active circuit theory, computer-aided design, microcomputer applications, and optimization theory. In addition he has been a Visiting Professor of electrical engineering at Rice University. His background in engineering education also includes several years of supervising courses and training programs for the Western Electric Co., Inc., and the teaching of a special engineering course for the Pacific Telephone and Telegraph Co. He has five years of industrial experience with the Western Electric Co.

Professor Huelsman received his bachelor of science in electrical engineering from Case Institute of Technology. He received his master of science in electrical engineering and his doctorate from the University of California at Berkeley.

In addition to the many papers he has published on active circuit theory, several of Professor Huelsman's 14 books have been translated into other languages, including Japanese, German, Spanish, and Russian. He has served as a consultant to various organizations, among them General Electric Co., Motorola, Inc., and the Burr-Brown Research Corp. He has served as Associate Editor of the *IEEE Transactions on Circuit and System Theory* and the *IEEE Transactions on Education* and was technical chairman of the IEEE Region Six Annual Conference. He is a member of the steering committee for the Midwest Symposium on Circuits and Systems. His other scientific, engineering, and honorary society memberships include Tau Beta Pi, Phi Beta Kappa, Eta Kappa Nu, and Sigma Xi. He has received the Anderson Prize of the College of Engineering and Mines of the University of Arizona for his contributions to education.

STANLEY V. MARSHALL

Stanley V. Marshall is a professor of electrical engineering at the University of Missouri at Rolla. Since coming to UMR in 1967, he has taught courses in electromagnetics and has conducted short courses in radar systems and in applied magnetics.

Professor Marshall received his doctorate in electrical engineering from the University of Missouri at Columbia in 1967. He received his master of science in electrical engineering also from UMC in 1965, and he received is bachelor of science in electrical engineering from Oregon State University in 1954. His experience in industry includes 10 years radar system evaluation with Bell Laboratories.

Professor Marshall is the co-author of *Electromagnetic Concepts and Applications,* published by Prentice Hall. It is a textbook for a junior-level course in electromagnetics.

CHARLES L. PHILLIPS

Charles L. Phillips is professor emeritus at Auburn University. He received his doctorate from the Georgia Institute of Technology in 1963, and has been at Auburn University since 1964. He has performed extensive research in digital control systems for NASA, the U.S. Navy, and the U.S. Army. He is co-author of two books published by Prentice Hall, *Digital Control System Analysis and Design* and *Feedback Control Systems*. His current interests are in undergraduate teaching and in writing undergraduate textbooks.

MUHAMMAD H. RASHID

Muhammad H. Rashid is a professor of electrical engineering at Purdue University, Calumet. Professor Rashid received his bachelor of science in electrical engineering from the Bangladesh University of Engineering and Technology. He received his master of science in information and systems engineering and his doctorate in electronics and electrical engineering from the University of Birmingham, England. Professor Rashid is a Fellow of the Institution of Electrical Engineers (London) and a Senior Member of the Institute of Electrical and Electronics Engineers. He is the author of two other books published by Prentice Hall, *Power Electronics* and *Electromechanics and Electrical Machinery*. In addition to writing these books, he has published numerous research reports and has refereed journal and conference publications. Professor Rashid is actively involved in teaching, research, and lecturing on control, motor drives, and power electronics.

MARTIN S. RODEN

Martin S. Roden is chairman of the Department of Electrical and Computer Engineering at California State University at Los Angeles. Professor Roden received his bachelor of science in electrical engineering *summa cum laude* from Polytechnic Institute of Brooklyn (now the Polytechnic Institute of New York). After five years doing research at Bell Telephone Laboratories, Professor Roden returned to California State University. At various times he has been department chair, associate dean, dean and associate vice president; however, his first love remains teaching, for which he was awarded the University's Outstanding Adviser Award. He is very active in the Institute of Electrical and Electronics Engineers, and has earned the IEEE's Outstanding Adviser Award. In addition, he is a Fellow of the Institute for the Advancement of Engineering. Professor Roden has authored and co-authored many books on communications, computer software, and electronics.

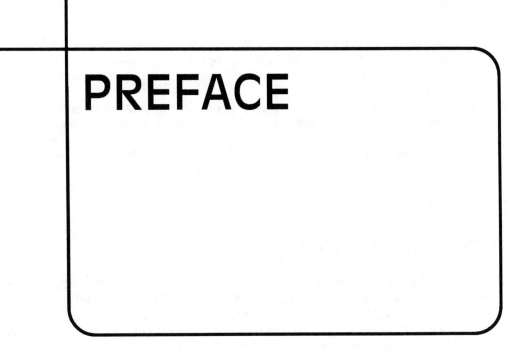

PREFACE

ABOUT THIS BOOK

There is often a large gap between the engineering design studied in school and the actual practice of engineering in industry. Little effort is made to bridge that gap in undergraduate studies, and engineering graduates are usually left to their own devices when it comes to developing procedures for successfully carrying out design tasks. This book, however, is different: it integrates the principles of engineering design with practical, hands-on, real-world experience. Its purpose is to provide a unified, methodical approach to engineering design projects. In its first four chapters, it examines project design principles; in the remaining chapters, it illustrates the application of the principles in six practice modules.

Planning and scheduling are vitally important aspects of an engineering project. Finishing the design and prototype in a reasonable time requires attention to many details. Without proper attention, even the project that is technically perfect can turn out poorly. Consequently, this book stresses how to plan a project and how to schedule a realistic completion date for the project.

WHO SHOULD USE THIS BOOK

This book is written especially for electrical engineering students who are planning and designing projects. Because of the broad scope of student projects, this book touches on many electrical engineering topics: digital, analog, electromagnetics, control, communications, and power.

The subject matter of this book is particularly important for students because their future depends on being able to solve the technological problems of society effectively. To get problem-solving experience, students need to practice design by doing projects throughout their years of education. To make the most of these design projects, guidelines on problem solving and on project planning and implementation can be most helpful. The guidelines in this book provide a method of carrying out a project from start to finish.

HOW TO USE THIS BOOK

This book is intended for use as a supplement to regular course material at all levels of the electrical engineering curriculum. It can be used for senior-level capstone design courses as well as for introductory-level projects. A light reading of this book without immediate application will provide no design practice; in order to benefit fully from the book, one must use it actively in projects of all types.

A number of projects drawn from various areas of electrical engineering are presented. Depending on student interest, projects may be selected and used in an undergraduate project course emphasizing design. Each of the project modules has enough information to give the student a feeling for how involved a design might become. In addition, each module provides background information to aid in an early search of design literature.

HOW THIS BOOK IS ORGANIZED

Engineering Design for Electrical Engineers is divided into two main parts: Principles and Practice. The principles in the first segment are quite generic and are intended to support design activity across the entire spectrum of electrical engineering. The practice segment is much more specific and presents design projects from six major facets of electrical engineering.

Chapter 1 introduces the concept of designing to meet customer needs. Engineering design involves two steps in meeting these needs: first, the project must be defined and planned; second, the project must be implemented. Problem solving is introduced as a tool to help identify the customer requirements as well as to help in all phases of the design process. The interplay of problem solving and project planning is essential for assembling the proposal at the end of the chapter. The proposal is the guiding document that contains the project definition, objectives, strategy, and step-by-step plan of action with a time schedule. The plan developed in the proposal is then used in Chapter 2 to complete a full project implementation. This implementation, beginning with the analysis of the specifications and constraints, covers the technical design of the product on paper and the construction of a working prototype.

Chapter 3 presents a number of design guidelines and rules that can help the student get started in a project. There is a vast amount of general knowledge that the practicing engineer takes for granted; this information is not nearly so obvious to the student or new graduate. Thus, Chapter 3 seeks to give the reader some measure of reality.

Every engineer writes reports and makes oral presentations relating to project work. Chapter 4 covers the essentials of recording the project in a lab notebook and of documenting the final design. The chapter also includes examples of various papers and reports such as the feasibility study, proposal, progress report, and engineering design report. Finally, the technical manual is presented as comprehensive user documentation for a major project.

Practice, the second half of the book, illustrates the reality of electrical engineering. Design projects are presented in modules from six diverse, yet fairly related, specialty areas. Each of these modules portrays a different aspect of electrical engineering by applying one or more of the design principles from the first half of the book. The differences between the modules affirms a legitimate range of interpretation of engineering design: In nearly every situation, there are many valid ways to engineer a product.

ACKNOWLEDGMENTS

My most enthusiastic thanks go to all my students who participated in the development of this book. It was truly refreshing to see their quick growth into engineering professionals over just a few short years. Time flies when you're having fun, and it seems like just yesterday when we began our many experiments together. We all keep growing, and I certainly thank them for my growth too!

My heartfelt thanks to all my contributors as well: Lawrence P. Huelsman, Stanley V. Marshall, Charles L. Phillips, Muhammed H. Rashid, and Martin S. Roden. With their enthusiastic support and interest in developing the material in Part II, this book has been not only fun, but exciting as well. We each approach engineering differently, and that creates a rich diversity for student inquiry.

Tim Bozik, my editor at Prentice Hall, has been more than just an editor: he has been a source of ideas, help, and always a source of inspiration. Debbie Young, my production editor, has been a delight to work with to bring this book into final reality.

Alan D. Wilcox

1

ENGINEERING DESIGN
A Creative Activity
that Requires Planning

Engineering design is fun! How else can you enjoy building a piece of complex equipment and expect to have it working in several days? If the entire circuit has not already been described in some magazine or book, you can always take parts of the circuit design from several sources and piece together a complete design ready to build. After a quick smoke test to see if you wired it properly, connect it to a computer. After a few quick patches, you can type a program from your favorite magazine and run it in a matter of hours. After the big bang test to see if you put all the code together correctly, you can congratulate yourself on a successful project!

Do you see a bit of yourself in this? We all have occasionally fallen into this approach, and generally it seems to work. It has survived the test of time to become an almost traditional way of developing new hardware and software products. Although not the most efficient way of doing a project, it does appear to get the job done.

Getting the job done is certainly important, but have you really done a proper engineering design? You have been creative and solved the problem, but you might also have abandoned sound engineering practice along the way. The "product" is probably one of a kind and probably unsuitable for another person to build or for a company to manufacture.

Whether you are a student about to start a major design project or a professional engineering on the job, this hobbyist technique is clearly not satisfactory. You need a systematic way of approaching engineering design so that you can complete your project on time and within your budget; in addition, your design must meet all specifications. In short, you must plan your project and plan it well.

1.1 DESIGN OVERVIEW

Engineering design is the creative process of identifying needs and then devising a product to fill those needs. As shown in Figure 1.1, engineering design is the central activity in meeting needs; these needs may be yours or a customer's. If you understand the requirements involved, then you can develop a creative design to satisfy them.

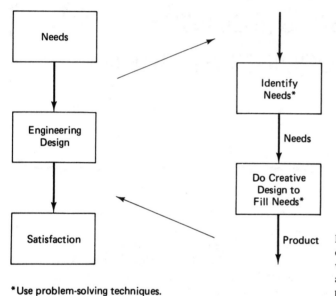

*Use problem-solving techniques.

Figure 1.1 Engineering design is the central activity in meeting needs. It involves identifying the needs and then creating a design to fill them; both require problem-solving techniques.

Figure 1.2 shows two parts of the creative design process. The first part of the process is making a project plan—outlining the various needs and reducing them to a set of specifications. The project plan is an administrative tool used for identifying the various tasks and indicating when to do them. The second part of the process, the project implementation, is designing and developing the final product. Both the project plan and the project implementation are necessary for an orderly product development.

In the context of engineering design, the project plan leads to a set of specifications and tasks. In a sense, you can consider it a nontechnical document, because it includes more concepts than technical detail. But this is no reason for overlooking it. For one think, the project plan may be easily summarized and put into the form of a proposal, which is used to communicate the design plan to others, perhaps to management or to a potential customer. For another, the project plan is an outline of intended work for the complete project. It functions as a road map for the entire creative design effort, making the difference between project success and failure.

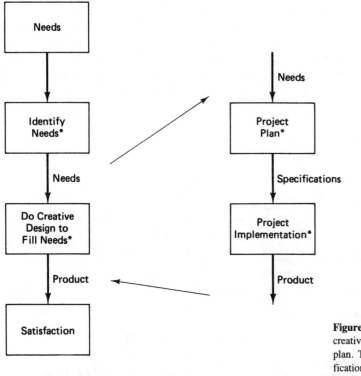

Figure 1.2   The essential first part of a creative design is to complete the project plan. The project plan produces the specifications that describe what is needed so it can be designed and built.

*Use problem-solving techniques.

The project implementation, on the other hand, involves the technical activity you would expect in a design project: specifications, hardware and software design and development, documentation, prototype construction, and testing. You can see that the hobbyist technique is only a small part of this implementation and consequently overlooks many essential aspects of the project. Because of these many details, the next chapter is devoted to doing the project implementation.

Both parts of the creative design process require problem solving. Determining the information that you need to set the design specifications is a problem. Likewise, it is an equally substantial problem to design the product. Both can be addressed by the same problem-solving techniques.

1.2 PROBLEM SOLVING

Problem solving is the process of determining the best possible action to take in a given situation. This process requires identification of the problem and a description of its causes. It then makes a systematic evaluation of various alternative solutions until one can be selected as the best. Although you have used problem-solving techniques in one form or another for years, you probably have not looked at them closely.

An outline of a problem-solving method suitable for engineering design is shown in Figure 1.3. It is important to note that this method is not limited to identifying the needs of a customer. It can be used in working through both the project plan and the project implementation. The general problem-solving activities of analysis, synthesis, evaluation, decision making, and action are the essence of engineering design.

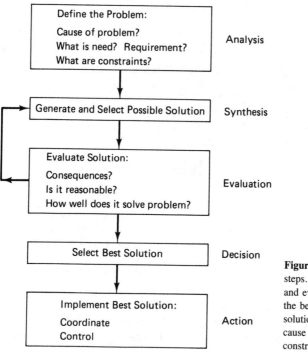

Figure 1.3 General problem-solving steps. The engineer must define a problem and evaluate a number of possibilities until the best solution can be selected. The best solution is never perfectly satisfactory, because it is a balance between needs and constraints.

How can you apply the problem-solving steps in Figure 1.3? Assume for a moment that you have a customer or client with a particular technical difficulty. Before you can even hope to solve the problem or offer any advice, you need to define the problem: ask when it first appeared, and then find out what caused it. When you try to define the problem better, be sure to separate the causes of the problem from its effects. Next consider possible solutions, and select the one that appears most likely to resolve the difficulty. Finally, put your solution into action, but be sure to stay in control to ensure its success.

A more specific example would be the following. Suppose that the owner of a local metal-working shop has asked you for your advice on buying a computer. You would begin by asking questions to determine what he wants a computer to do. Does he want a computer to simplify his job scheduling and inventory management so that he has more free time to plan his future business? Does he want to put all of his accounting on a computer so that he can have quick monthly reports? Has a friend told him that a computer will help business, and that "everybody needs a computer to be competitive"? What you are doing in asking these questions is analyzing the situation and defining the problem. Remember, if you you do not grasp the problem, then any solution will do. This is simply another way of saying, "If you don't know where you're going, then any road will take you there."

How do you find the information necessary to know the customer and his needs? Ask him! If he thinks you can help solve his current problem, he will be more than willing to tell you every problem his company ever had. Understanding his day-to-day operations is vital to defining the problem and its cause.

By the time you understand the problem and its cause, you are also likely to have some ideas on solutions. Make a list of possible solutions, select one, and evaluate its effectiveness. What consequences would you expect from this solution? Any decision you make will have both favorable and unfavorable consequences.

For example, if you were to select Brand-X computer to solve an accounting problem, you might find these consequences:

1. Computer hardware price reasonable.
2. Software price not too high.
3. This computer model might be discontinued soon.
4. Software might do for the company now, but might not do for a growing business.

Some consequences look good, while some seem to argue against Brand-X. What do you do about a list of consequences like this? Set aside for now and analyze Brand-Y and any other appropriate brands. Perhaps you might compare the brands by constructing a chart or developing a set of standard test programs.

While selecting and evaluating possible solutions to the problem, notice that you are gaining a deeper understanding of the problem. You are also reaching for solutions that were not apparent when you started. You are using facts and concepts to synthesize new ideas. In other words, you are being creative.

Finally, after gathering information and comparing various alternatives, you are ready to make a decision. Any decision, however, involves compromise. After comparing various computer brands, you may find two equally satisfactory choices. What do you do? How do you quantify your preference for the color of Brand-X, or the shape of Brand-Y? The final decision often depends on a feeling or preference, an intangible that you cannot define.

After making a decision, you must take action. As in Figure 1.3, the best solution is implemented, coordinated, and controlled. You accomplish this through project management. In the simple computer-selection example, if you were asked for advice on which computer to buy, then your job is done when you give the advice; no other action or project work is involved. On the other hand, if you were asked not only to make a selection, but also to purchase, install, and service the equipment, then you would have a project to implement. This project would require proper planning and close supervision to ensure its success.

1.3 PROJECT PLANNING

A project is a single job that can be accomplished within a specified time and within a certain budget. How this project actually gets done depends on your project plan. The project plan outlines the various needs and reduces them to a set of specifications. It also helps you to identify and schedule the various tasks.

What does this idea of a project plan mean to you, the student or engineer, as you begin designing a piece of hardware or programming a computer system? First, it means that you have an orderly way of conceptualizing the confusing array of information. Second, it means that you have an orderly way of completing the project. The project plan is the management tool that helps you do your job.

Look at the project-planning steps outlined in Figure 1.4. How can this outline help you do a better job? Instead of thinking of the project deadline as next year, think of it as next week. Go through the steps of the outline and make a list of the things you should do each of the next five days so that your ''one-week'' project is a success.

The first step in Figure 1.4 is to define the project. This is a statement of the goals you are trying to accomplish and is based on your understanding of the customer needs. These goals are an overall big picture describing your project. For example, suppose the customer needs a device that automatically measures temperature; after your analysis of

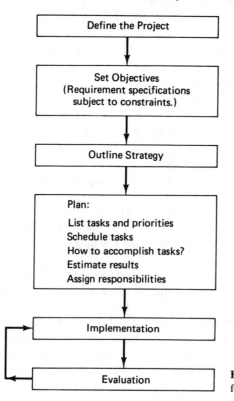

Figure 1.4   General outline of steps to follow when planning a project.

the needs, you conclude that a microcomputer-based temperature monitor is most appropriate. Thus, you might write your project definition:

> My project is to design, build, and test a meter that I can use to measure and record air temperature.

At this point, you are saying nothing about its performance (such as temperature range or accuracy); nor are you saying how you intend to build it (a microcomputer may or may not be necessary). Avoid locking yourself into a project goal that is too specific; stick to the big picture.

You get specific in the next step when you set your objectives. Your objectives should be specific measurable outcomes of your work. This is where you get into details about the performance of the device you are designing. The objectives are stated in several dimensions: required performance, time to complete, and total cost. For example, you might set these objectives:

> By the end of this month, my meter will be completely built and tested. It will perform to these specifications:
>
> - Temperature range -40 to $+100°C$
> - Accurate to within $1°C$
> - Display either Fahrenheit or Celsius temperature
> - Display minimum and maximum temperatures during last 24 hours
> - Calculate and display 24-hour average temperature
> - Calculate and display daily heating degree days
>
> In addition to these performance requirements, the meter will be portable and capable of battery operation. Parts for the prototype will cost less than $150.

After you have some solid objectives to work toward, you need to outline your strategy; that is, you need to form your concept of how to reach your objectives. Keep in mind that your strategy is your idea of how to achieve the objectives, not the details for actually achieving them. To reach the temperature meter objectives, you might form this strategy:

> To attain my objectives, I will breadboard a prototype model of the analog circuitry with the temperature sensor on the breadboard. Once I understand how it should work, then I will add an analog-to-digital converter plus an interface to a small microcomputer board. I should be able to handle all the calculations and display functions with the microcomputer. After I have it working properly, I will make a prototype printed-circuit board for the customer to evaluate.

Such a strategy is unique to you and your choice of a design solution. In terms of problem solving, your problem is to meet the required design objectives; your solution is to start with the breadboard and then build a circuit board. Another possible solution might be to do a complete design on paper first, breadboard it, and then interface it to the microcomputer. Whatever approach you choose depends entirely on you and your work habits. Thus, your strategy is a statement of how you intend to implement the best solution.

You implement your solution by using a plan. Depending on the size of the project, you may find the plan ranging from a simple list of tasks to a complex set of schedules involving many different engineers and departments within your school or company. For our purposes here, we will assume that the implementation is going to involve only one person: yourself.

The best place to start with your plan is to look closely at your strategy and list the major tasks. Early in the project you may not know all your tasks, but you can begin by listing the major tasks chronologically. Under each major task, you probably will think of some subtasks that are also necessary. Some of the major tasks will be high-priority items and must be listed. For example, you must have a breadboard and you must test the circuit for proper operation. Consider this as a possible plan to implement your strategy:

1. Get a breadboard and power supply for the protype.
2. Look for articles and designs on temperature measurement.
3. Select temperature sensor and A/D converter for first design.
4. Sketch tentative circuit and calculate circuit values.
5. Build the analog circuit and take measurements.
6. Connect the analog circuit to the A/D converter.
7. Test the circuit completely for proper performance.
8. Design the microcomputer interface logic.
9. Connect the microcomputer and test the interface.
10. Write a simple program to read the temperature.
11. More programs and tasks I cannot estimate now.

Can you start work with this list of tasks? Probably you can. However, you might want to consider how long each will take to complete. If you want to finish the project in a month, when must you complete each task? If you spend the first two weeks on only a few tasks, then you will probably not finish the project in time. You need to set your own deadline for each task.

One way of scheduling is to estimate how many days each task will take and when you should be done with each. As you work your schedule, though, you might lose track if you get ahead or fall behind schedule. To avoid this problem, you may want to use a bar chart graphical representation of your schedule, such as the one shown in Table 1.1.

The bar chart is one of the easiest ways to manage your work schedule as you progress through your project. The chart shows not only the tasks you listed when you

TABLE 1.1   BAR-CHART SCHEDULE OF TASKS NEEDED TO BUILD A SIMPLE TEMPERATURE METER

Tasks to Do	Week Beginning March			
	3	10	17	24
Get breadboard, etc.	**			
Get articles	***			
Select sensor and A/D	****			
Sketch circuit	*****			
Build analog and test		*********		
Connect analog and A/D		********		
Test completely		******		
Design interface			****	
Connect microcomputer			****	
Write simple program			*******	
Write more programs			*********	
Unknown extra tasks				*******

started your project, but also the times when you will actually start and finish each task. At a glance, you can tell which tasks overlap and may be done at the same time. For example, you might work on the "Build analog and test" task at the same time one of your team members works on "Connect analog and A/D." According to the Table 1.1 schedule, you should be working on these activities around March 10th.

Sometimes one crucial task must be completed before another can be begun. Unfortunately, a large bar chart does not lend itself well to indicating such a dependency. A small chart, however, can be flexible enough to show some key interrelationships. For example, before you can "Connect the microcomputer," you need to "Design the interface." You can show this dependency if you wish by using a small arrow, as has been done in Table 1.1. This expedient is quite adequate when you have a simple schedule.

The "unknown extra tasks" at the end of the chart reminds you that the schedule must be flexible and will probably be modified as you go along. At the start, you do not know all the things you need to do or how long each will take. The best you can do is estimate. Remember, though, that time must work to your schedule if you intend to finish on time, and the better you estimate, the less likely you will be in a crisis later on.

While you are creating your schedule, think about how you will accomplish each of the tasks. What results do you expect as you go along? Anticipate problems and act as early in the process as possible to avoid or deal with them. For example, if you think you might need precision components for the accuracy specified, then complete that part of the design early and order the parts so that they will be available when you need them in the circuit. Plan ahead! Also, think of contingency plans so that your project is not in jeopardy if, for example, your precision parts are unavailable.

Once you have a plan and a tentative schedule put together, implement it. Get to work! The implementation part of Figure 1.4 goes hand in hand with evaluation. Because the evaluation is done as you work on your project, you know how closely you are following your plan. Are your results meeting your objectives? Are you getting ahead of or falling behind schedule? Should you rethink and modify your schedule to reflect changes? If your project is in trouble, have you asked for help?

It is likely that someone will want to be apprised regularly of how well you are keeping to your schedule and whether you need help with any problems. Normally, you would update management with a monthly progress report. If you are in school, your professor might require several progress reports during the term. A progress report can take many forms depending on individual preferences, company policy, or customer requirements. In its simplest form, a progress report describes the current status of your project, the work completed, the work in progress, and your plans leading up to the next report. You should attach a copy of your schedule and mark your progress in each task. A sample progress report is shown in Table 1.2.

TABLE 1.2 SAMPLE PROGRESS REPORT COVERING THE SECOND WEEK OF THE TEMPERATURE-METER PROJECT

	PROGRESS REPORT Temperature-Meter Project—Week 2
Current status:	The analog design has been completed and successfully tested. There have been no delays and I am on schedule.
Work completed:	During the week since the last report, I completed the building and testing of the analog circuit. I used the temperature sensor and measured the output of its amplifier and plotted a graph of its response. I connected the A/D converter and tested its performance by varying the termperature sensor voltage.
Current work:	During the last day of this week I started work on the interface design and I am now in the middle of connecting it to the microcomputer board.
Future work:	During the third week I plan to finish the connection to the microcomputer board and to write a program to test the A/D converter. Then I plan to write a more complex program to display the termperature in either Celsius or Fahrenheit.

As you near the end of your project, you should be evaluating how well you are meeting all of your objectives. Review your progress reports and your schedule. Decide what last-minute action is necessary to correct any difficulties. Leave enough time at the end of the schedule to review your project and report on your technical accomplishments.

As mentioned earlier, you can easily summarize all the steps of your project plan in the form of the proposal, shown in Table 1.3. The proposal defines your proposed project, what you want to achieve, and how you plan on doing it. This example proposal is abbreviated and illustrates only the major topics you should include in a full proposal. If you are a student, you might find this proposal very useful for focusing your project and winning financial support to build it. If you are a professional engineer, the proposal is necessary to describe a project to a potential customer. Likewise, a proposal is valuable to gain support for possible areas of new-product development.

TABLE 1.3 PROPOSAL OF A PROJECT

	PROPOSAL Temperature Monitor
Project definition:	The goal of this project is to design, build, and test a meter than can be used to measure and record air temperature.
Project objectives:	At the end of four weeks, the temperature monitor will be completely built and tested. It will perform to these specifications: Temperature range of -40 to $+100°C$ Accurate to within 1 °C Display either Fahrenheit or Celsius temperature Display minimum and maximum termperatures during last 24 hours Calculate and display 24-hour average temperature Calculate and display heating degree days In addition to these performance requirements, the meter will be portable and capable of battery operation. Parts for the prototype will cost less than $150.
Strategy for achieving objectives:	The analog circuitry and temperature sensor will be prototyped on a temporary breadboard until its operation is fully understood. An analog-to-digital converter plus interface circuit will be added to allow unit to work with a microcomputer system. After temperature is being properly read by the computer, a number of display and calculation programs will be written.
Plan of action:	The various tasks needed to implement the strategy are as follows: Get prototype breadboard and power supply Look for articles and designs on temperature measurement Select temperature sensor and A/D converter Sketch tentative circuit and calculate circuit values Build analog circuit and take measurements Connect analog circuit to the A/D converter Test the circuit completely Design the microcomputer interface logic Connect microcomputer and test interface Write simple program to read temperature Programs and tasks I cannot estimate now The schedule necessary to finish the project in the required four weeks is attached. [Refer to Table 1.1 for schedule]
Reporting:	Weekly progress reports will be made. At the end of the project a complete engineering design and working prototype will be presented.
Budget:	Initial funding of $150 is necessary to purchase the prototype analog parts and the microcomputer.
Evaluation:	Verification of how well the prototype meets the design specifications subject to the constraints will be made weekly and at the end of the project. The final evaluation will be conducted by the design engineer and the customer.

1.4 SUMMARY

We all enjoy a quick, "fun" project: put together a circuit, add in some software, enjoy the results. Many times, though, we tend to fall into this hobbyist approach when doing a major project. The result is a product that might not always work when someone else operates it; worse, the product might not even be what the customer wanted.

Rather than using this inefficient hobbyist approach to a project, think first about the customer's requirements. Once you identify what the customer really needs, then you can develop a product that responds to that demand. Thus, engineering design is the creative process of devising a product to fill customer needs; it closes the gap between customer needs and satisfaction.

Problem-solving skills are necessary: you must find out what the customer needs—sometimes a major problem—and then do the actual design. The problem-solving approach can be applied to both; in fact, problem-solving applies to all aspects of engineering. The steps of defining the problem, selecting a possible solution, evaluating the solution, generating another possible solution, and selecting the best alternative can be used anywhere. The general problem-solving activities of analysis, synthesis, evaluation, decision-making, and action constitute the essence of engineering design.

A creative design that translates customer needs into a satisfactory product requires careful planning. This planning involves creating the specifications that describe the product. Furthermore, it involves designing and developing the final product itself. In contrast to the hobbyist approach, this planning leads to a well-considered project that ensures success.

The project and its plan for completion are completely described in the proposal. The proposal not only defines clearly what you want to achieve, but it also indicates what action you must take in order to finish on time. One part of the proposal, the schedule, can be of immense help as you work through a project. Rather than haphazardly designing and building, you can work more orderly and spend your time more efficiently.

EXERCISES

1. An old family friend just graduated from law school and started working at a local law office. The two attorneys at the firm asked your friend to find a way to automate the typing of legal documents. Using their electric typewriter for all letters and drafts had become increasingly unsuitable as their workload increased over the last several years. Knowing your interest in computers, your friend called you yesterday and asked if a computer is worth investigating.
   a. Who is the customer?
   b. What does the customer need for satisfaction?
   c. Define the problem.
   d. What constraints are there?
   e. List three possible solutions to the problem.
   f. Make a selection. How would you justify it to the customer?

    g. Who is responsible if your idea proves disastrous? Who is responsible if your idea is a great success?

2. Rather than move into a new house, you and your family are going to refurbish your present home. The heating system has needed repair every year and probably should be replaced if you plan on keeping the house. The winter heating season begins in about two months. Make realistic assumptions based on your past experience.

    a. Define the problem and constraints.

    b. List three possible solutions to the problem and the factors you must consider in making a decision.

    c. Which solution would you choose? Why?

    d. List the tasks needed to implement your solution.

3. Make the temperature-monitor proposal into a proposal for creating a device to monitor the local 115 VAC line voltage. There have been a number of complaints that the voltage drops down briefly (how briefly?) when the building's heat pump turns on. This drop is alleged to cause a problem with any computers that are running at the time. You want to find the maximum and minimum voltages as well as the time of day they occurred.

4. Your manager at the Wheel Works just walked into your office to tell you about an idea from the marketing department that could possibly become a product with sales potential. The idea is to install an electronic water-level indicator on the company's 200-gallon standard steel tank. Besides being able to delete the glass-tube level indicator on the side of the tank, an electronic indicator might even be adapted later to turn on an inlet valve automatically when the water level drops during usage.

    a. Define the problem. Make assumptions about the system.

    b. Make a proposal describing a creative solution.

FURTHER READING

LOVE, SYDNEY F. *Planning and Creating Successful Engineered Designs.* New York: Van Nostrand Reinhold, 1980. (TA174.L68)

MIDDENDORF, WILLIAM H. *Design of Devices and Systems.* New York: Marcel Dekker, 1986. (TA174.M529)

OSTROFSKY, BENJAMIN. *Design, Planning, and Development Methodology.* Englewood Cliffs, NJ: Prentice Hall, 1977. (TA174.087)

RAY, MARTYN S. *Elements of Engineering Design: An Integrated Approach.* Englewood Cliffs, NJ: Prentice Hall, 1985. (TA174.R37)

ROBERTSHAW, JOSEPH E., STEPHEN J. MECCA, and MARK N. RERICK. *Problem Solving: a Systems Approach.* New York: Petrocelli, 1978. (QA 402.R6.)

RUBINSTEIN, MOSHE F. *Patterns of Problem Solving.* Englewood Cliffs, NJ: Prentice Hall, 1975.

RUBINSTEIN, MOSHE F., and KENNETH PFEIFFER. *Concepts in Problem Solving. Englewood Cliffs, NJ: Prentice Hall, 1980.*

WICKELGREN, WAYNE A. *How to Solve Problems.* San Francisco: Freeman, 1974.

2

PROJECT IMPLEMENTATION
Bring Ideas to Reality

When you examined engineering design in the last chapter you saw how your needs or your customer's needs could be satisfied. First you used problem-solving techniques to identify needs. Then, after you identified the needs, you prepared a project plan that could be summarized in the form of a proposal. This proposal outlined all the necessary work and completion dates for each task.

This chapter shows how to use the project plan to complete the project implementation step shown in Figure 2.1. This step is important because it is a systematic way of finishing the project design within the given time and financial constraints. The approach presented here is just one of many ways to tackle the project implementation, and it may be easily modified to your own particular requirements. The focus is on the method of design rather than on the details of digital circuit design or computer programming.

As indicated in Figure 2.1, the specifications are used in the implementation phase of the engineering design to produce a product meeting your or a customer's needs. The project implementation involves two major steps: the technical design and the construction of a prototype. In the technical design step the circuit is created on paper; in the construction phase, the prototype (a working model) is built and tested.

When you look at the temperature monitor project in Chapter 1, you can see the evidence of some technical design work. Although the project plan is an administrative planning document, it contains enough technical effort to establish a set of reasonable

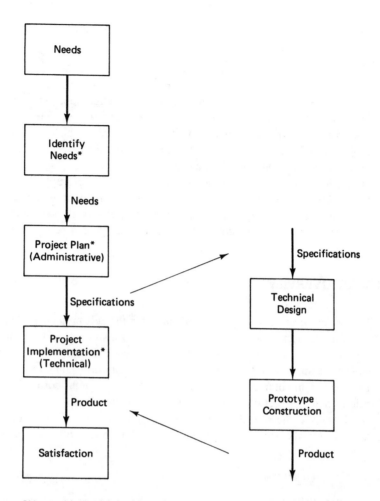

Figure 2.1 Engineering design involves identifying the needs of either you or your customer. Using problem-solving techniques, you can develop a project plan describing the specifications of the needed product. Then using these specifications, you can implement a project to build the product.

specifications and a realistic work schedule. Most of this design was conceptual, and unless you had built something similar in the past, you did not do enough detailed design to be absolutely certain of the results. Consequently, your strategy might be inadequate. However, the project plan does establish some feasible specifications and does provide a useful working document for the full design effort.

Although the proposal is adequate to describe your small project, a typical industrial or government proposal needs substantial design content. If your company is competing for a manufacturing contract, most of the design work, including the completed prototype, will probably be done before the proposal is finalized. You must be certain of your design and be able to estimate closely how much time will be needed to deliver a final product. If your company hopes to make a profit, there is little latitude for errors and radical design changes once the contract has been signed.

For your purposes in learning engineering design, once you have a documented and tested prototype, you will consider your engineering complete. However, a prototype that works and meets specifications is by no means a finished job if you are doing the project in industry. If your project is research-oriented, resulting in patents and further research, the prototype is only the beginning. Likewise, if your project is directed toward production, you have much follow-up work to do. For example, your design documentation will be used by drafting personnel to make assembly drawings and schematics. Also, you will be coordinating your protect with other electrical, mechanical, production, test, and quality-control engineers so that the final design can be manufactured successfully.

2.1 PROJECT OVERVIEW

The project plan provides an overall plan for the full project implementation. It establishes the project definition, its objectives, and a strategy for meeting those objectives; then it details a plan of action with a schedule for completion. Figure 2.2 shows these project planning activities (left column) with their corresponding project implementation activities (right column). "Analysis," in the right column, corresponds to "project definition" and "project objectives" in the left column. Likewise, "synthesis" corresponds to "strategy"; "technical design" and "prototype construction" correspond to "plan of action." On the surface you might think that project planning activities and project

Project Plan	Project Implementation
Project Definition Goal of the project	

Project Objectives
  Specifications
  Constraints
  Assumptions
	⟶ Analysis
	  Specifications
	  Constraints
	  Assumptions

Strategy
  Idea of how to solve the design problem.
	⟶ Synthesis
	  Generate design concept

Plan of Action
  List tasks (design, build, test)
  Schedule tasks
	⟶ Technical Design
	  Do various tasks

	Evaluation and Decision
	Prototype Construction
	Evaluation
	Documentation

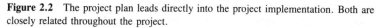

Figure 2.2 The project plan leads directly into the project implementation. Both are closely related throughout the project.

implementation activities are almost the same. There is a difference: when you carry out the project, you are *doing* the technical design and the prototype construction rather than *talking* about doing it.

Figure 2.3 shows the overall activities involved in the project implementation. Accomplishing each of these requires a number of steps and may appear somewhat confusing at first. The design sequence is one way of simply visualizing the process you use when designing a product. The major design activities and typical tasks are:

Analysis	Consider the product specifications and features. Allow for constraints related to environment, customer limitations, industry standards. Balance overall tradeoffs between specifications and constraints.
Synthesis	Generate a possible solution to the design problem, subject to the constraints.
Technical Design	Partition system into functional modules and define operation of each. Select ways of implementing each module; make tradeoff between hardware and software. Do the circuit design and computer programming, integrate into the system, and document the design so far.
Evaluation/Decision	Review the design. Does it meet the specifications? Is the design reasonable? Try another design and compare the two. Repeat until you can select the best compromise that meets specifications subject to the constraints.
Construction of Prototype	Build a prototype system. Test it and correct any hardware and software errors.
Evaluation	Review the system as built. Does it perform as designed? Does it meet specifications? Is it a reasonable solution to the problem?
Documentation	Gather design documentation and prepare a complete engineering design report.

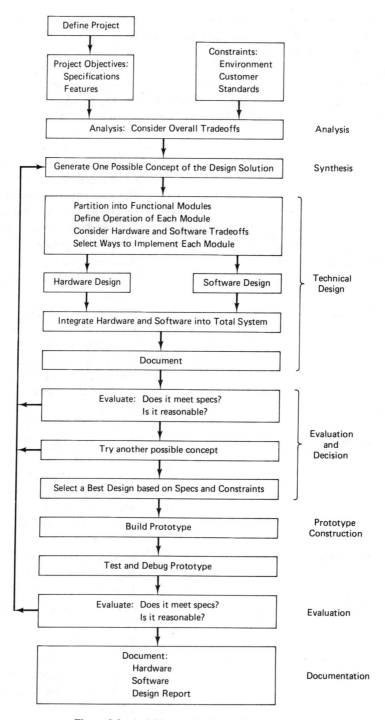

Figure 2.3 Activities involved in implementing a project.

These design activities are based on the work in the project plan, which by now should be complete. Although they are a systematic way of dealing with project implementation, they need not be followed rigorously: consider this morphology as a guide to design rather than as an inflexible absolute. In all probability, you will do a little of each step, skipping some steps until later, and even going back to the very beginning on occasion to rethink the problem with new insight.

2.2 ANALYSIS

You are analyzing when you break down a system into its component parts and examine each to see how it fits into the system. In this context, you are breaking down the problem statement, the specifications, and the constraints. Then you look closely at each of them to see that it fits well enough to solve the problem.

Begin your design analysis by studying the problem statement as given in the proposal. Investigate the background that led to the problem, and then paraphrase the problem in a sentence or two to ensure that you fully understand it. Review the product features and see if they are consistent with each other and with the specifications. Step back a moment, look at the total situation, and imagine that you have the product already completed as specified. Would it solve the problem? If so, is the solution reasonable? Does it make sense?

The specifications you accept at the start of the project will be your criteria for selecting among the design alternatives. Because the specifications are a statement of your design objectives, they must be as specific as possible so that you know when your design is good enough to start building it. Over-engineering a product is perhaps as bad as under-engineering: the product never gets built. As you examine the specifications, identify the top-priority requirements and be prepared to consider them first as you solve the design problem.

Resolve any problems with the specifications. Ideally, the specifications should describe the product exactly, but often a product might be over-specified. Trying to meet unnecessary specifications adds extra engineering and complexity to the finaly product. Similarly, specifications can be ambiguous. Ambiguity results when the writer uses poorly defined or imprecise terms. Specifications can also contradict each other, so that a design solution meeting one requirement would never meet the other.

Review each of the contraints or limits imposed on the product. Are they necessary and realistic, or could some of these limitations be relaxed? Find out how much room you have to work in before you get too involved. For example, if one of your constraints is that the product must be battery-operated and run for 72 hours at full load, find out whether 48 hours would solve the problem. Why? Because the extra battery life might add to the product cost, complexity, and design time. If you know which constraints are flexible, then you can ask for relaxation of certain limitations if necessary.

Some constraints, however, are absolutes. For example, various standards set by the Institute of Electrical and Electronics Engineers (IEEE) have been agreed upon concerning certain aspects of electrical design. If you are designing a product that must meet

IEEE Std-696, then your design cannot deviate from the limits written in the standard. If your design does not meet the standard on all points, then your product might not be compatible with other units in the system. If that happens, then the customer will be inclined to blame any system malfunctions on your product even though your violation might have been inconsequential.

Although standards can at times be an inconvenience, they do make the design job easier because you have a ready-made design outline before you even start. For example, IEEE Std-696 describes the physical and electrical specifications of a circuit board intended for use in a computer system. If you know that your design must conform to this standard, then you immediately know what physical space and what voltages are available for your circuit: the environment for your design will be an enclosure with a maximum of 22 connected devices. As you study the standard and begin to visualize your creation, you can work more easily toward a tentative design solution.

In addition to the explicit constraints, you are working within the implied constraints of a schedule and limited financial resources. These implied constraints are likely to affect your design decisions substantially. If you had all the time you wanted to complete a design, it would be a masterpiece. If only you had some extra finances, or the customer were willing to pay more, you could create a truly wonderful work of art. Think of the time-money limit as part of the engineering challenge: you would like to design the right product at a reasonable price in time to be useful.

With a set of workable specifications and standards, consider the tradeoffs that you should make between them. When you analyze the specifications, you consider whether each specification is consistent with the next; you consider each of the constraints in a similar manner. You also should investigate an overall tradeoff between specifications and contraints. Consider the battery-life constraint: perhaps you find that the 72-hour life is a "must," but that you can reduce product cost by modifying the specification in another area. The longer battery life might be required, but nothing is said in the specifications about a trickle-charge being used to recharge the batteries constantly before "battery-only" operation. If you can keep the batteries fully charged, then perhaps they can be the same size as the 48-hour-life batteries and still run for 72 hours. You might not be able to make the tradeoff even though the specification is "quiet" about recharging; on the other hand, you might be able to negotiate a specification requiring charging before use. If depends on the application and all the other variables involved.

The analysis of specifications is never complete. After completing all the steps to implement a project, you will find that another iteration of the analysis improves your understanding. Even though you understood the problem, the objectives, and the constraints, another look can add substantially to the success of your work. In design, you never fully know the situation.

2.3 SYNTHESIS

In the synthesis portion of implementing your project, you are seeking to create and define one concept of the problem solution. Your initial strategy in the proposal described one concept that you believed would work, and from there you developed a project plan. After a complete analysis, you might refine that concept to synthesize a better approach.

As you conclude your analysis, you will also have a number of other ideas for solving the problem. Write them all down, even though some of them seem extreme or impractical. Sketching each of your ideas helps you to visualize a potential solution to a design problem. Sort through this assortment of design ideas and pick one that you think will best meet the specifications. This idea might very well be the concept that you use for your final product design; however, you may yet discover a better one. At this point, you make your selection expecting to do a technical design and then an evaluation. You might do several designs before final selection, and each time you go through a design you will have better ideas on how to solve the original problem. This iteration helps refine your concepts into better designs.

Using the concept that best fits the specifications, begin by sketching a block diagram of the system. You can do the block diagram easily by asking what the total system does and drawing one big block with an input and an output. Then look inside the block and draw several small blocks that describe how to use the input to create the output. This is a top-down design approach similar to the software concept of writing a program by starting with the top level module followed by writing its support modules. Consider the temperature monitor from the last chapter where you saw a proposal (Table 1.3) containing specifications and a plan for design. For the monitor, draw one big box with temperature as an input and display as an output. Then, to obtain the smaller blocks inside, look at the proposal strategy. The strategy (concept) includes a sensor, an analog-to-digital (A/D) converter, an interface, and a microcomputer. You can draw the block diagram of this system as shown in Figure 2.4 to express your strategy for solving the measurement problem.

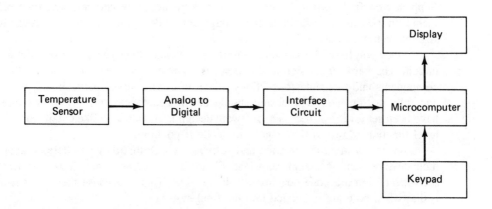

Figure 2.4 Block diagram of the temperature-measurement system. The diagram is a result of partitioning the design into functional modules.

2.4 TECHNICAL DESIGN

The technical design phase begins with the block diagram of the desired system and ends with the hardware and software description of the product. The design is on paper in sufficient detail to fully predict how well the product will meet the specifications. For this reason, all your circuit designs and computer programs must be well-documented.

A system block diagram can be drawn as in Figure 2.4 to help understand a computerized design. Block diagrams can be used for any other system as well, be it a power system, a communications network, or a control system. As you draw each of the blocks in the system, you are in effect partitioning the system into functional modules. Each module has a purpose, and you should define each according to its operation, inputs, and outputs. For example, the purpose of the A/D converter block is to convert an analog voltage to an equivalent digital value. To operate properly, it must be told when to do a conversion, and it must be able to notify the computer when it finishes.

When you partition the system into modules, you actually imply a tradeoff between hardware and software. According to the product concept, the temperature monitor will acquire data and pass it without modification to the computer. If any corrections must be made to compensate for nonlinearities in a thermocouple, for example, the solution must implement them in software. Another concept for solving the measurement problem might have done the compensation in hardware before the A/D converter. Consider the various tradeoffs as you review the design.

The next step in the design is selecting a way to implement each module. Draw a block diagram for each of them to the same level of detail as shown in Figure 2.5 for the A/D converter module. Then for each module, see if you did a similar design in the past. Can you use your previous work in your current design? Likewise, see if the design has been published in a magazine, book, or manufacturer's application note. For example, how would you implement the A/D converter module? You could build it using transistors and op-amps or perhaps use a single integrated device for the whole A/D function. Suppose you find such a device that meets your accuracy and response-time requirements. In this case you might sketch a rough circuit design like Figure 2.6 to use for the A/D converter module.

Once you have all the modules roughly sketched, then you can design the detailed circuit. The hardware design at this point is completed to the final circuit with all the components and their interconnections shown in detail. Actual parts should be selected and fully documented. The design should be in accordance with any design rules that have been set for the project. The software design is also done in like detail from the top-level functions down to flow charts and code if possible.

As you design the hardware and software, watch that they parallel one another in their development. Although shown in Figure 2.3 as separate activities, hardware and software design are done concurrently if possible. This is because they must work together when both are integrated into the final system.

Documentation is vital to the success of the hardware and software design. Throughout the analysis, synthesis, and technical design stages of your project imple-

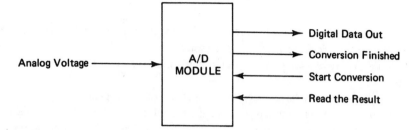

Figure 2.5 The analog-to-digital (A/D) module. This sketch shows more detail than the overall block diagram of the system shown in Figure 2.4.

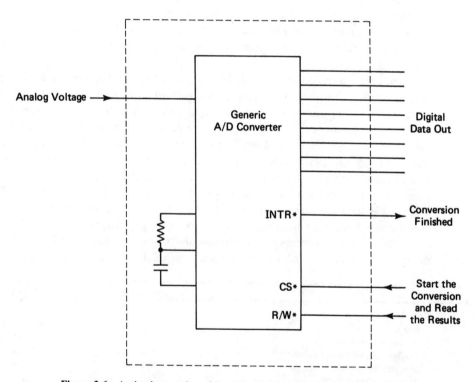

Figure 2.6 An implementation of the A/D Module. This is a rough circuit that needs additional design effort to be operational.

mentation, you should be maintaining a laboratory notebook. The lab book serves as a permanent reference document of your ideas, plans, and designs as you work through the project. As you make design decisions, you should record the rationale for each decision in the lab book. Also, include in the lab book all the information to make design decisions and to formalize a final design.

2.5 EVALUATION AND DECISION

The evaluation following the technical design stage is intended to see if the hardware and software will perform together as a system and meet the specifications. The evaluation should also reveal what the expected performance should be if the system were actually built.

Suppose you have recently finished a complete paper design of the temperature monitor using the functional modules illustrated in Figure 2.4. You would like to know if your design will meet or exceed the required specifications given in the proposal in Table 1.3. Consider, for example, the requirement for accuracy to within 1°C. To find out how well you meet this accuracy specification, you get the worst-case performance data on the temperature sensor and A/D converter from the manufacturer's data sheets. Also, ask yourself where other errors could come into the system, estimate their size, and add the errors. Your answer will not be exact, but it will be useful. Is the amount of error greater or less than 1°C? If it is greater than 1°C, you know you have more design work ahead to improve accuracy.

For each of the product specifications, you might want to make a small chart like that in Figure 2.7 to help you compare the performance of each design. Include cost, development time, and other possible requirements in addition to the specifications. After you have done one or two designs, you will sense what to expect for a final product and whether or not the original requirements were reasonable for the price. You might find that no design can be completed within your budget in the time available. What do you do then? Perhaps you need to rethink your approach entirely: delete the microcomputer and implement the logic with large-scale integration (LSI) components. Perhaps you need another meeting with your customer to review what you can deliver versus the specification that is required; there may be room for negotiation.

The evaluation process goes on continually as you perform the technical design and documentation. As you begin your design, you might find that a particular technical

	Design 1	Design 2
Specification		
Range −40° to + 100°C	−40° to +90°C	−40° to + 100°C
Accuracy within 1°C	2°	1°
Display Fahrenheit and Celsius	F only	Both OK
Min/max temperature reading	yes	yes
Average temperature	yes	yes
Heating degree-days	no	yes
Portable	yes	yes
Cost	$60	$200
Time to develop final prototype	3 weeks	6 weeks
Special test equipment required?	no	logic analyzer

Figure 2.7   A simple chart with the project specifications showing how one design compares with another.

approach cannot meet the specifications. Rather than waste time carrying the design further, estimate its performance, put it in the comparison table, and work up another possible solution to the design problem. Doing this speeds up your technical design substantially, and you have a more diverse selection of alternatives for comparison.

After you complete several designs, your comparison chart will help you decide which design to build as a prototype. The specifications are your decision criteria. Given two designs that meet the specifications equally, you then consider cost, maximum performance, maintainability, reliability, and other values important to you or your customer. The actual selection you make, however, should meet the required specifications.

2.6 PROTOTYPE CONSTRUCTION

The purpose of building a prototype is to demonstrate that your paper design is correct and to reveal any oversights that might hinder the product's performance. You can easily use your completed prototype in a number of different experiments to adjust the design and verify its performance.

When you build your prototype, build it module by module. This holds whether you use wire-wrap, a prototype board, or solder for your actual construction. Hardware can be constructed and tested one module at a time just as you might write a computer program one module at a time. The reasoning is this: if you build one small module, apply power, and test it fully for proper operation, then you can use it as part of a larger subsequent module. If any problems develop with the larger module, then you know the difficulty is probably in the circuit you just added. This modular approach to building and testing hardware is far easier than wiring the entire circuit and then trying to diagnose an elusive malfunction in the system.

After you have an operational prototype, test it fully over all the ranges of the specifications. Find and fix any problems that occur as you test the unit. Keep accurate notes in your lab book—this is especially important when you are testing and debugging the prototype. Be able to explain why the unit behaves as it does. Does it perform the way you designed it?

2.7 EVALUATION AND DOCUMENTATION

The evaluation following construction of the prototype is intended to demonstrate that the hardware and software do in fact work together properly and meet the specifications. Unlike the evaluation you did on the prototype, this more formal evaluation will probably involve other persons from different departments in your company. In addition, depending on the product and the arrangements, the customer might receive a copy of the test results.

The results of the prototype testing should prove the merit of your design concept and its implementation. If something was overlooked or a specification was changed late in the design cycle, then you might have to redesign even now. Figure 2.3 shows the evaluation going back to start with another concept, but in reality you go back only as far as necessary to correct the problem.

While the prototype is being tested, you should be finishing your final design documentation on the project. Review your lab book and outline your technical design report. Plan on covering the design concept, the reasons for your technical choices, the hardware and software design, the prototype construction, and the operation of the proto- type. Besides treating the design details, you should also include a description of how to test the unit and what results should be expected. Later, when your design goes into production, either you or a test engineer will need this test information to write the test plan for the manufactured units.

2.8 SUMMARY

Chapter 2 shows how to finish the project systematically by following a number of engineering design steps in sequence. First, identify needs by using problem-solving techniques, and then prepare a project plan. You can summarize the plan in the form of the proposal. The proposal outlines each task and its completion date and can be used to focus the project implementation. Using the specifications and design concept in the project plan, you can complete the project within the given time and financial constraints.

The activities of analysis, synthesis, technical design, evaluation and decision, prototype construction, evaluation and documentation are presented as a flowchart in Figure 2.3. The sequence is one way of approaching the project implementation and may easily be modified to suit your own needs. View the various activities as guides for aiding your design rather than as restraints. You will probably begin each step and then on occasion return to the start to rethink with a new understanding of your project.

When you analyze, you are breaking down the problem statement, the specifica- tions, and the constraints to see how well they fit together to solve the problem. Because your planned design must meet the specifications, resolve any problems with them such as ambiguity, contradiction, and over-specificity; resolve any similar problems with the stated constraints as well. If you are designing to conform to a particular industry stan- dard, be sure that your specifications are consistent with its requirements.

In the synthesis portion of the project implementation, you are attempting to create and define one concept of the problem solution. After considering a number of ideas, pick one concept that appears likely to fulfill your specifications the best. Then sketch a block diagram that expresses the concept.

You use this block diagram in the technical design phase to complete a paper design of your project. Each block in the diagram is a functional module; you can describe each according to its operation, inputs, and outputs. Select how you can imple- ment each module in hardware and software, and then design the circuit and program in detail.

The evaluation following the technical design is intended to determine if the hard- ware and software will perform together as a system that meets the specifications. Make a comparison chart to establish which of your design alternatives is most satisfactory. When you have several possibilities, use the specifications as your criteria for deciding which design to build as a prototype.

The purpose of building the prototype is to demonstrate that your paper design is correct and to uncover any oversights that might adversely affect the product's performance. Construct the prototype module by module so that you can test each section as you build it. When you have all the modules interconnected, fully test and debug your finished prototype.

The final evaluation after you debug the prototype is intended to demonstrate that hardware and software work together as a system and that they meet specifications. The documentation should result in a technical design report during this phrase of the project. This report should cover design concept, reasons for your choices, and the design, construction, and operation of the prototype.

EXERCISES

1. During the heating season, fuel-oil distributors make customer deliveries based on how cold the weather has been rather than filling tanks on a weekly or biweekly basis. Needless frequent deliveries increase costs, so it is desirable to wait until the customer tank is nearly empty before filling it. Ideally, a typical 275-gallon tank should be refilled when it gets to within 20 to 50 gallons of being empty.

Hot-Spot Oil company presently estimates a "k-factor" for each customer to help decide when to deliver oil. The k-factor is an empirical number of degree-days of heating the customer gets from each gallon of oil. Heating degree-days equal 65 minus the average temperature during 24 hours; for example, if the average temperature yesterday was 20°F, then 45 degree-days of heating were required. Suppose Hot-Spot estimated Jack Smith's house at $k = 5$ degree-days per gallon: the 45 degree-days of heat required yesterday used 45/5, or 9 gallons of oil.

If Hot-Spot Oil can keep data on daily heating degree-days, then they can estimate how much oil Jack Smith is using, If Jack has a 275-gallon tank, then that means he can heat for a maximum of 275 times 5, or 1375 degree-days. If each day averages 20°F, then Jack will run out of oil in about 30 days ($1375/45 = 30+$). To be on the safe side, Hot-Spot will probably deliver about 5 days before they estimate Jack will run out of oil. This is equivalent to about 1100 degree-days accumulated since the last delivery.

Hot-Spot Oil came to you recently, and you both worked out some specifications for a way to calculate yesterday's number of degree-days each morning when they come to work. For Jack and their other customers, they can total the degree-days and figure out when to make deliveries. The specifications you worked out are: measure temperature from -40 to $+70$°F, calculate the average temperature from 8 A.M. to 8 A.M., calculate the number of degree-days, and display the result for them to write down.
   a. Define the problem.
   b. List the specifications above and add three more specifications you might want to include for a better definition of the job.
   c. List three constraints.

     d. List three possible ways to solve the problem.

     e. Do a rough sketch of each way you listed.

     f. Select the best approach and do a block diagram of the system.

     g. Using your block diagram, partition the system by function.

     h. Do a detailed block diagram of each module.

     i. Do the circuit design for a least one module.

     j. Describe how you would build your prototype.

     k. Describe an alternative way of constructing the prototype.

2. Make up a problem and specify a product that you can design. Do a rough proposal and then all the implementation steps from problem definition through prototype description (steps a–k in Exercise 1). Polish the proposal after completing these steps. Your deliverable to the customer is a completed proposal.

     As a topic for this problem, pick something from either your own background or the following list of ideas:

     Computer-controlled speech synthesizer
     Programmable music organ
     Waveform generator
     ASCII display of serial or parallel data
     Joystick or mouse for computer cursor control
     Printer buffer
     Clock with alarm
     Data modem
     Morse code generator
     Programmable power supply

FURTHER READING

ARTWICK, BRUCE A. *Microcomputer Interfacing.* Englewood Cliffs, NJ: Prentice Hall, 1980. (TK 7888.3.A86)

ASIMOW, MORRIS. *Introduction to Design.* Englewood Cliffs, NJ: Prentice Hall, 1962. (TA 175.A83)

CAIN, WILLIAM D. *Engineering Product Design.* London: Business Books Limited, 1969. (TA 174.C3)

COMER, DAVID J. *Digital Logic and State Machine Design.* New York: Holt, Rinehart and Winston, 1984. (TK 7868.59C66)

DAVIS, THOMAS W. *Experimentation with Microprocessor Applications.* Reston, VA: Reston Publishing, 1981.

FLETCHER, WILLIAM I. *An Engineering Approach to Digital Design.* Englewood Cliffs, NJ: Prentice Hall, 1980. (TK 7868.D5F5)

GREGORY, S. A. *Creativity and Innovation in Engineering.* London: Butterworth, 1972. (TA 174.C7X)

HARMAN, THOMAS L., and BARBARA LAWSON. *The Motorola MC68000 Microprocessor Family: Assembly Language, Interface Design, and System Design.* Englewood Cliffs, NJ: Prentice Hall, 1985. (QA 76.8.M6895H37)

HAYES, JOHN P. *Digital System Design and Microprocessors*. New York: McGraw-Hill, 1984. (TK 7874.H393)

KLINE, RAYMOND M. *Structured Digital Design*. Englewood Cliffs, NJ: Prentice Hall, 1983.

PROSSER, FRANKLIN P., and DAVID WINKEL. *The Art of Digital Design, second edition*. Englewood Cliffs, NJ: Prentice Hall, 1987.

ROBERTSHAW, JOSEPH E., STEPHEN J. MECCA, and MARK N. RERICK. *Problem Solving: A Systems Approach*. New York: Petrocelli, 1978 (QA 402.R6)

SHORT, KENNETH L. *Microprocessors and Programmed Logic*. Englewood Cliffs, NJ: Prentice Hall, 1981. (QA76.5.S496)

WINKEL, DAVID, and FRANKLIN PROSSER. *The Art of Digital Design*. Englewood Cliffs, NJ: Prentice Hall, 1980. (TK 7888.3W56)

3

DESIGN GUIDELINES AND IMPLEMENTATION

In the first chapter, you examined engineering design and considered how customer needs lead to your project proposal. This proposal sketches the required work and shows when each major task must be completed. Then, in the second chapter, you used the project proposal to complete the project implementation. The chapter showed you how to finish the project systematically by following a number of engineering design steps in sequence.

Chapter 3 provides a number of guidelines for executing the technical design. These guidelines or design rules are the conventions established for carrying out designs that are not only technically sound but also consistent with the designs of team members working on the same project. In addition to providing technical guidelines, this chapter presents a number of *heuristics*, or rules of thumb, that may be applied to the design process. These heuristics serve to moderate the paper design with a measure of common-sense reality. Finally, the concept of designing for testability is described.

This chapter also includes information on how to implement a project. First, some prototyping alternatives are considered for building a breadboard model of the project. Then, several testing and troubleshooting strategies and techniques are examined for use in project development.

The technical design you did in Chapter 2 involved using a block diagram of one particular concept. Before building a prototype, you expected to go through the design of several different concepts, and you hoped that one of them would meet the specifications subject to the constraints. When you did the technical design using your block diagram, you probably did it rather haphazardly and did not concern yourself with following any particular rules. If the numbers worked together, then you were happy enough to finish.

When you follow design rules, however, your work goes easier and is more orderly. For these rules to make sense, though, some additional detail beyond the original ideas in Figure 2.3 might be helpful. Figure 3.1 shows how the technical design can be expanded and used to go from a block diagram to a complete paper design.

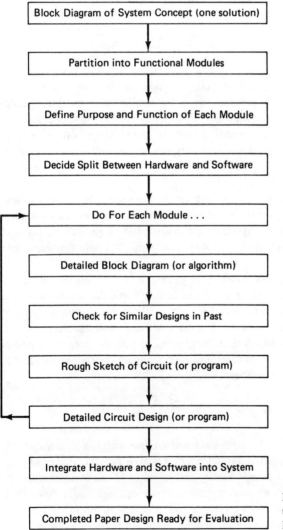

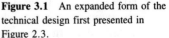

Figure 3.1 An expanded form of the technical design first presented in Figure 2.3.

Starting with the concept, you can partition your system into functional modules and describe the purpose and function of each module. At the same time, you can decide on how to split the various functions between hardware and software. Then, for each hardware and software module, you can draw a block diagram or write an algorithm and do a detailed circuit design or working program. The design rules in this chapter typically apply when you do the detailed circuit design or the program.

Heuristics, on the other hand, apply anywhere in design engineering, from the original problem-solving steps through to the detailed circuit design. Heuristics are techniques or rules of thumb that help solve a problem, but are not themselves technically justifiable. They are a blend of past experience, logic, common sense, and nonsense that give the engineer some direction in solving the problem at hand.

3.1 TECHNICAL DESIGN RULES

After you have a block diagram of your intended circuit, you will probably want to quickly check some of your previous work for similar designs. Many times you can locate a useful circuit in your own notes, in a magazine, or in a text and save some time for extra effort on the more innovative parts of your design job. This is not to say, however, that you can simply select a handy circuit and put it in your system without analysis; even if the circuit appears to fit exactly, you should always verify that it does indeed meet your specifications.

Based on your understanding of the circuit requirements, draw a rough sketch of the circuit. At this point, the idea is not necessarily to have a working circuit. You want to get an idea of how many components are involved and how they all fit together in the module. Pinpoint areas you think are difficult or might cause problems later in your design.

Finally, using the rough sketch as a guide, do a detailed circuit design. As you work on the design, you might be unsure of how a particular device works; find out— take it to the lab with the data book and try it out. While you do the design work, review the following design rules as a guide. The rules will help you transform the rough circuit sketch into a technically sound design. In addition, if you are working with other designers on a large project, the design rules will help maintain consistency so that the various systems modules will work together.

3.1.1 Hardware Design Rules

Each discipline or major field within electrical engineering has its own set of hardware issues that should be considered as you begin a design project. For example, in digital design one must decide on a logic family and whether to use synchronous or asynchronous sequential circuits. In an analog design, however, one might consider topics like measurement accuracy and standard values for resistors, capacitors, and inductors. In spite of the differences, though, some overlap between fields is normal.

There are a few general hardware issues that all electrical engineers should consider. Some of these are worst-case design, computer simulation, the effect of temperature, reliability, and product safety.

Worst-case design means that you develop your circuit or system while accounting for component values that would produce degraded performance. Normally, when you design, you specify components with a certain value: a 1000-ohm resistor, for example. We know, however, that a resistor can deviate from its specified nominal value by a tolerance of, say, 5%. This means the true value of the resistor is somewhere between 950 and 1050 ohms. How does this affect your design? Suppose that 950 ohms results in a loss of performance, but your system is still within its overall specifications? What about other parts? Do they cause similar performance degradation?

If you sense that worst-case design implies hard work, you are right. This is a good argument in favor of using a computer to simulate the performance of your design. To simulate the operation of your system, you specify the circuit topology and the nominal values and tolerances of the various components. The computer can then calculate how well your system works for many random combinations of the parts involved. In addition to covering the manufacturing tolerances. you can also include variations in component values due to temperature changes.

Always consider temperature in your designs. Regardless of what hardware you create, it does not always live in a controlled environment. Electrical devices eventually are packaged in a box, cabinet, or perhaps epoxy cement, which tend to prevent heat from dissipating, which in turn causes the temperature of the devices to rise. As devices get hotter, their characteristics change, and that can severely affect system performance. If you doubt that temperature can vary much, put a temperature sensor inside the cabinet of a computer that stays on all day. You'll see that it gets quite warm in the cabinet.

Temperature not only affects performance, but it affects reliability, too. Think of that same above-mentioned computer: how do you suppose the computer's overall reliability is affected by constant temperature cycling every night when the power goes off? Might the thermal stress cause a failure in the future? Reliability is a major issue, just as you might suspect. How much are you willing to pay to guarantee a very low failure rate? For example, consider a small power supply that must be in constant service. First, we must estimate how hot it becomes while in service. Next, we must estimate whether the components will not only survive, but also stay within their design tolerances over time. Even if we decide they *can* survive, can we be certain of a low failure rate? Not really, but we can improve our odds by "burning in" newly manufactured supplies. This means to power-up and leave the units on for days (even weeks); units still functional at the end of the burn-in are presumed more reliable than unstressed units.

Product safety ties in with reliability in a sense. A unit that fails will affect the system in some manner, hopefully with degraded performance rather than a spectacular display of pyrotechnics. The idea of "fail-safe" simply means that if a device fails, it should do it in a safe manner. For example, if a power supply fails, it should shut off output completely rather than allow an excessive output voltage. If the 120-V line shorts to the cabinet, a fuse should blow rather than present a lethal voltage on the cabinet. If you design anything but the smallest, simplest, lowest-voltage system, always think safety! Even small, simple systems can be hazardous, especially health-care products, so think safety!

3.1.2 Software Design Rules

When you program a computer, regardless of the language you use, each program can be treated like hardware. That is, programs can be interconnected and used as building blocks to solve a particular problem. Visualize a program as you would hardware: it has inputs and outputs, and performs a particular function in the system. In the same sense, your programs can be modularized, and perhaps used over and over, to save substantial design time as your project evolves.

In order to make your programs into modules that you can call as needed, you should do a top-down design of your software system, just as you did for your hardware design. This top-down design can be drawn easily in the form of a structure chart, as shown in Figure 3.2. Consider each block as a functional module within the system and define the purpose of each. Start with the purpose of the main program: what does it do and what are its inputs and outputs? Then, for the main program to accomplish its purpose, a number of supporting tasks are necessary. The process becomes more detailed as you get down to the next level in the structure chart.

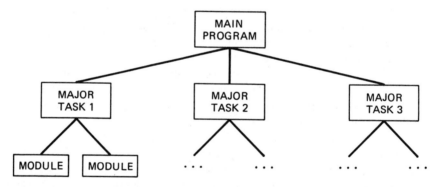

Figure 3.2   The form of the structure chart used in a top-down program design.

The easiest way to visualize the process of breaking down a program into modules is to think of the main program as in the form of a menu of tasks that can be selected. Each of the tasks is a subroutine within the program and can be selected from the menu for execution. Once a task has been selected, it needs to call on a number of supporting modules or routines during execution.

If you think of each of the blocks of the structure chart as subroutines, you can see the advantage of making each module as straightforward and specific as possible. With one function per module, you can combine them in just the same fashion as you design hardware. Not only that, but you can write the code for the module and test it thoroughly before "building" it into the larger body of the main program.

Rules on software design

A module should:

1. Have one purpose.
2. Be as general as possible for use in other applications.
3. Be reliable. (Provide worst-case test data to demonstrate.)
4. Have a length less than two pages.
5. Contain one statement maximum per line of program.
6. Have one entry point and one exit point.
7. Be internally documented with ample comments.
8. Contain a heading with name of module, date, revision number; list of external modules and variables; public labels and variables; description of input and output variables; and note of any registers that are changed during a call to the module.

In general:

1. All constants should be defined at the beginning of the main program or in a library related to the appropriate module.
2. Routines, parameters, labels, storage area, and all calling procedures should be consistent with each other.
3. Avoid absolute addresses if possible. Use relative addressing. Program for easy relocation of module. Ideally, your module should execute wherever you place it in memory.

3.2 DESIGN HEURISTICS

Your design up to this point has probably been somewhat conventional: define the problem and specifications, synthesize several possible solutions to the problem, select the best solution, and then implement it. Although these are the general steps in the engineering design process, they seem somewhat pedestrian. Where is the creativity and flexibility to innovate?

In reality, when you first begin a design task, you do not understand the problem. You cannot decide which specifications are critical to the design or even decide which job to do first. Why not follow some rule of thumb, or heuristic, that can help you get moving in the right direction as you feel your way into a better understanding of the problem?

By its very nature, a heuristic is a guide based on past experience and common sense. A heuristic is not a rule that can be conclusively proven, because the heuristic might not even be correct in certain situations. Therefore, when you use heuristics to help speed your design work, remember that they do not guarantee a correct answer and that you must still work out a proper design. The advantage of the heuristic is in helping you decide on which design might be worth your time and effort.

The following list of heuristics are a collection of useful rules for general engineering as well as digital design. Some are obvious, some are obscure, but many should be useful.

3.2.1 Engineering Heuristics

1. Don't reinvent the wheel: read data sheets and application notes.
2. Reduce your problem to something you've solved before.
3. If you can't meet the specs, negotiate; don't hide the problem.
4. Always have an answer; you have to start somewhere.
5. Change one variable at a time when you adjust your design.
6. Develop circuits and programs module by module; debug as you go.
7. Build a quick simple circuit for experimentation; understand it.
8. Keep your designs simple.
9. Use multifunction integrated devices when possible.
10. Talking aloud to yourself helps spot errors.
11. If you find you made a mistake, figure out why.
12. Solve the right problem.
13. Act rather than react; think ahead to prevent problems from cropping up; don't spend your day fighting fires.
14. Read the fine print at the bottom of data sheets.
15. When in doubt, don't guess; look it up and be sure.
16. On time management:
    - Keep a daily do-it list with priorities for each task.
    - Do critical or difficult tasks as soon as possible.
    - Schedule unfinished tasks for a definite day in the future.
    - Keep a time log of your work and review your progress.
    - Don't procrastinate—a project gets late one day at a time.

3.3 DESIGNING FOR TESTABILITY

When you design a product, your main concern is probably to make a prototype that works. Certainly, you will be designing to meet the product specifications, but what about the extra "convenience" features that might not be explicitly included in the specifications? How much extra product cost is reasonable if testing can be simplified by adding an extra test module? The benefit from such design goes beyond the design engineer to include test and service personnel and perhaps the customer.

To get a sense of how designing for testability is important, select some equipment in your lab and try testing it. For example, suppose you select a small microcomputer board and want to use an oscilloscope to see several of the control circuits. Your first problem: where to hook the scope ground clip? Rather than force the test person to clip onto an integrated circuit (IC), perhaps a few inexpensive ground stakes could have been provided. As you work through your testing, jot down your ideas on what features would make the test job easier.

Consider the following list of features for a new design. The idea is to make the design easy to test during the development process and easy to troubleshoot later after the system is complete.

1. *Display Lights.* Include a light-emitting diode (LED) or equivalent to indicate the status of your system. For example, in a microprocessor system, an LED to indicate a halted computer can be quite useful. Similarly, an LED to show a normally running system is helpful.

2. *Built-In Test Circuits.* Simple test circuits can usually be designed in easily for little extra cost. For example, in a microprocessor system, a reset switch is extremely useful for troubleshooting, but is not always provided.

3. *Test Points.* Provide states for ground and power so you can connect a logic probe or oscilloscope easily. Add connections to access major signals in the system.

4. *Test Jumpers.* Provide a means of breaking vital circuits between modules by removing jumpers. You might want to test a circuit in isolation from other modules, and jumpers can be quite useful for opening a circuit.

5. *Test Sockets.* If space or cost is at a premium, a test socket should be provided for connection to your circuit board. For example, some automobile manufacturers provide a socket for a mechanic to connect a diagnostic computer to aid in servicing.

6. *Board Layout.* When you lay out a circuit board, allow room around the various devices to connect test equipment. Also, be sure to locate serviceable components where they can be reached. For example, if you design a computer system, do not physically locate the sockets for the EPROMs underneath other modules.

3.4 BREADBOARDING

Throughout the whole cycle of engineering design, you work by modules to gradually create a new product. After completing an overall system design, you design, build, and test the first module; next you design the second module, and so on. You continue adding modules until the whole system is finished. The concept is simple and quickly leads to a fully-tested and working prototype system.

Typically, when an engineer designs a new product, a prototype model is constructed by either the engineer or a technician on the support staff. After the prototype has been debugged, a preproduction model might be built, and finally a production model is completed. The production model is the final product and probably uses a multi-layer printed circuit board (PCB) and takes advantage of the latest manufacturing technology. The prototype, however, is not usually as sophisticated: it might be constructed using a solderless breadboard or be wire-wrapped on a protoboard.

The prototype you build and test is really a design-concept verification; it only needs to work! The purpose of the prototype is to help you hammer out the final design, and to do that it must be flexible and simple. The method of construction you use depends on your preference and any guidelines your company might impose. Some of the possibilities are:

- Solderless breadboard
- Wirewrap board
- Solder parts onto kludge PCB
- Solder parts onto top surface of bare PCB
- Lay out and make a custom PCB; solder parts onto it.

3.5 TROUBLESHOOTING THE SYSTEM

Troubleshooting is problem solving applied to fix a defective hardware or software system. You probably do not automatically think of troubleshooting in quite this way, but look back at the problem-solving steps shown in Figure 1.3. These steps can be reformulated along the lines indicated in Figure 3.3. The overall approach to fixing a system is to pinpoint the problem and generate several ideas of what might be causing it. After that, pick the most likely cause and repair it.

The concept sounds simple on paper; in reality it is a bit more difficult. For example, you might not notice some symptoms and never even guess the real cause of the problem. Some problems are heat-related: you might test the system and find it good for hours, but then later see it fail after it heats up. Even worse, intermittent component failures can leave you wondering if there is even a problem in the first place.

Avoid the "shotgun" method, in which you guess many solutions and try them all while hoping for a fix. Rather, attack the problem systematically even if the process seems somewhat slower. Use a large measure of common sense when you have a defective system.

3.5.1 Strategies

- *System Swap.* If your system absolutely must continue in operation even if repairs are necessary, the strategy of replacing the entire system might be appropriate. Although costly, this minimizes downtime and might allow for more relaxed troubleshooting. Examples of where a system swap should be considered are computers in communications systems, health equipment (such as heart monitors), and military gear.

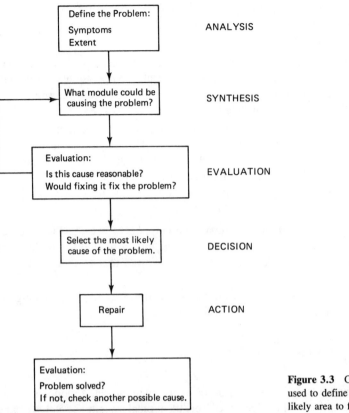

Figure 3.3 General troubleshooting steps used to define a problem and select a likely area to find a defect.

- *Board Swap.* A less-costly strategy for troubleshooting a system is to replace the defective board or boards. The repair task is more complex because a skilled person must determine which board in the system is bad before replacing it. This approach requires keeping an inventory of good replacement boards in stock.
- *Repair.* The common strategy for troubleshooting is to repair the system or board. Unless you plan on throwing out a defective system or board, a skilled person ultimately must fix it. In addition to the cost of labor, the system might be out of service for some time.

3.5.2 Repair Techniques

Assuming that the repair strategy is appropriate in your case, remember that your engineering approach has been to design, build, and test by modules. If the unit needing troubleshooting has been built by modules, then your task is considerably easier: identify the defective module and then the fault within the module. Even if the system is not modularized especially well, you can still do troubleshooting. In either case, consider the following sequence for troubleshooting.

1. *Define the Problem.* What are the symptoms and their extent within the system? When? Where? To answer these questions, make an operational check and a visual check of the system. Look for the obvious: check the fuse, plug in the power, be sure all the cables are connected.

2. *Cause of the Problem.* What modules could cause the symptoms you observe? Localize the problem to one or more modules. Use the bracket technique if several modules are connected in series: if the module on the left is good, and the module on the right is also good, then the middle one must be bad.

3. *Select the Module.* After localizing the problem, pick the module most likely to be at fault.

4. *Repair the Module.* Find and repair the component causing the module failure. Apply an input signal and trace through the circuit to find the faulty component. Measure voltages, check signal waveforms. Test or replace individual components as necessary.

5. *Evaluation.* Make sure you solved the original problem without creating new problems; be sure that the system works completely.

3.5.3 Microcomputer Repair Techniques

A microcomputer system is a collection of many interconnected modules, as shown in Figure 3.4. In addition to the microprocessor, the typical system has a clock, a read-only memory (ROM), a random-access memory (RAM), an input-output (I/O) port, a reset circuit, address decoders, and a power supply. The connections between the modules are

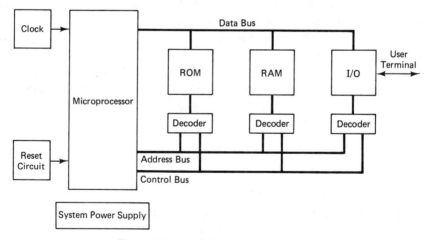

Figure 3.4 A typical microcomputer system.

groupings of related wires called buses; for example, the data bus might have 8 wires or 16 wires, one for each data bit used by the microprocessor.

To repair a microcomputer, the clock, reset circuit, some memory, and the microprocessor (collectively referred to as the *kernel*) must run properly. Once the kernel runs, all the other modules can be tested one at a time until the system runs correctly.

You can think of the system kernel as shown in Figure 3.5. All it contains is the microprocessor and enough memory to execute a program. Its normal operation is to put an address on its address bus, set the controls to read an instruction, read in the data on the data bus, and then increment to the next address. The feedback path between the processor and memory complicates the test and repair of the system.

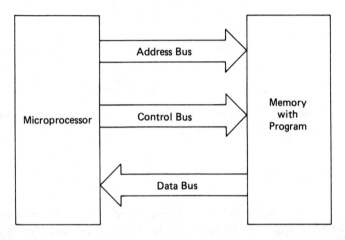

Figure 3.5   The "kernel" of the system is comprised of the clock, the reset circuit, some memory, and the microprocessor. The kernel is the essential minimal hardware required for program execution.

Freerunning the processor

If you break the normally-closed loop between the microprocessor and memory, as shown in Figure 3.6, you can freerun the processor. Freerunning means that the processor is allowed to execute a do-nothing instruction (call it a NIL) continually. Instead of fetching program code from memory, the NIL instruction can be jammed on the data bus. Thus, when the processor reads the data bus for an instruction, it fetches the NIL, executes it, increments the address, and reads the next NIL. This cycling repeats over the entire address range of the processor; when it reaches the end of its address range, it simply starts over again.

Unless the clock is missing or the processor is defective, there is no reason why an inoperative system will not freerun. This means that you can troubleshoot many system components such as ROM, RAM, and I/O. When freerunning, you can observe all the address lines as they count up to their maximum, and you can see their effect on address decoders and the inputs to all the memory devices.

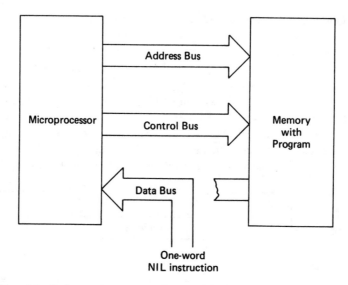

Figure 3.6 To freerun the processor, the normal feedback path from memory is disconnected and a do-nothing NIL instruction is substituted.

Scope loops

A helpful oscilloscope technique you might utilize to troubleshoot a microcomputer is the scope loop. The problem with the scope is that it cannot be easily synchronized: repeating patterns are not normally found on the processor buses. The solution to this is to create a repeating pattern that allows scope synchronization.

If the processor executes a short program over and over, then you have just the repetition you need for a stable scope trace. For example, if you write a program at memory location 1000 that jumps to memory address 1000, you might have the one-line program.

JUMP 1000

When this "program" executes, it repeats fast enough for you to synchronize your oscilloscope. You can then look at various address, data, and control lines with a second trace on the scope.

The obvious drawback with this approach is that the system must function well enough so you can write the program in the first place. An alternative is to program some scope-loop programs in an EPROM (erasable programmable ROM) and substitute your test EPROM for the normal system ROM.

3.6 SUMMARY

Design rules are the procedures or conventions established to direct your project. These design guidelines, rather than being confining, can help you make your design effort more orderly and technically sound. They also help make your work consistent with the designs of other team members working on the same project. This is important so that you can complete your project within your available time and budget.

Software can be designed following the same general approach that you use when you design hardware. You can do a top-down modular program design just the same as you would design a hardware system. Each of the modules has an input and an output and perform a specific function. A structure chart is an easy way of visualizing how the various software modules in the system relate to one another. As you write each of the modules, you can test and debug them as you go, just the same as you test and debug hardware.

Engineering heuristics are rules of thumb that you can use in a fairly intuitive sense to solve engineering problems. They cannot be proven, and some might not even work in a particular situation. They can, however, speed your design work by giving you a feel for what might be important in the design. At the very least, heuristics can usually get your initial calculations approximately correct. Instead of getting bogged down in a deep theoretical design issue, you can speed your work with the common-sense practicality of the heuristic.

By applying both technical design rules and engineering heuristics, you can work much more effectively to finish a design problem. The guidelines will help you do a technically sound design that is consistent with the design work of other team members. The guidelines will also help make the work go faster and, as you use more heuristics, make design engineering an enjoyable challenge to your creativity.

Throughout your design, you should always keep product testability in mind. If at all possible, add in test features so that your design and development can progress smoothly. Test features that you find useful will likely make testing during product manufacturing considerably easier.

When you do engineering design, building and troubleshooting a prototype is important because it validates your design concept. The experience you gain when you troubleshoot your new product can also be extremely valuable in you gaining a broadened understanding of the theory supporting the design.

There are a number of ways of troubleshooting a product. Assuming that you cannot just throw away a defective system or board, a reasonable approach is to use the problem-solving steps you learned in Chapter 1. If you must troubleshoot a microcomputer-based product, you can apply the same general steps. Freerunning and scope loops are useful techniques that can help make the troubleshooting go much faster.

EXERCISES

1. Recently you were asked to design an air-pressure measurement system and build a prototype model on a solderless breadboard. Use Figure 3.1 as a guide and complete the following:
   a. Draw the block diagram of the system.
   b. Partition into functional modules.
   c. Define the purpose and function of each module.
   d. Decide how to split tasks between hardware and software.
   e. Do the detailed block diagram for each module.
   f. Sketch a rough outline of the complete design.

2. After meeting with your supervisor, you were asked to go ahead with construction of the prototype above.
   a. List three relevant hardware design rules.
   b. List three relevant software design rules.
   c. What are some applicable engineering heuristics?

3. Make a list of five "testability" features you would like to include in your prototype. Give a reason for and a reason against including each feature in a final design.

4. Suppose you built the air-pressure measurement system described above. It uses an A/D converter between the measurement circuit and a computer. You don't know it, but four data-bus wires between the A/D converter and the computer are broken. Describe how you would find and repair the problem.

5. Sometimes a microprocessor system fails to run, and troubleshooting and repair are necessary. List features that should be designed into a new product that would make this service easier and faster. For example, you should be able to check the system clock with an oscilloscope, so you would provide a ground stake near the clock circuit for the scope's ground clip.

6. To take advantage of freerunning, must the computer circuit be modified in some way? For your favorite processor, describe how you can make it freerun. Do it and verify your results in lab.

7. What is a scope loop? Write one on your computer and describe how you can use it in troubleshooting. Try it out with an oscilloscope and describe its limitations. Describe how to overcome sweep-stability problems such as those caused by direct-memory access (DMA) devices.

FURTHER READING

FLETCHER, WILLIAM I. *An Engineering Approach to Digital Design.* Englewood Cliffs, NJ: Prentice Hall, 1980. (TK 7868.D5F5)

KOEN, BILLY VAUGHN. "Toward a Definition of the Engineering Method." *ASEE Engineering Education* (Dec. 1984) 75(3): 150-155.

LENK, JOHN D. *Handbook of Advanced Troubleshooting.* Englewood Cliffs, NJ: Prentice Hall, 1983. (TK 7870.2.L46)

MANGIERI, ADOLPH. "Wire-Wrapping and Proto-System Techniques." *Byte* (May 1981) 6(5): 152-170.

ROBBINS, ALLAN H., and BRIAN LUNDEEN. *Troubleshooting Microprocessor-based Systems.* Englewood Cliffs, NJ: Prentice Hall, 1987. (TK 7895.M5R63)

WILCOX, ALAN D. *68000 Microcomputer Systems: Designing and Troubleshooting.* Englewood Cliffs, NJ: Prentice Hall, 1987. (QA 76.8.M6895W55)

WILCOX, ALAN D. "Bringing Up the 68000—A First Step." *Doctor Dobb's Journal* (Jan. 1986) 11(1): 60-74

WINKEL, DAVID, and FRANKLIN PROSSER. *The Art of Digital Design.* Englewood Cliffs, NJ: Prentice Hall, 1980. (TK 7888.3W56)

4

PROJECT COMMUNICATION

In the first two chapters, you examined engineering design and considered how customer needs lead to a project plan. Then you used the project plan to complete the project implementation by systematically following a number of engineering design steps in sequence. The third chapter provided guidelines and some heuristics for doing the technical design. The concept of designing for testability and some prototyping alternatives were also considered. Finally, several testing and troubleshooting strategies and techniques were examined for use in project development.

In contrast, Chapter 4 is about written and oral project communication. The emphasis here is not on the technical development of the product; rather, it is on recording facts about the product and being able to describe it to both technical and nontechnical people. The material here is divided into three main areas: the project documentation you keep and use yourself, the written reports you make for others, and oral presentations you make about the project.

When you think of project communication, always keep two important points in mind:

- Audience
- Purpose

When you write or speak about your project, you think of your intended audience (other engineers, management, or perhaps the customer) and what they need to know. Your purpose might be to inform them about your project or maybe to convince them to buy the completed product. Thus, to communicate effectively, write or speak to a specific group of people and focus on their specific needs.

4.1 BASIC PROJECT DOCUMENTATION

The basic documentation related to your project does not usually get written up and reported to someone. That is, the various notes you take and raw data you collect generally stay with you. This documentation, however, does form the basis for many reports you need to make, and you might be required to produce it on occasion.

4.1.1 Information Files

Some of the most basic facts about a project can be found in your own information files of magazine articles. Consider this: engineers regularly receive a host of trade magazines that describe new products, discuss design applications, and give tutorials. What happens? Often the magazines pile up waiting to be read at some convenient moment that never seems to come. After the stack gets over a foot high, it gets in the way and goes either to a bookcase ("never throw out something that might be useful") or to the trash can ("but throw out under pressure").

As a student, you are already beginning to have to deal with a barrage of information from periodicals, and though you may have no use for most of the information now, you can readily see that some of it may be quite useful in the future. Therefore it is important to learn now, as a student, how to deal with it. So, as an alternative to the above scenario, you might want to make a number of file folders labeled by subject topics (analog, batteries, filters, memories, programs). When a trade magazine comes, scan it quickly, tear out and file the useful articles, and throw out the remainder of the magazine. Later on, when you need to locate specific information about batteries, for example, pull the "batteries" file and see what you have. After a year or two, you have an impressive selection of useful material that can get you moving on new projects. *This works.*

4.1.2 Product Design Information

In addition to collecting various magazine articles, you should also gather specific information on design with specific products. Manufacturers of components provide not only data manuals (which you should always keep), but also application notes (AN's) explaining how you can design with their products. These "ap-notes" can save you from reinventing the wheel (i.e., spending a lot of time working out something that's been done before) and can help you keep a project moving. File them in a folder by manufacturer or by topic with magazine articles.

For example, suppose you need to design an analog data-collection system. You look in your "analog" folder and find Motorola's AN900, which is "Using the M6805 Family On-Chip 8-bit A/D Converter." The note includes a description of analog-to-digital converters, the circuit for a temperature-measurement system, program listings, and 6805 microcomputer information. Although this ap-note is specific to a particular situation, you can benefit greatly by examining it closely: it might give you a new perspective on how to approach your data-collection project.

4.1.3 Laboratory Notebook

The laboratory notebook is your workbook in which you record the tasks you do each day. All your ideas and thoughts on your project should be included in it, beginning with the project concept, through the written proposal, and ending with the final report. Consider it your primary "idea book" in which you write down everything that seems even remotely useful.

Physically, your lab book should be a bound notebook with consecutively numbered pages; it should not be a loose-leaf notebook, because pages can be removed and easily lost. Allow several pages at the beginning for a table of contents. All writing should be in ink rather than in pencil; date each page as you use it. Never tear out pages or obliterate any material. If you make an error, never erase it or blank it out: cross it out with a line and place the correct information beside the error. If a whole page is in error, put a large "X" through the page. Later, when you review your notes, you can see your errors and perhaps avoid making the same kind of mistake again.

Your lab notebook should be neat. In the interest of neatness, though, never write down information on a scrap piece of paper with the idea of copying it later into your lab book. Loose paper gets lost easily; even if not lost, copying into the lab book might introduce errors. The lab book must always contain original data.

Roughly speaking, there are two basic approaches to lab notebooks: a strictly "legal" version and a relaxed "comfortable" version.

The *legal* version is a lab book written so that it can be used in a court of law to establish your claim to patent rights. This means that you scrupulously record every detail of your work in the book and afterwards have a knowledgeable colleague witness and sign your notebook pages with you. Leave no blank pages, and never go back and add material to pages already witnessed. Your lab book is evidence if you ever need to prove in court when you first worked on an invention.

The *comfortable* version is a lab book written without excessive concern for all the legal details. Of course, you should still write all your work in the lab book, but you might find it more convenient to use just the right-hand pages. Save the left-hand pages for graphs, for equations you might want to find easily, or for various marginal notes to yourself. You might also find the left-hand pages useful for rough sketches of ideas to check into later during the project.

Whether you use a strictly legal notebook or something less formal depends on the nature of your work and the policies of your school or employer.

Figure 4.1 illustrates a typical page of an informal lab notebook. The circuit shown is just one of many modules in a large system, so there are a number of signals that refer to other pages in the lab book. Using a ruler helps make the circuit appear neat; as changes get made, though, the drawing gets somewhat cluttered. This drawing was also used to wire a prototype: as each wire was connected, a yellow highlight pen was drawn over the diagram to indicate a complete circuit. The assignment of gate pin numbers was made for convenience while wiring.

You might find it helpful to tape photocopies of manufacturers' data sheets into your lab book so you can refer to the information easily. Besides, you might need to use your lab book several years later when you do a similar design; by that time, the data manual you used originally might be replaced, lost, or changed. Your lab book should be as complete a record as possible of all that goes into your design; it should be able to stand alone.

If you find a technical article that is especially relevant to the lab work you are doing, tape it into your lab book for easy reference. Be sure to note its bibliographic information and where you found it. Generally, however, you will find it more helpful to collect relevant articles and file them by topic rather than putting them into the lab book. Depending on the nature and size of your project, you might want to keep the lab book and article files together and not mix the articles in with any others you might be saving in your information files.

The organization you follow when you actually enter information in your lab book depends on the nature of the problem. If you have a short "experiment" to perform, you will find the outline shown in Table 4.1 helpful. Notice that it follows the pattern of problem solving presented earlier. Does it make sense to use Table 4.1 for a large experiment that might take weeks to complete? Yes, because with a sizable job, it is easy to lose sight of your objectives and to waste time working on some minor detail. As with any design work, the outline is only a guide, and it should be modified to fit your particular situation.

If you begin your lab book with the original project concept and thoughts leading up to the proposal, then you will be able to focus quite clearly on your objectives. Break up a large project into manageable tasks, work each task as shown in Table 4.1, then write a short summary for each task as you complete it. Each of these summaries can be used later as part of your progress reports or as part of the final project report.

In addition to the table of contents at the beginning of the lab book, you might want to prepare an index. As you work, you gradually fill more and more lab books, and it becomes increasingly difficult to locate information. Rather than search through every page in all your lab books, a short index at the end of each could be quite a help in finding what you *know* you wrote.

Keeping your lab book neat and complete takes time. However, that time is well spent. In addition to its value as a record of your designs and data, it is your daily idea book of useful information.

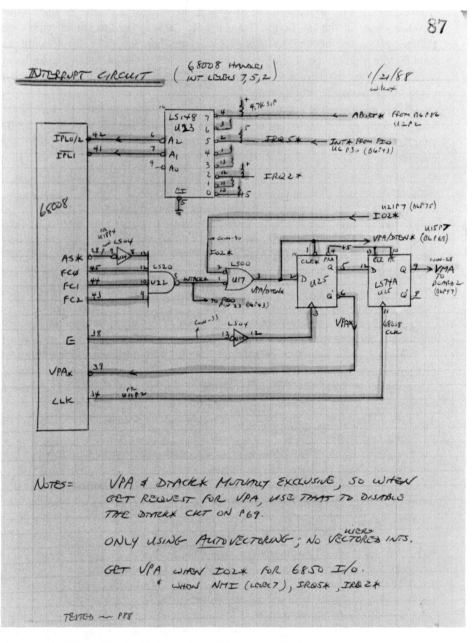

Figure 4.1 A typical page from a laboratory notebook.

TABLE 4.1 AN OUTLINE OF A TYPICAL LABORATORY EXPERIMENT.

Problem Statement	Briefly state an overview of what you are trying to accomplish. What is the problem or purpose of the experiment. Significance?
Objectives	List specific measurable outcomes of your experiment.
Background	Outline of relevant theory or practice. Include references for sources of information.
	Relate present problem to past work.
	Do an analysis of the present problem. (Do diagrams, equations, derivations, simulations.)
	What results are expected? (The analysis should give preliminary answers to each of your objectives stated above.)
Experiment Design	Plan how to obtain the data necessary to verify or disprove your analysis.
	Sketch equipment configuration and test circuits you need to attain each objective above.
Experiment	For each objective, connect equipment in accordance with your plan and make measurements and observations. Put your data in tables if appropriate.
	Note the model and serial number of the equipment you actually use for the experiment in case you need to verify data or expand the scope of your experiment later.
Evaluate Results	Analyze the data collected. What does the data indicate? Plot graphs of data if appropriate. Are there interrelations that explain what happened?
	For each objective, interpret the results and compare with the expected results. Why are there any differences between actual and expected?
Conclusions	What is your answer to the original problem?

4.1.4 Daily Log

When you work on a project, you need to attend meetings, contact various vendors, and talk to people inside and outside your school or your company. Keep a daily log of all this activity. A simple spiral-bound notebook will do fine.

On the left-hand page, jot down a list of "things to do"; on the right-hand page, make an entry for each phone call you made, meeting you attended, or action you took. For calls, write the date, telephone number, person contacted, topics discussed, and decisions arrived at. If you need to take further action, put the task on the left-hand sheet; later, you can scan the left sheets and make sure all the loose ends are accounted for. For meetings, make only brief dated notes that you were at a certain meeting; if you need details, you can refer to your regular meeting notes.

There are several reasons for a daily log. The most important is to keep track of what you've been doing and commitments made. Forgetting to do some particular task might not be in your best interest! You also need to make periodic progress reports; the log provides the information when you write your report. Another reason is that the contacts you make (name and phone number) can be forgotten or lost easily; after a month of working a project, you can quickly forget the name of the person you spoke to several weeks earlier about your stock of formgates.[1]

A personal reason for a daily log is your own career progress. Review what happened during each month and summarize your work (what you accomplished, what you learned). The daily log provides the raw data for you to quickly recall the month's activities. By reflecting on the work completed, you can watch your career unfold and make corrections as needed.

4.2 WRITTEN REPORTS

In industry, there are a host of different reports and papers you will write during the course of a project. The material in this section represents some of the most important that you might need to consider. Assuming that you have identified some customer needs and have written tentative specifications, a feasibility study will help you and your company decide whether you should go forward with a project. Then, if the project appears feasible, you might need to prepare a proposal to management or to an outside sponsor for funding. A periodic progress report is normally expected to help management monitor the project. Depending on the nature of the project, you might need to write a design report documenting your project. Finally, you might be required to prepare a technical manual for customer use.

4.2.1 Feasibility Study

After you recognize a problem or identify a customer's needs, you will probably outline a plan or design to meet those needs. But before you get involved in a lengthy design project, you should find out whether the project is even *worth* doing by making a feasibility study. The purpose of the feasibility study is to assess the economic and social value of a proposed venture and its probability of success.

A feasibility study is an analysis of a particular problem, the evaluation of alternatives, and the selection of the most reasonable solution. To help make a decision among various possible options, you need to consider not only whether you can technically build a product, but also whether your company can sell it at a competitive price and still make a profit. In addition, a large study might involve a recommendation to add more factory workers; you need to consider the social price if the plan goes astray and your company has a major layoff.

For the discussion here, assume that the feasibility study is to help your company decide whether to manufacture a particular product. Consequently, you will write a feasibility report to management. To do this, review the problem-solving steps presented in Chapter 1:

- Analysis of Problem
- Synthesis of Possible Solutions

---

[1]A *formgate* is like the ubiquitous *widget*, but was coined by your author.

- Evaluation of Alternatives
- Decision
- Action

Compare these general steps with the feasibility study outline shown in Table 4.2. Notice that the study is nothing more than applied problem solving! But now your perspective is global, because you need to consider more than just engineering issues.

TABLE 4.2   AN OUTLINE OF THE MAJOR SECTIONS OF A PROJECT FEASIBILITY STUDY

Executive Summary	Overview of the project and recommended course of action.
Project Statement	Concise statement of the project. Background of the problem showing why the project is necessary.
Market Analysis	Description of the marketplace: past, present, and future supply and demand. Does market exist or can it be developed? Evaluate all alternatives.
Technical Analysis	Description of project and how to do it; is it technically possible? Availability of the required facilities, equipment, labor, and material. What are the major technical problems? Evaluate all alternatives.
Financial Analysis	Projected sales, income statement, balance sheet, cash flow. What investment is required? Is it affordable? Risks and expected return on investment. Will the project be profitable? Evaluate all alternatives.
Social Analysis	What are costs and benefits to environment? Jobs created or lost? Evaluate all alternatives.
Recommendations	Proposed course of action and rationale. Consequences of action and assessment of how well the action will solve the original problem.
Implementation	Objectives, strategy, and plan of action. Schedule of required tasks and responsibilities for action.

After a brief executive summary of the project, the feasibility study begins with a general statement of the problem or project. Next, market, technical, financial, and social aspects are considered; each of these sections individually examines the problem, possible solutions, and the reasonable alternatives. Finally, the decision or recommendations you make are based on how you weigh each of the market, technical, financial, and social factors. If you conclude that the project is feasible, then finish the feasibility study with a discussion on how to implement your recommendation.

4.2.2 Proposal

After you write the complete feasibility study and decide to design and manufacture your product, the next step might be to write a proposal. Basically, a proposal is just a request for financial support so you can carry out your project. If the proposal is to your own management, a simplified proposal such as the one in Table 1.3 will probably be quite adequate. Although it does not get into the background issues leading up to the project, it does define the project and explain how to reach the objectives.

On the other hand, suppose that you need a proposal to obtain the support of a customer? In such a case, you will need to write a sales proposal; its purpose is to convince the customer that you have a product or service that solves a particular problem. Therefore, a sales proposal must be persuasive. The proposal should lead to either acceptance of your offer or at least to an opportunity for you to make a sales presentation to the customer. Start with an attention-getter, an overview, and benefits to the buyer. Explain the work or product you propose, how and when to complete the tasks, and the costs involved. Finish with a persuasive summary.

If your proposal is directed toward the government and seeks support for research, the format is much more structured. The exact style depends on the nature of the proposal and the specific requirements of the funding agency.

The outline shown in Table 4.3 provides a basic framework for a proposal that could be submitted to either a customer or to a government agency. You might also have to make separate sections on reports, your company and facilities, and references. Compare the proposal outline with the project planning steps in Chapter 1.

TABLE 4.3 AN OUTLINE OF A TYPICAL PROPOSAL

Overview	Purpose of the project, technical approach, significance, benefits.
Problem Statement	Statement of what is proposed.
Background	What caused the problem, its significance, and why a solution is necessary. Prior work done and how the proposed work will solve the problem.
Project Objectives	Scope of work: objectives for the project, the required product specifications, limitations, and assumptions.
Strategy	Concept of the approach to reach each of the objectives. Details of the proposed work.
Plan of Action	List of all tasks to carry out the strategy, all scheduled completion dates, who is responsible for each. Chart of project schedule with expected delivery dates.
Results	Description of how to report progress, how to document results, and how to verify that the project objectives were met.
Budget	Estimate of costs and investment for personnel, facilities, and equipment. Method and timing of payments.
Personnel	Qualifications of key personnel involved in the project.

4.2.3 Progress Report

A progress report or status report is normally made every week or month to help your manager monitor your project. It is, as outlined in Table 4.4, a report that tells where you are in your project, what you completed, and where you go next. You should attach a copy of your bar-chart schedule to the report and mark the progress of each task.

In addition to your schedule, you might want to attach documentation on key design issues or discoveries you made since the last report. This information might be useful for other team members or for future work by others. Be sure to note where

TABLE 4.4   AN OUTLINE OF A PROGRESS REPORT

Current Status	What is the situation now?
Work Completed	What work has been done since the last report?
Current Work	What is being done now?
Future Work	What is planned next?

additional information can be found; for example, give the page numbers where information can be obtained in a certain lab book.

If some aspect of your project is in trouble, it should be mentioned in your progress report. For example, if some component critical to construction of a prototype assembly is missing and will be delayed a month, your manager needs to know; perhaps the part can be expedited or a substitute located for you. Reporting bad news is no fun, but risking a disaster on your own is worse.

You might have responsibility for more than one project. When you write multiple progress reports, indicate how much time you applied to each project. Your company accountant probably already requires you to report time spent on each project, but your manager should not have to search in other documents to see how your time was spent.

Finally, when you write a progress report and have no visible "progress" toward task completion, what can you report? It may be that preparatory work took more time than expected; it still had to be done though, and doing it does represent progress. Thus, you report on work being done, even if it seems somewhat unexciting until you finish a task or two.

4.2.4 Engineering Design Report

Depending on the nature of your project, you might need to write an engineering design report. The purpose of the report is to tell your manager or the customer what work you have completed. It documents your design project and explains the rationale supporting your engineering decisions.

Table 4.5 shows an outline of a typical engineering report. The details of what you should include in your engineering report depend, as always, on your intended reader and the purpose for the report. As presented here, the outline can be used to tell your manager how you approached your design project and why you made certain decisions. Documenting the reasoning behind your decisions is especially important: you or someone else might need to address similar problems in the future.

4.2.5 Technical Manual

A technical manual is similar to an engineering design report in that it completely documents your design project. It does not, however, explain the rationale supporting your engineering decisions that led to the finished product. Its purpose is to provide the customer with enough information to set up, use, and fix your product easily.

TABLE 4.5   AN OUTLINE OF A TYPICAL ENGINEERING REPORT

Abstract	Concise summary of the essential points in report: purpose or problem, method, results, conclusions, recommendations.
Introduction	Background, problem or need, purpose of report, overview.
Methodology	Engineering design, construction, operation.
Results	Results of the engineering. Compare with expected results.
Conclusions	Interpret the results; what does it all mean?
Recommendations	Based on engineering so far, where to go next?

When you write a technical manual, design it so that the reader can use it efficiently. If the material is arranged logically and facts can be found easily, then your manual will be effective and helpful. Remember that your reader probably has no previous experience with your product, and points that are obvious to you might be quite obscure to someone else.

As shown in Table 4.6, the complete technical manual contains the information necessary to install, operate, understand, and troubleshoot the product. This information comes from your laboratory notebook and related material. If your lab book was written with short summaries at the end of each major design task, then they can be used in the technical manual with only a little revision.

In Table 4.6 the *introduction* is intended to clarify the rationale behind your product. It presents the nature of the problem addressed and how your product solves the problem. Any relevant background information and how product relates to it should be discussed. Give a brief description of your product including its features and limitations. Your introduction should provide enough information so that a reader can determine if your product will solve his or her particular need.

The *installation* section should provide all the information needed to connect and test your product for proper operation. Sketches are useful to illustrate the equipment setup and to show the settings for any switches and jumpers. Consider the possibility of putting in a very brief "hook-it-up-quickly" section; this is for the reader who skips the instructions unless the product fails to work as expected.

A special section of the installation instructions should cover system checkout. Illustrate several different software and hardware configurations and how the equipment responds for each setup. If the installer has been having difficulty, an indication of correct performance will be quite valuable.

The *operation* section covers all the details of how to use your product. You might find a tutorial section and a reference section helpful in explaining the operation of your system. The tutorial section will aid the inexperienced user by illustrating some practical instructions on each of the product features; the reference section will help the knowledgeable user find needed information quickly. If you are doing a major product, the tutorial and reference sections may easily be separated from the technical manual and used alone by a nontechnical operator. Include a section on how to resolve operating difficulties. For example, if the user makes a single incorrect datum entry, explain how it can be corrected without reentering all the data.

TABLE 4.6 AN OUTLINE OF THE MAJOR SECTIONS OF A TECHNICAL MANUAL

Title Page	Title of project or product, author, date.
Introduction	Purpose of the product: What problem was solved?
	Importance: Background information and how the product relates to prior designs.
	Features: Description of unit and how it solves the problem.
	System Configuration
Installation	Hardware Setup and Requirements
	Equipment Interconnections
	Switch and Jumper Settings
	Location drawing of switches and jumpers
	Function table of switches and jumpers
	Connectors
	Location and assignments
	Table of signals at each connector
	Software Organization and Requirements
	Memory Map
	I/O Map
	System Checkout Instructions
Operation	Operating Instructions
	Operating Difficulties (How to Resolve)
Circuit Description	Theory of Hardware Operation
	Block diagram of system and modules
	Explanation of functional modules
	Timing diagrams
Software Description	Theory of Software Operation
	Structure Chart of System
	Description of Algorithms
	Flowcharts
Troubleshooting	Explanation of How to Troubleshoot Product
	Chart of symptoms and possible causes
	Sample hardware and software test-data readings
References	Documents Related to the Product
Appendix	Specifications
	Schematic Diagram
	Component Layout
	Jumper and Switch Index
	Parts List
	Data on LSI Devices
	Program Listings

    The *circuit description* section explains all the technical aspects of your hardware. After an overview of the product, present a block diagram of the system and its division into various functional modules. Show each of the modules individually and explain how each operates. If appropriate, include timing diagrams and segments of the circuit diagram to help the reader understand the design. By explaining the hardware design in detail, the technical reader can repair the equipment himself or herself rather than send it back to the manufacturer if service is required.

The *software description* presents the system programs and how they work together with the hardware. A program structure chart, or a flowchart equivalent, can help the reader understand system functions easily. Include a description of the algorithms and their flowcharts as necessary. By providing these details, the user can correct any software bugs and keep the system running. Depending on the reader and the nature of the system, you might include program listings in the appendix of your manual.

The *troubleshooting* portion of your technical manual is also intended to help the technical reader repair your product. The most helpful information you can give is a chart describing various symptoms of hardware and software malfunctions. For each of the symptoms, give a list of several possible causes and how to fix them. Keep it brief: a checklist at the workbench is far more valuable than page upon page of theory. Show several test setups, and give a number of typical voltage and oscilloscope patterns at critical points.

Much of the troubleshooting outline can come from your own experience in getting the prototype working properly. You probably already know which parts are critical and what the symptoms are if they fail. Additional information can be gathered for high-risk parts by replacing a good part with a defective one and noting the effect on the product. Open some critical circuits or cause some shorts in signal paths for additional troubleshooting data. If your system uses a microprocessor, include diagnostic programs to test various modules such as memory, I/O, and any external devices connected to the system.

TABLE 4.7 A SAMPLE OUTLINE OF A SOFTWARE DOCUMENTATION PACKAGE

Problem Statement	Concise statement of the problem. Include a description of input variables required and outputs that will be provided by program.
Program Description	Overview: The approach to the problem's solution. Describe the strategy used to solve the problem. Include equations.
	Assumptions: What assumptions were made about the problem or the solution method?
	Variable List: Include list of names and descriptions of each of the input, process, and output variables.
	Data Structures: Sketch how the data is represented. This might be on several levels of abstraction: the problem level, the system level, and the machine level.
	Limitations: What parts of the problem are not programmed completely? How does the program handle undesired events such as out-of-range data or system faults? Areas that need more design in the future?
Program Design	Structure Chart: Describe the overall plan of how the program is constructed.
	Algorithms: Use pseudo-design language (PDL) to describe how the program works.
	Flow Chart: Illustrate portions of the program with a simple flow chart.
Program Listing	Provide a complete listing of the program. The program should be internally documented and start with a heading containing the name and function of the program, your name, and the date. Include comments to explain each major section of code. Tell how to compile and link all the program modules together.
Test Data and Results	Provide sample output that will illustrate correct operation of the program for normal and abnormal inputs. Include test data verifying the program at its design limits.

The *references* section cites all the documents related to your product. The idea is for the reader to know what other material must be included with the design manual for a complete documentation package. You may also want to cite reference articles or tutorials for the reader to study.

The *appendix* includes all the charts, tables, diagrams, programs, and background material related to your design. It is a collection of vital information required to describe and completely build your product.

When you assemble the technical manual, you can easily delete the software details and put them in a separate document. An outline of a typical software documentation package is shown in Table 4.7. For many products, it is convenient to give a brief explanation of the software in general and then to refer the reader to a software manual. Because software tends to be updated with new revisions more frequently than hardware, a separate manual is easier to keep in order. This is especially true in a large project in which different groups of designers are responsible for hardware and software.

4.3 ORAL REPORTS

In addition to the diverse written reports that you will prepare, you can also expect to make oral presentations quite frequently. Most often, these will be simple unrehearsed progress reports given to your manager and your fellow project engineers. At other times, however, you will need to speak to upper management or customers, and it will be essential that you come fully prepared.

Table 4.8 lists a checklist of issues that you should consider when you need to make an oral report. As you start to prepare a talk, you should find out as much as you can about your audience and why you need to make a presentation for them. Are you informing them about a situation or persuading them to buy or fund a project you would like to pursue? These facts should dictate how you organize the various topics and supporting material.

After you have the topics outlined, sketch visual aids that can help illustrate your ideas. Ask yourself which might be most suitable in your talk: transparencies, movies, videotape, posters, or actual equipment. Transparencies for an overhead projector are convenient, quick, and they have a bonus: you can put notes to yourself on the margin.

Avoid trying to *read* a presentation; be natural and conversational when you speak. Note cards work, but only if you stick to simple keywords that help you remember your topic sequence. You should, however, have a solid well-practiced introduction that puts everything in perspective for your audience. Similarly, your closing should summarize all the main points and conclude with your recommendation if appropriate.

Being nervous before a presentation is normal. The best remedy is knowing your material. You have an advantage in that regard: you know more about your topic than anyone else or you would not have been selected to speak. Rehearse your talk, be sure you can operate the equipment, and investigate the room where you will speak. Finally,

TABLE 4.8 PREPARATION FOR PRESENTATIONS

Audience Analysis	Who is the audience? What do they already know about the topic? What do they need to find out?
Purpose	Why give the talk? Inform or persuade? What is the main point?
Outline	Plan topics and support for each. Organize topics logically.
Visual Aids	Prepare illustrations.
Notes	Put keywords on cards or on margin of transparencies.
Introduction	Orient the audience to the problem or issue; give needed background.
Closing	Summary and recommendations.
Rehearsal	Practice; do full dress rehearsal.
Equipment	Know equipment; have it ready.

TABLE 4.9 PRESENTATION CRITERIA

Introduction	Tell audience what to expect, how talk is organized. Purpose clear?
Topic Ordering	Are topics in logical sequence?
Topic Explanation	Are topics explained well?
Closing Summary	Closing summarizes points well?
Purpose Accomplished?	Is audience informed or persuaded?
Correctness	Facts and theory correct?
Visual Aids	Appropriate, well executed?
Timing	Presentation within time limit?

when you do address your audience, remember they are listening for a reason; if you concentrate on their needs, then the presentation will be successful.

Criteria that you can use to rate your presentation are shown in Table 4.9. When you rehearse, have a friend comment on each point. Did you introduce your subject well? Did you order your topics in a logical sequence and explain them adequately? Did your closing statements bring the whole presentation together and succesfully accomplish the purpose of the talk? Did you have all your facts right? Did the visual aids get the ideas across effectively? Did you stay within your allocated time limit?

During your presentation, you should maintain eye contact with the audience. A professional appearance can help instill audience confidence in you and make the presentation much easier. Your interest in the subject, plus your enthusiasm for what you have to say, can help the audience get involved and interested too.

4.4 SUMMARY

Engineering involves more than designing a product that satisfies customer needs. Documentation and communication are both essential to build not only the first prototype, but also to manufacture production quantities. In addition, without good documentation and communication, the customer cannot effectively use your product and will not be likely to purchase again.

Successful project documentation and communication requires you to consider your audience and why they should read or hear your message. Are you communicating with your company management, the customer, or both? Is your purpose to inform or to persuade?

Basic project documentation is composed of the notes you make and raw data you collect. These are, for example, information files, product design information, laboratory notebooks, and your daily log. Although this material generally stays with you, it forms the basis for a number of written and oral reports you will make.

The feasibility study, proposal, progress report, engineering design report, and technical manual are some of the most important documents you might need to write. The feasibility study can help your company make an informed decision on whether to start a project. Then, if the project looks viable, you might write a proposal to obtain funding for the job. A progress or status report is usually expected so that management can monitor how well the project is progressing. Finally, an engineering design report or a technical manual provides overall documentation of the finished task.

Oral presentations, both informal and formal, are quite commonplace. Your topic might be related to any of the written documents already prepared during a project: the oral presentation is your chance to explain what you did. Be prepared! Your written work might be excellent and show great technical insight, but if you come across poorly in an oral presentation, it throws your writing into question. In fact, a poorly prepared presentation or two can put your professional credibility in jeopardy as well.

FURTHER READING

ALLEY, MICHAEL. *The Craft of Scientific Writing.* Englewood Cliffs, NJ: Prentice Hall, 1987. (T11.A37)

BROWNING, CHRISTINE. *Guide to Effective Software Technical Writing.* Englewood Cliffs, NJ: Prentice Hall, 1984. (QA 76.9.D6B76)

CLIFTON, DAVID S., JR. and DAVID E. FYFFE. *Project Feasibility Analysis.* New York: John Wiley & Sons, 1977. (HD 47.5.C57)

MALI, PAUL, and RICHARD W. SYKES. *Writing and Word Processing for Engineers and Scientists.* New York: McGraw-Hill, 1985. (T11.M335)

MIDDENDORF, WILLIAM H. *Design of Devices and Systems.* New York: Marcel Dekker, Inc., 1986. (TA 174.M529)

OLSEN, LESLIE A., and THOMAS N. HUCKIN. *Principles of Communication for Science and Technology.* New York: McGraw-Hill, 1983. (T11.O54)

RATHBONE, ROBERT R. *Communicating Technical Information.* 2nd ed. Reading, MA: Addison-Wesley, 1985. (PE 1475.R37)

ROSENBURG, RONALD C. "The Engineering Presentation—Some Ideas on How to Approach and Present It." *IEEE Transactions on Professional Communication,* Vol. PC-26, No. 4, pp. 191-193, Dec. 1983.

SHERMAN, THEODORE A., and SIMON S. JOHNSON. *Modern Technical Writing.* 4th ed. Englewood Cliffs, NJ: Prentice Hall, 1983. (T11.S52)

WEISS, EDMOND H. *How to Write a Usable User Manual.* Philadelphia: ISI Press, 1985. (QA 76.165.W45)

WEISS, EDMOND H. *The Writing System for Engineers and Scientists.* Englewood Cliffs, NJ: Prentice Hall, 1982. (T11.W44)

5

DIGITAL MODULE
Temperature Monitor
Clock Board

Alan D. Wilcox
Micro Resources Company

INTRODUCTION

The purpose of this digital module is to illustrate digital design by examining two specific projects. Each project is typical of design work you can finish in a single semester as an undergraduate engineering student.

The first project, a temperature monitor, is a combination of analog and digital electronics. The project emphasizes identifying the customer needs and planning the tasks so everything can be completed in 4 weeks. The design culminates in a technical manual that describes the product and how to use it.

The second project, a clock board for a computer system, is primarily digital. In contrast with the temperature monitor, it concentrates more heavily on project implementation than on project planning. It illustrates how a successful design can be easily completed using the specifications in an industry standard.

SUGGESTED PROJECT TOPICS

Many digital projects can be done in conjunction with a small computer for data collection, display, or control. In the following list of project topics, consider how you might combine digital logic with some type of computing system.

- Speech synthesizer
- Melody generator
- Temperature controller
- Morse code generator
- Morse code receiver and character display
- Logic gate tester
- Stepper motor controller
- Programmable power supply
- EPROM programmer
- Digital filter
- Programmable frequency or function generator
- Tachometer
- Light intensity meter and controller
- Electronic lock system
- Elapsed-time meter
- Telephone dialer
- DTMF tone generator and decoder
- Parallel-serial converter (or vice versa)
- FIFO interface to computer system
- Data modem
- Digital DC voltmeter or ammeter
- Digital RMS voltmeter

EXAMPLE PROJECT: TEMPERATURE MONITOR ————————

The purpose of this module is to unify the design sequence from need identification
through documentation. Parts of this material appeared in Chapters 1 and 2; they
appear here in their normal chronology and culminate in a technical manual describing
the final product.

In this project, assume that you are a design engineer at an electronics company;
there is no company policy against your doing an occasional moonlight job. The temperature monitor project does not involve the ''formality'' of reports to management or
involved budgets. In fact, the customer wil pay for the parts you need as you go; at the
end of the project you expect only nominal compensation for your efforts (and perhaps a
tank or two of oil!)

NEED IDENTIFICATION

During the winter, fuel-oil distributors make customer deliveries based on how cold the weather has been rather than on a weekly or biweekly basis. Needless deliveries increase costs, so it is desirable to wait until the customer's tank is almost empty before refilling it. Ideally, a typical 275-gallon tank should be refilled when it gets to within 20 to 50 gallons of becoming empty.

Hot-Spot Oil Co. presently estimates a "k-factor" for each customer to help decide when to deliver oil. The k-factor is an empirical number of degree-days of heating the customer gets from each gallon of oil. Heating degree-days equal 65 minus the average temperature during 24 hours; thus, if the average temperature yesterday was 20°F, then 45 degree-days of heating were required. Suppose Hot-Spot estimated Jack Smith's house at $k = 5$ degree-days per gallon: the 45 degree-days of heat required yesterday used 45/5 or 9 gallons of oil.

So if Hot-Spot Oil can keep data on daily heating degree-days, then they can estimate how much oil each customer will use. If Jack Smith has a 275-gallon tank, then that means he can heat for a maximum of 275 times 5, or 1375 degree-days. If each day averages 20°F, then Jack will run out of oil in about 30 days (1375/45 = 30+). To be on the safe side, Hot-Spot will probably deliver about 5 days before Jack is likely to run out of oil. This is equivalent to about 1100 degree-days accumulated since the last delivery.

The owner of Hot-Spot Oil came to you recently, and you both worked out an automatic way to calculate yesterday's number of degree-days. It appears that he needs a device that will monitor the outside temperature, calculate degree-days, and print a paper tape indicating the latest 24-hour cumulative degree-days. Every morning the paper tape can be checked and its answer added to the degree-days accumulated for each customer since fillup. Then, when a customer's total reaches a certain threshold, say 1100 as above, it is time to make an oil delivery to that customer.

PROJECT PLAN

Sketch a plan for the project in your lab notebook. Based on your discussions with the customer, you decided on a product concept and some preliminary specifications. The monitor should measure temperature from −40 to +70°F, calculate the average temperature over the most-recent 24 hours, calculate the degree-days, and print the results on a paper tape.

Begin outlining the major parts of a proposal in your lab notebook. The idea is to get your thinking down on paper so you can plan for a successful project and write a proposal to the customer. In this case, the proposal should be submitted to the customer after you do some prototyping.

PROJECT DEFINITION.   My project is to design, build, and test a meter that I can use to measure and record air temperature.

PROJECT OBJECTIVES

- Measures temperature from -40 to $+70°F$ (maybe higher)
- Accuracy within 1°F
- Displays in either Fahrenheit or Celsius
- Displays minimum and maximum temperatures in last 24 hours
- Calculates and displays daily heating degree-days
- Prints on a paper tape the daily degree-days

PROJECT CONSTRAINTS

- Should cost less than $150 for parts
- Must be built and tested before the heating season

STRATEGY.   To attain my objectives, I will build a prototype model of the analog circuitry with the temperature sensor on a solderless breadboard. Once I understand how it should work, I will add an analog to digital converter plus an interface to a microcomputer board. The microcomputer should be able to handle all the calculations and display functions. After I have it working properly, I will make a prototype printed-circuit board for the customer.

PLAN OF ACTION

1. Get a breadboard and power supply for the prototype
2. Look for articles and designs on temperature measurement
3. Select a temperature sensor and A/D converter
4. Sketch a tentative circuit and calculate circuit values
5. Build the analog circuit and take measurements
6. Connect the analog circuit to the A/D converter
7. Test the circuit for proper performance
8. Design the microcomputer interface logic
9. Connect the microcomputer and test the interface
10. Write a simple program to read the temperature
11. Write the remaining programs for degree-days and printer

The schedule I must follow to complete the project before winter looks like this so far:

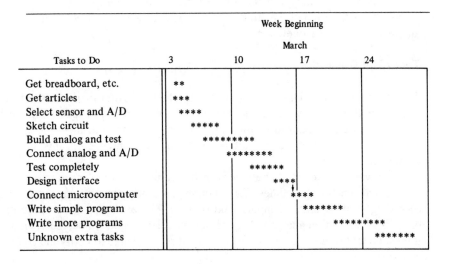

| | Week Beginning | | | |
| | | March | | |
Tasks to Do	3	10	17	24
Get breadboard, etc.	**			
Get articles	***			
Select sensor and A/D	****			
Sketch circuit	*****			
Build analog and test	*********			
Connect analog and A/D	********			
Test completely	******			
Design interface	****			
Connect microcomputer	****			
Write simple program	*******			
Write more programs	*********			
Unknown extra tasks	*******			

PROJECT IMPLEMENTATION

Before you get to this point, you should complete the need analysis and then synthesize several potential design alternatives. (Refer to Chapter 2, Sections 2.2 and 2.3 for additional information.) Once you have a reasonable design concept selected, draw its block diagram as in Figure 5.1 and begin the project implementation.

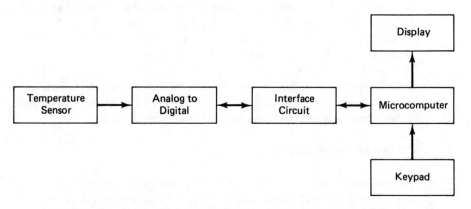

Figure 5.1 Block diagram of the temperature-measurement system. The diagram is a result of partitioning the design into functional modules.

The project implementation involves two major steps: the technical design and the construction of a prototype model of the circuit. The technical design is when you do a complete paper design of the project; the construction phase is when you build a first unit and test it for proper operation.

Technical Design

The technical design phase begins with the block diagram of the desired system and finishes with the hardware and software description of the product. The design is on paper in sufficient detail to predict how well the product will meet the specifications. For this reason, all your circuit designs and computer programs must be well-documented.

As you draw each of the blocks in the system, you are in effect partitioning the system into functional modules. Each module has a purpose, and you should define each according to its operation, inputs, and outputs. For example, the purpose of the A/D block is to convert an analog voltage to an equivalent digital value. To operate properly, it must be told when to do a conversion, and it must be able to notify the computer when it finishes.

When you partition the system into modules, you actually imply a tradeoff between hardware and software. According to the product concept, the temperature monitor will acquire data and pass it without modification to the computer. If any corrections must be made, to compensate for nonlinearities in a thermocouple for example, the solution must implement them in software. Another concept for solving the measurement problem might have done the compensation in hardware before the A/D converter. Consider the various tradeoffs as you review the design.

Once you have all the modules roughly sketched, then you can design the detailed circuit. The hardware design at this point is completed to the final circuit with all the components and their interconnections shown in detail. Actual parts should be selected and fully documented. The design sould be in accordance with any design rules that have been set for the project. The software design is also done in like detail from the top-level functions down to flow charts and code if possible.

As you design the hardware and software, watch that they parallel one another in their development. Although shown in Figure 2.3 as separate activities, hardware and software design are done concurrently if possible. This is because they must work together when both are integrated into the final system.

Prototype Construction

The purpose of building a prototype is to demonstrate that your paper design is correct and to reveal any oversights that might hinder the product's performance. You can easily use your completed prototype in a number of different experiments to adjust the design and verify its performance.

When you build your prototype, build it module by module. This holds whether you use wire-wrap, a prototype board, or solder for your actual construction. Hardware can be constructed and tested one module at a time just as you might write a computer program one module at a time. The reasoning is this: if you build one small module, apply power, and test it fully for proper operation, then you can use it as part of a larger subsequent module. If any problems develop with the larger module, then you know the difficulty is probably in the circuit you just added. This modular approach to building and testing hardware is far easier than wiring the entire circuit and then trying to diagnose an elusive malfunction in the system.

DOCUMENTATION

Proposal

When you first started the sketch of the project plan in your lab notebook, you outlined the major parts of a project proposal. The purpose of the proposal is to communicate a definition of the project, its objectives, and the strategy for meeting those objectives; then it details the plan of action with the schedule for completion. In all likelihood, it seeks to convince someone that the project is worth pursuing. The following small proposal to Hot-Spot Oil does all of this.

The proposal should be written after enough work has been done so that you can write with some authority on the project. In the Hot-Spot project, you might need to breadboard only enough to convince yourself that the project is in fact well-conceived and worth undertaking. For many large government and industry proposals, a prototype might be built and tested *before* the proposal is written.

PROPOSAL
Temperature Monitor

Project definition:	The goal of this project is to design, build, and test a meter that can be used to measure and record air temperature.
Project objectives:	At the end of four weeks, the temperature monitor will be completely built and tested. It will perform to these specifications:
	Temperature range of -40 to $100°C$
	Accurate within $1°C$
	Display either Fahrenheit or Celsius temperature
	Display minimum and maximum temperatures during last 24 hours
	Calculate and display 24-hour average temperature
	Calculate and display heating degree days
	In addition to these performance requirements, the meter will be portable and capable of battery operation. Parts for the prototype will cost less than $150.
Strategy for achieving objectives:	The analog circuitry and temperature sensor will be prototyped on a temporary breadboard. An analog-to-digital converter plus interface circuit will be added to allow the unit to work with a microcomputer system. After the temperature is being properly read by the computer, a number of display and calculation programs will be written.
Plan of action:	The various tasks needed to implement the strategy are as follows:

Get prototype breadboard and power supply
Look for articles and designs on temperature measurement
Select temperature sensor and A/D converter
Sketch tentative circuit and calculate circuit values
Build analog circuit and take measurements
Connect analog circuit to the A/D converter
Test the circuit completely
Design the microcomputer interface logic
Connect microcomputer and test interface
Write simple program to read temperature
Programs and tasks I cannot estimate now

The schedule necessary to finish the project in the required four weeks is attached.

Reporting: Weekly progress reports will be made. At the end of the project a working prototype will be presented.

Budget: Initial funding of $150 is necessary to purchase the prototype analog parts and the microcomputer.

Evaluation: Verification of how well the prototype meets the design specifications subject to the constraints will be made weekly and at the end of the project. The final evaluation will be conducted by the design engineer and the customer.

Progress Reports

Normally, an oral or written progress report would be given to your engineering manager or project team members; a weekly report is typical. Customer progress reports are less frequent and their form and scope vary widely depending on the customer and contract.

The progress report for Hot-Spot will probably be just a chat on the telephone to indicate that you are moving forward.

If you were making a small written report to your technical manager, however, the progress report might take the form of the following:

PROGRESS REPORT
Temperature Monitor Project-Week 2

Current status: The analog design has been completed and successfully tested. There have been no delays and I am on schedule.

Work completed: During the week since the last report, I completed building and testing the analog circuit. I used the temperature sensor and measured the output of its amplifier and plotted a graph of its response. I connected the A/D converter and tested its performance by varying the temperature sensor voltage.

Current work: During the last day of this week I started work on the interface design. I an now in the middle of connecting it to the microcomputer board.

Future work: During the third week I plan to finish the connection to the microcomputer board and to write a program to test the A/D converter. Then I plan to write a more complex program that will display the temperature in both Celsius and Fahrenheit.

Technical Manual

The project documentation for Hot-Spot may be in the form of a user's manual that tells how to set up and operate the equipment. The customer really has no interest in any of the technical details of the project; if anything goes wrong, you get to respond with the service.

Assume for a moment that the customer is quite knowledgeable technically: you might be required to provide more than just setup and operation instructions. For illustration then, consider the following technical manual directed to a technical reader.

TEMPERATURE MONITOR TECHNICAL MANUAL: ————— HOT-SPOT OIL COMPANY

INTRODUCTION

The purpose of the temperature monitor is to measure and record outside air temperature every hour each day and then calculate heating degree-days over a 24-hour period.

During the heating season it is necessary to know how cold the weather has been each day so that timely oil deliveries can be made. Deliveries made too frequently result in extra driver time and truck mileage as well as extra administrative billing costs. On the other hand, a late delivery can result in delivery driver overtime and in possible loss of customers. If the heating degree-days can be totaled since the last oil delivery, then it is possible to estimate when the next delivery should be made. The temperature monitor provides the basic information needed to make this estimate.

The temperature monitor is a small self-contained unit that can be placed on a desk or other convenient location in the office. A single wire with a temperature sensor on the end is put outside and connected to the monitor. The monitor runs on standard house current, but has an internal battery to retain data in case of power failure. The temperature and degree-days are displayed on the front panel; the time and latest 24-hour cumulative degree-days are printed each hour on a paper tape in the unit.

After setting up the monitor, the paper tape can be checked each morning to see how many heating degree-days were needed during the last 24-hours. This reading can be added to the total degree-days accumulated for each customer since fillup. When the customer total reaches a certain threshold, say 1100 degree-days, it is time to make an oil delivery to that customer.

INSTALLATION

As shown in Figure A, place the temperature monitor in a convenient location where it will be used during normal daily operation. Plug the power cord into a wall socket.

Install the temperature sensor outside in a shaded spot and run the wire into the building to the monitor. Attach it to the connecter on the rear of the unit.

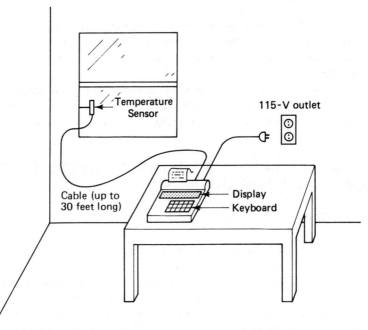

Figure A   Temperature monitor setup for normal operation.

Press the button marked "test" on the front panel. The monitor will check itself and the sensor you just connected. It will display "OK" in several seconds at the end of the test and you can begin normal operation. If you do not get the "OK" display, refer to the Troubleshooting section in this manual.

OPERATION

To begin operation, push the "start" button on the front panel. You will see a display of the present outside temperature. No data will be recorded on the paper tape until after an hour has elapsed. The correct present outside temperature will be displayed continuously.

To set the time, push the "set time" button on the front panel. Press four numbers on the keyboard for the correct time. All time is maintained in 24-hour format; that is, 1:00 PM is 1300, 11:00 PM is 2300, etc. Example entries:

Time is →		Press →	
	7:00 A.M.		0700
	11:35 A.M.		1135
	8:40 P.M.		2040

To set the time at which the data logging is done, press the "start log" button on the front panel. This should be done on the hour if you want your time and degree-day prints recorded on the hour. If you prefer the prints recorded hourly on the half-hour, then press the "start log" button when the time is half-past the hour.

Note that the first day's reading of degree-days will not be correct until 24 hours have passed. After that, the display always shows the correct heating degree-days regardless of when the data log is printed. Every hourly printout will correctly represent the degree-days during the most recent 24 hours.

CIRCUIT DESCRIPTION

The temperature monitor measures the current temperature and continuously displays the temperature and the latest 24-hour heating degree-day summary. Every hour the time and degree-days are printed on a paper tape in the unit. The monitor uses a microcomputer to perform the control of the system and do the various calculations.

The temperature monitor is composed of a number of subsystems as shown in Figure B. The temperature sensor is connected to the analog-to-digital (A/D) converter; the output of the A/D converter is interfaced to the microcomputer itself. The operation of the keypad, display, and paper-tape printer are all controlled by the microcomputer.

The temperature sensor, the analog circuits, and the digital interface control for the A/D converter are shown in the schematic diagram of the unit.

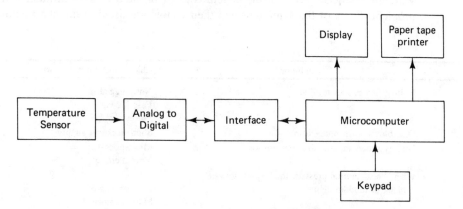

Figure B Block diagram of temperature monitor.

SOFTWARE DESCRIPTION

The temperature monitor software is contained in permanent memory in the microcomputer section. The programs handle all the operations necessary to inialize the unit, to test for proper performance, to set the time, to set the logging time, to read and display temperature, to calculate and display heating degree-days, and to print temperature and degree-days.

The software functions are shown in the structure chart. The temperature monitor software is divided into four main modules: SELF-TEST, SET-TIME, SET-LOG-TIME, and RUN. When the computer is first turned on, the SELF-TEST code should be executed to verify the system operation and to initialize data memory. The SET-TIME module is used to set the system internal time clock. The SET-LOG-TIME module is used to set when each hour the temperature data is printed on the paper tape. The last module, RUN, is used to control the normal system operation.

When the RUN module is executed, the outside temperature is read once each second, averaged over the last 16 seconds, and the average saved in memory. Each hour all these averages are averaged again and used to calculate the hourly degree-days using the formula "degree-days" = 65 − average hourly temperature in Fahrenheit." The most recent hourly degree-days are saved in memory and averaged together to display and record on the paper tape.

TROUBLESHOOTING

The temperature monitor has an internal self-test feature that will indicate the possible cause of various problems. To use, press the "test" button on the front panel; the display will either indicate "OK" if the system is ready or indicate an error number if there is a problem. Some of the symptoms and their causes are listed in the chart below:

Condition	Possible cause/source of error
Nothing happens at turn-on	Not plugged in
	Fuse blown
	Power supply
Fuse blows when plugged in	Short in power supply
Display shows random digits at turn-on	Microprocessor
	Main memory
When "test" button pressed, the display shows . . .	
blank or random digits	Microprocessor
	Main memory
01 (Memory error)	Data memory
02 (No temperature)	Temperature sensor
	Analog amplifier
	A/D converter
03 (Printer)	Printer out of paper

REFERENCES

This manual contains the technical information on the temperature monitor analog and interface circuits. The circuit diagram and parts layouts for both of these subsystems are provided in the appendix to this manual. Information on the microcomputer subsystem and the computer program listings are not provided; they may be obtained from the factory on special order.

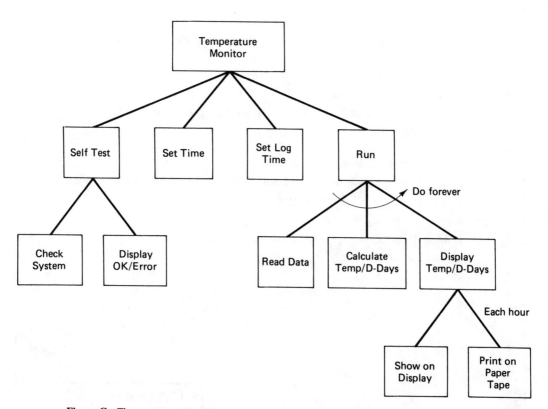

Figure C   The temperature monitor system's software structure chart.

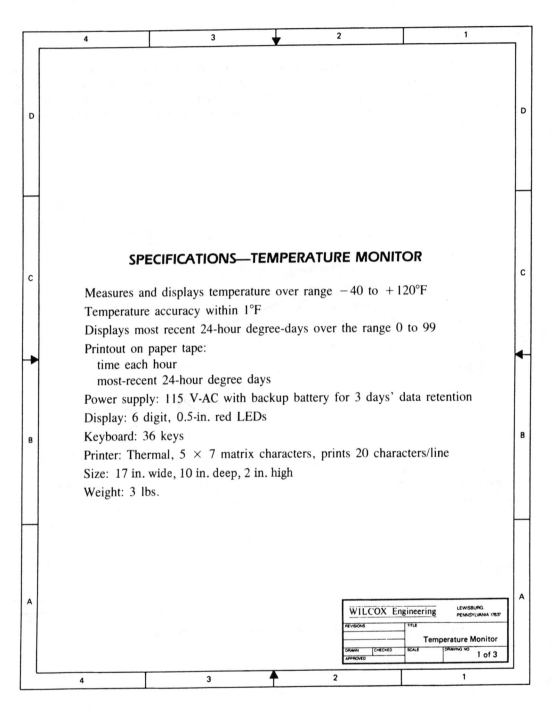

SPECIFICATIONS—TEMPERATURE MONITOR

Measures and displays temperature over range -40 to $+120°F$

Temperature accuracy within $1°F$

Displays most recent 24-hour degree-days over the range 0 to 99

Printout on paper tape:
  time each hour
  most-recent 24-hour degree days

Power supply: 115 V-AC with backup battery for 3 days' data retention

Display: 6 digit, 0.5-in. red LEDs

Keyboard: 36 keys

Printer: Thermal, 5×7 matrix characters, prints 20 characters/line

Size: 17 in. wide, 10 in. deep, 2 in. high

Weight: 3 lbs.

WILCOX Engineering   LEWISBURG. PENNSYLVANIA 17837

REVISIONS   TITLE
Temperature Monitor

DRAWN   CHECKED   SCALE   DRAWING NO
APPROVED   1 of 3

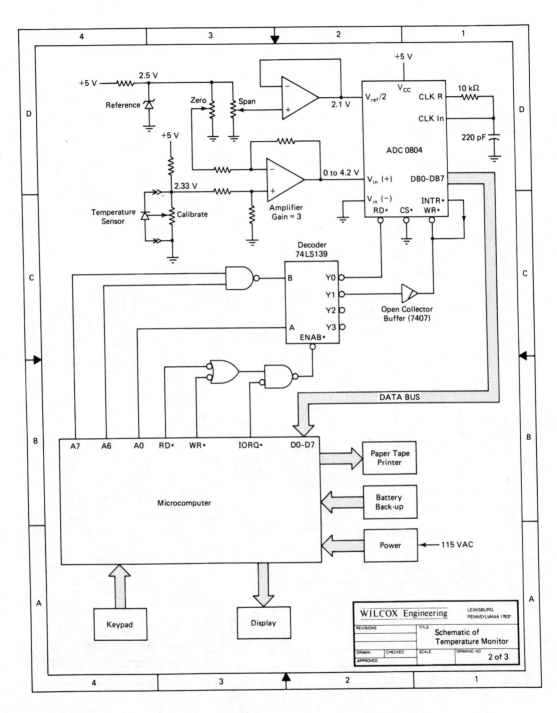

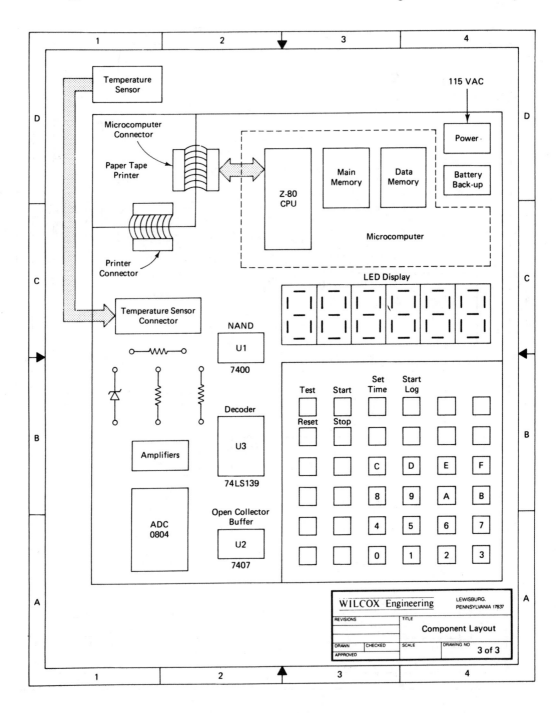

EXAMPLE PROJECT: CLOCK BOARD

The primary purpose of this module is to illustrate the complete design sequence from need identification through documentation. The secondary purpose is to introduce the use of an industry standard in designing a product.

Throughout the entire design sequence, notice how the modular approach is applied to not only the design, but to the construction and testing as well. Simple test equipment can be used for most design and development. The idea in this project is to keep everything as unsophisticated as possible.

The industry standard used here is the IEEE Std-696, which is the S-100 microcomputer bus. Designing to this standard, or to any standard for that matter, eases the burden of design: many technical details are already decided and do not require extra time on your part. However, your design must comply with the standard or run the risk of causing system malfunctions or complete system failure.

For our purposes, suppose you are a design engineer in a small design and manufacturing company and that you work directly with customers. A customer will normally meet with the sales and engineering managers first, and then you will be assigned to handle all the details of the project. When you first meet the customer, about all you can be sure of is that your company management thinks you can solve the customer's problem. Your role is to find out what the customer needs and then work out a solution to the problem. Although the customer will probably pay for a portion of your engineering time, assume your company expects to profit by building and selling several hundred units of the circuit you design.

NEED IDENTIFICATION

On first meeting and talking with your customer, you find that he needs a real-time clock that will operate in an S-100 (IEEE Std-696) computer system running at the maximum system clock speed of 6 MHz. The clock should be able to keep time and date as well as provide a means of interrupting the system on either a regular basis or at a predetermined point in time. It should maintain an accuracy within seconds per month with or without system power. Except for initially setting the time and date, the operator should not have to interact with the clock in any way.

The clock should operate as a slave on the bus without affecting normal system operation; likewise, there should be no changes required in the system software. Data transfer between the clock and system should use I/O-mapped ports. The handshaking should use the S-100 RDY line, and because the processor operates at 6 MHz, some wait states may be used if necessary. Clock interrupts to the system should be switchable to use any of the S-100 vectored-interrupt lines.

Although the customer is planning to write his initial programs to poll the clock for the time, the clock should be able to use any of the vectored-interrupt lines to implement a future real-time multitasking executive. In the long term, this could involve multiprocessing with a new 6-MHz 68000 central processing unit (CPU) board in the system. For the near term, however, the software will only set and display the time and service interrupts.

During these discussions with the customer, you discovered that he was really looking for two things: first, a clock in his system so that he could have a ''time'' function in his programs, and second, a future capability of using the clock interrupts in an advanced system being planned. If your clock design is a success, then there is a high probability that your company will have the contract to develop the advanced system as well.

PROJECT PLAN

At this point, you have a good idea of what your customer wants, and already you have a few ideas on how you can do the clock design. Before going out to the lab bench to build some models, plan your project! You have a job to do, so make a project plan for your own use to keep you on target as you do the project. Put this project plan directly into your lab notebook as you start work.

First, write your project definition as you understand it. Capture the essence of the big picture:

PROJECT DEFINITION.   The goal of my project is to design, build, and test a prototype real-time clock board meeting the IEEE Std-696.

Next, write your project objectives. These are the specific measurable outcomes of what you intend to accomplish by the end of your project. Allowing at least a page or more in your lab book, you can write these objectives as your product specifications.

PROJECT OBJECTIVES
- Time: hour, minute, second
- Calendar: day of week, date, month, year
- Periodic interrupts: 100 ms and 1 s
- Wake-up interrupts at preset times
- Accuracy 0.01 %
- Operating temperature 20 to 40°C
- Power supply: +8 V (200 mA, rechargeable battery)
- Meet IEEE Std-696
- Use readily available parts, easy to build and test
- No system hardware or software changes required

Once you have your project defined and have a set of objectives written in your lab book, figure out the strategy of how you can do the job. Avoid getting into the details of how to reach objectives, even if you think you know the answers. When you write the strategy, double space and allow yourself a full page in your lab book. Remember, this is a working document that you will want to refer to as you go along.

STRATEGY.   The strategy of how to meet the clock objectives is to do a complete design on paper of the entire clock. This will be followed by building a prototype and testing it as each module is completed.

Finally, make your plan of action to get the project accomplished. Go through your strategy and find major items that need to be done and write yourself a "do-it" list. Refer to Chapter 1 and outline a step-by-step plan in your lab book along with your best estimate of how long each step will take. Sketch a tentative bar chart of the various tasks so you have some deadlines to meet.

Notice the sequence you followed when you started the clock project. After identifying the customer's needs, you wrote a project plan in your lab book that contained:

- Project Definition   (the goal)
- Project Objectives   (requirements and constraints)
- Strategy   (how to reach objectives)
- Plan   (action needed to implement strategy)

Now that you know where you should go, you can begin the implementation of the project. Remember that doing the planning as you start the project might seem like lost time, but in reality you are saving time by focusing your overall effort directly on the problem.

PROJECT IMPLEMENTATION

As you learned in Chapter 2, the project implementation involves two major steps: the technical design and the construction of a prototype model of the circuit. The technical design phase is when you do a complete paper design of the project; the construction phase is when you build a first unit and test it for proper operation.

Technical Design

When you begin the technical design, you should analyze the constraints and the specifications you intend to meet. Review the standards that you expect to use in your design and see that you understand what will be required; be sure to work from the standard itself and not someone else's summary of it. You want to synthesize a design concept that is a best balance between the required specifications and the various constraints.

First, analyze the product specifications in detail and categorize each requirement by function. Try to describe what your clock board is supposed to do; when you do this, avoid any statement about how to do it. You might use this list when you divide up the product by function:

1. What does the clock board do?

2. How well must it perform?

3. What system interactions are required?

4. What operator attention is needed?

5. What hardware interface is required?

After you finish answering these questions, you will probably have a functional specification similar to Figure 5.2. This specification describes the product as you see it at the moment. As you synthesize a solution to the design problem, you will add more technical details later that describe the actual circuit as it evolves.

Functional Requirement	Keep time: hour, minute, second
	Keep calendar: day, date, month, year
	Provide periodic interrupts to system
	Provide wake-up interrupts to system
Performance Requirement	Maintain 0.01% accuracy
	Operate between 20 and 40°C
	Use less than 200 mA at 8 V supply
System Interaction	Operate with 6 MHz system bus
	Assert interrupts when required
	Set interrupt modes
Operator Interaction	Set initial time and date
	Inquire for time and date
	Set interrupt modes
Hardware Interface	Compatible with IEEE Std-696
	Operate as slave on the bus

Figure 5.2 The initial functional specification of the clock board. More details will be added as the design develops.

Next, sketch a system block diagram and then do a top-down design of the modules within the system. You might begin with a sketch of the system as shown in Figure 5.3a. After seeing the board in its proper frame of reference, go into more detail as in Figure 5.3b. Ask yourself what the board needs for inputs (power, someone to set the time at least once, etc.) and what it provides as outputs (time, interrupts, etc.). Note that these inputs and outputs match the functions you described in the functional specification in Figure 5.2.

At this point you can combine both sketches in Figure 5.3 to begin the block diagram of the clock board as shown in Figure 5.4. Now you are synthesizing a concept for the solution to the design problem. One possible concept is to use a CMOS LSI clock such as the National Semiconductor MM58167A real-time clock. The advantage of using CMOS is that you can operate the clock with a small battery over extended periods of time.

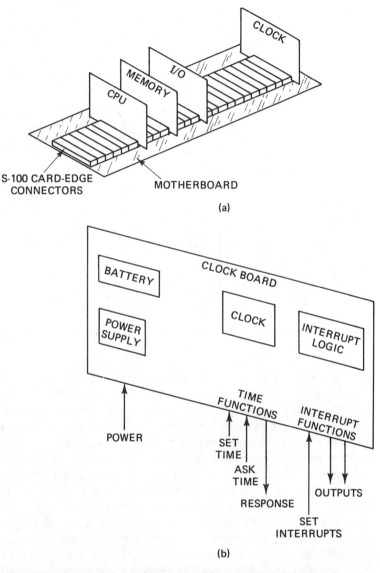

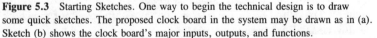

Figure 5.3 Starting Sketches. One way to begin the technical design is to draw
some quick sketches. The proposed clock board in the system may be drawn as in (a).
Sketch (b) shows the clock board's major inputs, outputs, and functions.

   The block diagram for the system designed around this clock IC is shown in Figure
5.5. The design using this clock IC can be partitioned into several major modules that
include the clock, address decoder, data-bus interface, interrupt switches, and power
supply. Once divided into modules, the hardware can be easily designed in much the

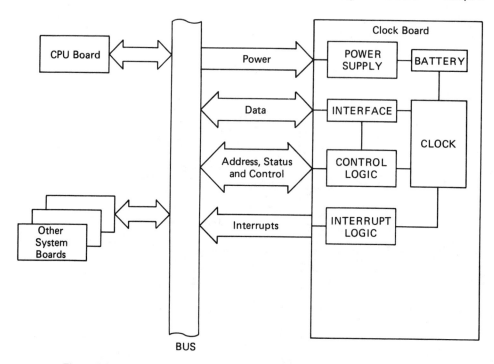

Figure 5.4   Block diagram of the system plus some rough detail on the clock board design.

same way software is developed; that is, the hardware design can be done top-down, bottom-up, or most critical first.

The appropriate design method in this case is to consider the most critical section first. Everything depends on the clock IC, and its requirements should be considered before all else. The block diagram of the MM58167A, Figure 5.6, shows that the IC uses 5 address lines (32 different address) and a chip select, has a single bidirectional data bus and separate read/write controls, two interrupt outputs, and a power-down control. Each of these requirements can be designed individually at this point and result in the implementation shown in the circuit schematic in Figure 5.7.

When you use I/O mapping (as opposed to memory mapping) for the clock data transfer, you have a maximum of 256 ports. Only the lower eight bits of the address bus need decoding, and five of these are internally decoded by the clock IC. For maximum flexibility, you can use DIP switches to select the three most significant bits of the I/O address. The output of the decoder is used as a chip-select for the clock and is used by the read/write qualifier circuit.

The S-100 data bus in-and-out lines are buffered with a pair of 74LS244s connected directly to the clock IC. The buffer for data-in (DI from the processor's viewpoint) is strobed using the I/O read qualifiers pDBIN, sINP, and the chip-select CS. The data-out buffer is strobed using pWR*, sOUT, and the chip-select CS. During a typical

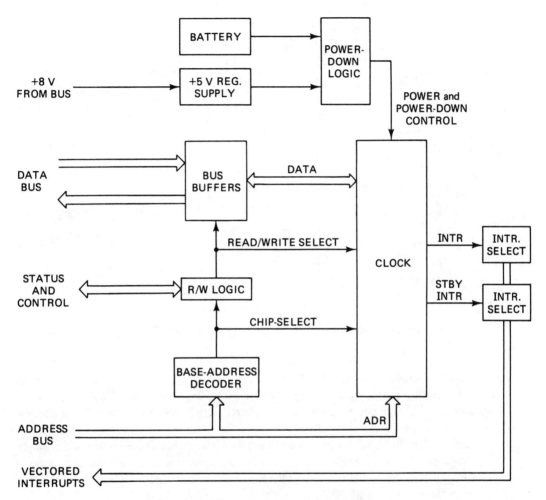

Figure 5.5 Block diagram of real-time clock board.

read bus cycle, for example, the proper address is placed on the address bus, sINP asserted, and then pDBIN asserted to strobe the DI buffer and the clock RD* input. In the typical write bus cycle, the address is put on the bus, sOUT asserted, and then pWR* asserted to strobe the DI buffer and the clock WR* input.

Timing.   A basic read or write bus cycle has three bus states (BS1, BS2, and BS3), each of which takes 167 ns in a 6-MHz system; consequently, a bus read or write

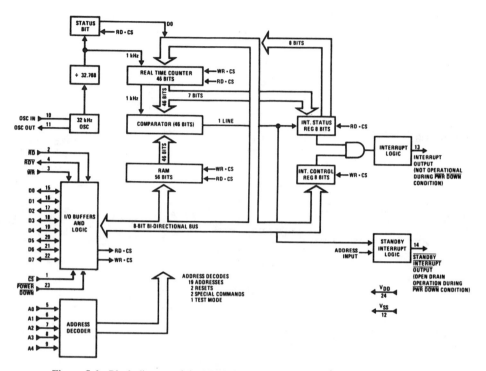

Figure 5.6   Block diagram of the MM58167A real-time clock. (Courtesy National
Semiconductor Corp.)

normally completes within 500 ns. However, for I/O devices that require substantial
access times, the bus cycle can be extended by adding a number of wait states, as in
Figure 5.8. To find out if wait states are required during any read or write bus cycle, the
bus master (the CPU) samples the RDY line at the rising edge of the system clock in Bus
State 2 (BS2). If the RDY line is found low, then a wait state (BSw) is inserted immediately after BS2; if the RDY is still low a bus state later, then yet another wait state is
inserted. Wait states continue to be added until RDY finally goes high; at that point, the
bus cycle concludes with BS3.

The MM58167A clock requires wait states in the bus cycle because of its slow
access time. For a clock-read operation, the time required from a valid address until the
output data is valid might range from 500 ns to the specified maximum of 1050 ns, far
longer than the time required for a normal bus cycle (i.e., 167 ns × 3 = 500 ns). The
read cycle of a typical 6-MHz IEEE-696 system is shown in Figure 5.8, with approximate times to scale. Notice that the example timing diagram includes a total of three wait
states to make up for the slow access time.

The normal S-100 requirement is that the RDY line be low at the end of BS1 if
waits are required in a bus cycle. In the clock case, however, this is impossible: the clock

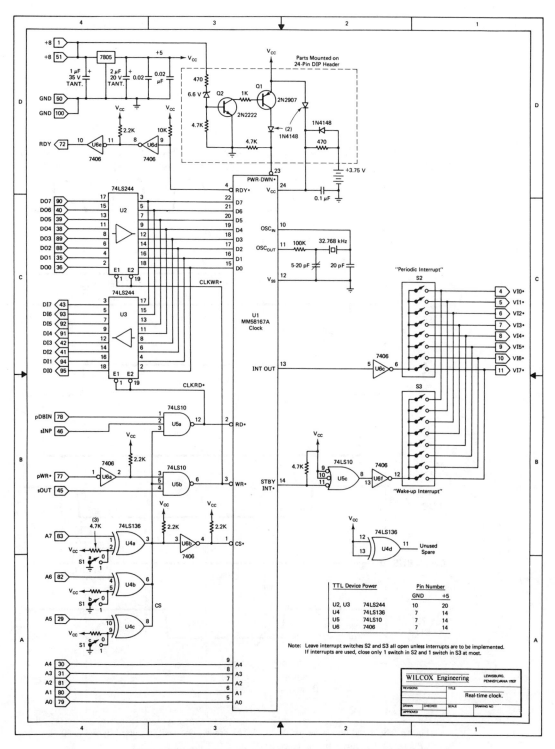

Figure 5.7 Real-time clock schematic drawn on zonal-coordinate paper.

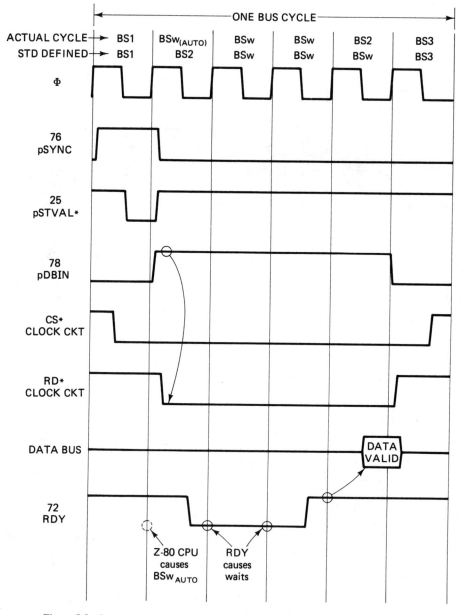

Figure 5.8 Read bus cycle for the clock. As drawn, one wait is caused by the Z-80 CPU board; the others by the clock RDY line.

is not even being read until BS2, so it cannot respond until about a cycle later. In a case like this, the CPU board itself has to add in a wait state automatically if an I/O access is being made. Doing so allows the clock to have until the end of BS2 to get RDY pulled low. As shown in Figure 5.8, the clock holds RDY low to get two more wait states in the bus cycle. When the clock data is finally valid, the RDY line is allowed to go high, and the data is read by the processor in BS3. To finish BS3, pDBIN is negated, which raises the clock RD* input, and the address deselects the clock.

Figure 5.9 shows actual bus timing data using a Z-80 CPU board as bus master. The CPU has been set to add in a single wait state. RDY is pulled low by the clock about 50 ns after the start of BS2; this is 167 minus 50 or about 120 ns before it *must* be low. The IEEE Std-696 calls for a 70-ns setup time before the rising edge of the next system clock, so you can see there is about 120 minus 70 or 50 ns margin here— that is, if RDY were later by more than 50 ns, then RDY would not meet the standard's setup-time specification. Your system would probably work even if the setup time were reduced to, say, 20 ns, but you would not be able to guarantee a general-case performance.

The write bus cycle timing requirements for the clock are quite similar to the read timing described above. As in the read, a total of two wait states must be included to allow sufficient time for RDY to be pulled low during the write operation.

Power-down design. The power-down design is quite critical in the actual operation of the clock. If PWR-DWN* is not asserted to a low-voltage level at least a microsecond before the system power is removed, then the contents of the clock memory

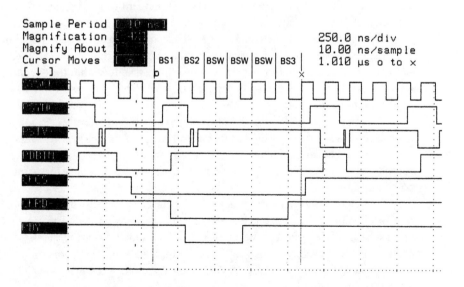

Figure 5.9 Actual bus data using a commercial Z-80 CPU board.

might be anything (or nothing) when normal system power is restored. Futhermore, when the power does come back on, PWR-DWN* must be held LOW until all bus signals are valid.

A common way of accomplishing this is to use a zener diode to set a reference threshold voltage to control a transistor switch. Consider the circuit in Figure 5.7 when the system is off: Q1 and Q2 are both off. When the system power comes on, nothing happens until the system bus voltage reaches about 6.6 V. Then the zener conducts, turns on Q2, which then turns on Q1. When Q1 goes on, voltage is applied to PWR-DWN*, which activates the clock chip for normal operation. A system bus voltage greater than 6.6 V is enough to allow near-normal output from all 5 V regulators, so all bus signals should be valid by this time. When the system is turned off, the system voltage drops down gradually enough so that when it passes below 6.6 V, the zener and Q1/Q2 can drop the PWR-DWN* to a low voltage before the bus signals become invalid.

A small 3.75-V, 20-mAh nickel-cadmium rechargeable battery is used to maintain clock operation when system power is off. Specified current consumption of the clock is on the order of 10 to 20 μA using the battery with series-blocking diode. The 470-Ω resistor provides a trickle charge of 0.5 mA to about 2 mA, depending on the state of the battery and component tolerances. For an average of several hours a day use, this resistor keeps the battery charged between 3.8 and 4.15 V with no difficulties.

Logic circuits.   IEEE Std-696 (Sec. 3.7) states that a card may not source more than 0.5 mA at 0.5 V nor sink more than 80 μA at 2.4 V on most system signal lines. The effect of this is that only one LS-TTL gate per card can be connected to each line of the address bus. The address decoder uses a 74LS136 exclusive-or, which sources a worst-case maximum of 0.8 mA at 0.4 V. This should cause no operational problems in any practical sense, and the appropriate design tradeoff is to use the 74LS136 rather than add extra hardware to buffer the address bus to be strictly within the specification. You might want to check with your customer to verify that this tradeoff will not cause a problem later in the system.

The pull-up resistors for the open-collector 7406 are selected to maintain proper logic levels and currents. The design tradeoff is to let the various resistors be high for lower current consumption, or to let them be low for more speed at the expense of the current. As drawn in Figure 5.7, the pull-up resistors are designed for as much speed as possible.

The clock standby-interrupt output can be used to implement the ''wake-up'' interrupt specification; to do this, an extra noninverting gate is needed. The spare 74LS10 and the last spare 7406 gate can be used to get this output from the clock board without adding another package. This particular output does not have the flexibility of the programmable output but is useful to indicate a match between real time and present time for a wake-up alarm.

Prototype Construction

The second half of the project implementation is the construction of the prototype model of the circuit. Although the paper design is done and appears correct, you still must build the prototype and demonstrate its proper operation. In the technical design, it is easy to overlook some specifications, and your prototype will help you find and correct these oversights.

First do a rough sketch of where the major functions will be physically located on the prototype circuit board. Then build the prototype module by module, much as you did the technical design by modules or functions. In the design phase, the most critical section was the clock, and you did its circuit first. After the clock, you did the address decoding, bus control, interrupts, and power-down. When you build, however, construct from the bottom-up so you can debug as you go along.

What you would like to have as you build the prototype is a working, error-free circuit that can help you catch flaws in your paper design. Start with a simple but necessary function on the clock board: the power supply. All the parts on the board need power, so build that module first and check it out. Once you have power available, then you can do the address decoder and check it out too. Next, do the bus buffers and continue with the rest until you have a complete circuit.

How do you do the testing and then the debugging if there is a problem? Test the first module, the power supply, with a multimeter for shorts when you finish its wiring. Then plug the board into an S-100 system and turn on the system power. Measure the +5 V from the regulator and see that it appears at the proper places on your prototype board. If you find a problem with your supply, trace the circuit back to see that the system +8 V is coming into your circuit. If it is, with only the 7805 regulator in the supply, then either the 7805 is defective or its output is shorted. You should have found the short earlier with the multimeter, so fix the regulator. When all is satisfactory, turn off the system, remove the board, and start wiring the next section.

Build and test the address decoder next. Wire up the four logic gates that produce the clock chip-select CS*. Set the three switches to a clear I/O port address (A0 hex, for example) and plug the board back into the system. Apply power and boot up your system as you do normally. If your system cannot boot, the problem must be related to the A7 through A0 address inputs you connected on the clock board. Use your logic probe and check to see if one or more of the address lines is being held high or low. If the system booted normally, use the logic probe and check for CS*. You should find activity here because the address bus hits the address A0 (and all the combinations of 101x xxxx) many times each second.

Following the same approach, build and test the read-and-write strobe qualifier circuits RD* and WR*. Boot your operating system and use the logic probe to make sure CS* still has activity. Check RD* and WR*: they should be negated (i.e., HIGH). Using your operating system debugging program (for example, CP/M's DDT), execute a small one-line program that will assert RD*. If your system is running with a Z-80, you might execute an instruction

IN A, (A0)

This will cause the Z-80 to place A0 on the address bus and then read the data at that I/O port into the accumulator. Relate your circuit to the read bus cycle in Figure 5.8: the combination of pDBIN and sINP and the correct address will cause RD* to go LOW just once. You should see this pulse on your logic probe as you execute the instruction. You can do a similar test for WR* by executing the instruction

OUT (A0),A

This will cause the Z-80 to send the accumulator data out to the I/O port A0. Each time you execute this instruction you should see the pulse on your logic probe.

If you have an IEEE Std-696 68000 CPU board in operation, you know that it does memory-mapped I/O. That is, rather than IN or OUT, the 68000 normally exchanges data with other system devices by reading or writing to memory addresses. A certain block of the 68000's 16-Mb address space should be decoded on your 68000 board for I/O purposes. For example, suppose the address range FF0000 to FFFFFF hex is designated for I/O devices. You could expect that the S-100 sINP and sOUT would respond properly and you could write your test code just as you would for memory accesses. For example, you might use

MOVE.B $FF00A0,D0

to do a read from port A0. The data would be stored in D0. Then use

MOVE.B D0,$FF00A0

to write D0 data out to port A0.

After you have RD* and WR* working properly, you can build and test the data bus buffers. With nothing in the clock socket, you will not be able to read or write actual data. You will, however, be able to boot your system and see that the buffers are being properly strobed when you execute the same programs you used to test RD* and WD*. If you want, you can test for proper reading by temporarily connecting arbitrary logic HIGH and LOW values to the data lines at the empty clock socket: execute an IN A,(A0) and see if you read the correct data into the Z-80 A register. Remove the temporary wires and execute an OUT (A0),A instruction to check if data is getting to the clock socket. When you do this instruction, you should be able to use your logic probe to see a pulse at each data pin on the socket.

Finish the rest of the clock board following the same approach: build a module, test it, build another module, and test it too. When you have the board finished, you will fully understand how it works and will be confident of how well it meets the specifications. Notice that the only test equipment you needed to get the clock board in operation was your multimeter and logic probe. You might have used an oscilloscope and executed scope-loop programs to check the various timing waveforms and be sure they were within specifications.

For illustration, the entire real-time clock was prototyped on a Vector 8800V wire-wrap board as shown in Figure 5.10. The interrupt switches (S3) for the wake-up interrupt are located beside the main interrupt switches (S2). Less than a third of a standard S-100 board is required for all the circuits. The transistor power-down circuit is wired on the 24-pin component-carrier at the lower-left edge of the board by the battery. Plastic "wrap-ID" panels were used on the back of the board for each IC socket to make component and pin identification easier.

Figure 5.10   Prototype model of the real-time clock.

DOCUMENTATION

When you started the clock project, you began by writing your project definition, objectives, and strategy in your lab notebook. After writing out a step-by-step plan of action, you did all your circuit design in the notebook. Then, as you started building and testing the prototype, you put more information in your lab book. By the time you had a working prototype meeting specifications, your lab book had probably become quite full. Of all the information, the most important is your test data and your notes on how you corrected any problems.

What you do next really depends on your actual situation. If your customer wants to try the prototype in his system so he can write some software for it, then all you may need to give him is a single sheet showing the address and interrupt switch settings. More likely, however, you will need to provide more information than that.

Suppose you learn that the design is entirely satisfactory and that your company will probably sell several hundred of the clock boards. The information in your lab book will be necessary so you can provide sketches for your drafting personnel and a parts list for purchasing. As your board finally moves into manufacturing, you will need to verify production test data with your original design. If you were diligent in keeping your lab book up to date, then you should have no problems.

FURTHER READING

BREEDING, KENNETH. *Digital Design Fundamentals*. Englewood Cliffs, NJ: Prentice Hall, 1989.

COMER, DAVID J. *Digital Logic and State Machine Design*. New York: Holt, Rinehart and Winston, 1984. (TK 7868.S9C66)

FLETCHER, WILLIAM I. *An Engineering Approach to Digital Design*. Englewood Cliffs, NJ: Prentice Hall, 1980. (TK 7868.D5F5)

HAYES, JOHN P. *Digital System Design and Microprocessors*. New York: McGraw-Hill, 1984. (TK 7874.H393)

KLINE, RAYMOND M. *Structured Digital Design*. Englewood Cliffs, NJ: Prentice Hall, 1983.

MANO, M. MORRIS. *Computer Engineering: Hardware Design*. Englewood Cliffs, NJ: Prentice Hall, 1988 (TK 7885.M27)

PEATMAN, JOHN B. *Digital Hardware Design*. New York: McGraw-Hill, 1980.

WAKERLY, JOHN F. *Digital Design Principles and Practices*. Englewood Cliffs, NJ: Prentice Hall, 1990.

WINKEL, DAVID, and FRANKLIN PROSSER. *The Art of Digital Design*. Englewood Cliffs, NJ: Prentice Hall, 1980. (TK 7888.3W56)

6

ANALOG MODULE

Lowpass Filter
Three-Phase
Analysis Program

Lawrence P. Huelsman
University of Arizona

INTRODUCTION

The purpose of this analog module is to illustrate analog design by examining two specific projects. Each project is typical of design work you can finish in a semester or less as an undergraduate engineering student.

The first project, a lowpass analog filter, is a component in a signal transmission system that uses PCM (pulse-code modulation) to encode and transmit an analog signal. The design includes selecting the type of filter, determining the order, making a simulation of the filter, and providing the necessary construction and testing.

The second project is the design of a program for the analysis of three-phase power transmission systems. The design includes defining the structure of the program and the user interface, writing the code, and testing the operation of the program.

SUGGESTED PROJECT TOPICS

Many other analog projects can be done in connection with a program such as SPICE, which provides a simulation capability well-suited to analog circuit design. Still other types of analog projects might require the design of software and the use of a personal computer to accommodate the processing of design data. Some examples of both types of projects are given in the following list.

- Lowpass, highpass, and bandpass passive filters
- Active-RC filter realizations
- Synthesis methods for specified network functions
- Approximation of magnitude, phase, and delay characteristics
- Sinusoidal steady-state analysis of functions and circuits
- Time-domain analysis of functions and circuits
- Operational amplifier circuits
- Symbolic analysis
- Sensitivity determination
- Applications of optimization

EXAMPLE PROJECT: LOWPASS FILTER

The purpose of this module is to unify the design sequence from need identification through final design. The various sections of this material appear in the normal chronology introduced in the earlier chapters of the text.

In this project, assume that you are the owner of a small custom-filter design company that specializes in designing and building filters for single-quantity applications. The designs are frequently used as prototypes for large-scale production, but this type of operation is outside the scope of your company. You have one employee, a technician, who can run computer programs, construct prototype models, keep parts inventories, and use and maintain your test equipment. You are approached by a customer who wants you to construct a filter that will meet certain specifications. You are to design the filter for him.

NEED IDENTIFICATION

Your customer is involved in the design of a PCM (pulse-code modulation) system for encoding analog signal information into a digital form so that it can be transmitted over a pair of wires. In a typical PCM system, the analog input signal first passes through a lowpass filter called an *anti-aliasing filter*. The filtered signal is then sampled by an encoder and converted to digital form. The sampling process used by the encoder produces sidebands that are located near multiples of the sampling frequency. If the signal information entering the encoder has frequency components greater than half the sampling frequency, the lower sideband will be superimposed into the actual passband occupied by the signal. Thus it constitutes an error signal that cannot be distinguished electronically from the input signal, and as a result, a distortion of the input signal occurs. The function of the lowpass filter is to prevent this aliasing from occurring by limiting the frequency content of the analog input signal. Your customer has completed the design of his PCM system with the exception of the lowpass filter component. He wishes you to design a suitable filter that will meet the specifications that he will provide.

PROJECT PLAN

Outline a plan for the project in your laboratory notebook. Based on your discussion with your customer, you decide on the use of a passive filter which will use RLC components (resistors, inductors, and capacitors). The plan should include sections defining the project, giving the project objectives and constraints, and developing an overall strategy and plan of action.

PROJECT DEFINITION.   My project is to design, verify the design by simulation, and build a lowpass filter that can be used in a PCM (pulse-code modulation) system with a sampling rate of 8 kHz.

PROJECT OBJECTIVES
- Lowpass passband of 0 to 3.3333 kHz.
- Lowpass stopband starting at 4 kHz.
- Maximum ripple of the passband magnitude characteristic of 1 dB with a tolerance of ± 5%.
- Minimum stopband attenuation of 28 dB ± 5%.
- Input and output (source and load) resistors of 150 Ω.

PROJECT CONSTRAINTS
- Standard component values are to be used to avoid the expense of custom designed parts.
- The design is to be completed in six weeks.

STRATEGY.   To attain my objectives, I will use the specifications given in the Project Objectives section above and apply standard approximation techniques and tables to design the filter. The design will be verified by computer simulation. Next I will modify the values of the filter elements to match standard component values. At this point a further simulation should be made to check the effect of the changes in the component values. Once the final design is verified, components can be ordered and the filter can be constructed and given an electrical test.

PLAN OF ACTION
1. Translate the specifications and tolerances given in the preceeding Project Objectives section to a graphical representation.
2. Frequency- and impedance-normalize the specifications.
3. Locate references for approximation tables to determine the type of magnitude characteristic and the order of the filter.
4. Select the filter approximation.
5. Locate filter design tables to determine the normalized element values of the filter.
6. Verify the design by simulating the magnitude characteristic of the filter.
7. Frequency- and impedance-denormalize the values of the filter elements and simulate the denormalized filter characteristic.
8. Locate tables of standard component values.

9. Replace the design values with the closest standard component values and repeat the simulation.
10. Check the effects of the +/- tolerance variations on the standard component values on the overall filter specifications.
11. Revise component values if necessary.
12. Order component parts of the filter.
13. Construct the filter.
14. Test the filter.

The schedule I must follow to complete the project in six weeks looks like the following:

Tasks to Do	1	2	3	Week 4	5	6
Graph specifications	*					
Normalize specifications	*					
Get approximation data	*					
Select approximation	**					
Get filter data	*					
Design filter	*					
Simulate filter	***					
Denormalize filter	**					
Simulate filter	**					
Get standard values	*					
Make standard design		*				
Simulate design		**				
Analyze tolerance		****	**			
Revise design		****	**			
Order components			***			
Construct filter				*****	*	
Test filter				*	****	
Unknown extra tasks					*	*****

PROJECT IMPLEMENTATION

The project implementation involves two major steps, the technical design and the construction of the filter. The technical design step is where you develop a complete paper design of the project, including simulation of its properties. The construction step is where you build and make a final electrical test of the filter itself.

Technical Design

The technical design phase begins with the acquisition of approximation information and finishes with the design of the filter. A necessary part of the design is the simulation of the filter configuration after the various steps of normalization, denormalization, and substitution of standard component values. Further simulation is necessary to establish the effect that component tolerances will have on the limits given for the specifications and to determine whether any redesign is necessary.

Construction

The actual construction of the filter satisfies two goals. It provides a final verification of the correctness of the design, and it provides the hardware that is to be furnished to the customer.

DOCUMENTATION

Proposal

When you prepared the outline of the project plan in your laboratory notebook, you also outlined the major parts of a project proposal. The purpose of the proposal is to communicate a definition of the project, its objectives, and the strategy for meeting those objectives. The proposal also details the plan of action with the schedule for completion. It also usually seeks support of some kind.

The proposal should be written after enough work has been done, so that you can write with some authority on the project. In the lowpass filter project that we are considering here, since the general subject of filter design is well known, only a small amount of feasibility determination need actually be done before writing the proposal.

PROPOSAL
Lowpass Passive Filter

Project definition:	The goal of the project is to design, simulate, build, and test a filter to be used as an anti-aliasing filter in a PCM (pulse-code modulation) data transmission system.
Project objective:	At the end of six weeks, the filter will be completely built and tested. It will meet these specifications:
	Lowpass passband of 0 to 3.3333 kHz.
	Lowpass stopband starting at 4 kHz.
	Maximum ripple of the passband magnitude characteristic of 1 dB with a tolerance of $+/-$ 5%.
	Minimum stopband attenuation of 28 dB $+/-$ 5%.
	Input and output resistors of 150 Ω.
Strategy for achieving objectives:	Standard approximation and filter design tables will be used to implement the design. The design will be modified to accommodate standard element values. Simulation of the design and electrical testing of the filter will be used to verify the filter performance.
Plan of action:	Translate the specifications and tolerances given in the Project Objectives section to a graphical representation.
	Frequency- and impedance-normalize the specifications.

Locate references for approximation tables to determine the type of magnitude characteristic and the order of the filter.

Select the filter approximation.

Locate filter design tables to determine the normalized element values.

Verify the design by simulating the magnitude characteristic of the filter.

Frequency- and impedance-denormalize the values of the filter elements and simulate the denormalized filter characteristic.

Locate tables of standard component values.

Replace the design values with the closest standard component values and repeat the simulation.

Check the effects of the $+/-$ tolerance variations on the standard component values on the overall filter specifications.

Revise component values if necessry.

Order component parts of the filter.

Construct the filter.

Test the filter.

Reporting: Weekly progress reports will be made. At the end of the project a completed and tested filter will be presented.

Budget: Designer work hours, computer simulation charges, and technician work hours will be billed at standard rates every two weeks.

Evaluation: Verification of the way in which the project is progressing and the current status of the filter design will be made weekly. The final evaluation of the filter will be conducted by the designer and the customer.

Progress Reports

Since this is a relatively small project, the weekly progress reports will probably just consist of a phone call to the customer reassuring him that the project is on schedule and that no unforeseen difficulties have been encountered. If you were a design engineer for a large company, you would probably make a weekly written progress report to your technical manager. It might have the following form:

PROGRESS REPORT
Lowpass Filter Project—Week 1

Current Status: The approximation and normalized design have been completed. There have been no delays. I am currently on schedule.

Work Completed: During the week I completed the approximation and determined that a fifth-order elliptic filter would meet the specifications. The element values for the denormalized filter have been determined, and the filter has been successfully simulated.

Current Work: I have started the modification of the filter design so as to be able to use standard element values.

Future Work: During the second week of the project I plan to study the effect of component tolerances on the overall design.

Technical Manual

The project documentation for the lowpass filter will consist of a single page describing the design and the specifications that were to be met. On the following pages, a circuit diagram of the filter will be presented showing the element values and the tolerances. This will be accompanied by the data obtained from the electrical test of the filter. This would usually be in the form of a graph showing the gain as a function of frequency. Since the filter is to be used as one component of a large system, no user's manual would normally be required. An example of the documentation follows.

LOWPASS FILTER DESIGN REPORT. This report describes a lowpass filter designed for use as an anti-aliasing filter in a pulse-code modulation (PCM) data transmission system.

Design Specifications:
Lowpass passband of 0 to 3.3333 kHz.
Lowpass stopband starting at 4 kHz.
Maximum ripple of the passband magnitude characteristic of 1 dB with a tolerance of ± 5%.
Minimum stopband attenuation of 28 dB ± 5%.
Input and output resistors of 150 Ω.

Comments:
A fifth-order elliptic filter was chosen as the result of the approximation studies. This filter realizes the design specifications and is of considerably lower order than other types of approximations. The design is shown in Figure 6.1. Standard component values with the specified tolerance were used in constructing the filter. Test data taken from an electrical test of the filter over a range of 0 to 6.67 kHz is shown in Figure 6.2. From this data it is seen that the filter meets the specifications.

EXAMPLE PROJECT:
THREE-PHASE ANALYSIS PROGRAM

The purpose of this module is to unify the design sequence from need identification through final design. The various sections of this material appear in the normal chronology as introduced in the earlier chapters of the text.

In this project, assume that you are a software consultant who specializes in developing custom programs for single users. You have no other employees. You are approached by a customer who needs a program that meets certain specifications. You are to design the program for him.

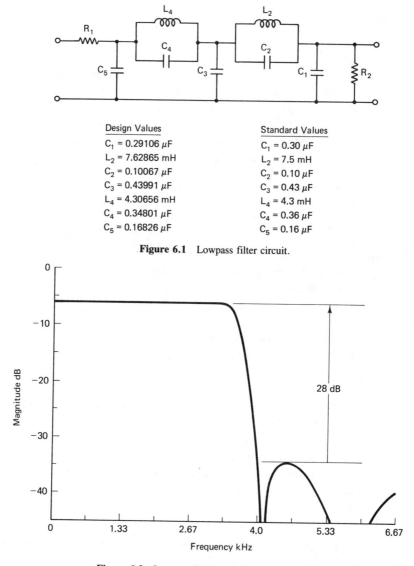

Figure 6.1 Lowpass filter circuit.

Design Values

$C_1 = 0.29106 \, \mu F$
$L_2 = 7.62865 \, mH$
$C_2 = 0.10067 \, \mu F$
$C_3 = 0.43991 \, \mu F$
$L_4 = 4.30656 \, mH$
$C_4 = 0.34801 \, \mu F$
$C_5 = 0.16826 \, \mu F$

Standard Values

$C_1 = 0.30 \, \mu F$
$L_2 = 7.5 \, mH$
$C_2 = 0.10 \, \mu F$
$C_3 = 0.43 \, \mu F$
$L_4 = 4.3 \, mH$
$C_4 = 0.36 \, \mu F$
$C_5 = 0.16 \, \mu F$

Figure 6.2 Lowpass filter magnitude characteristic.

NEED IDENTIFICATION

Your customer is involved in his own consulting business, namely, the analysis of power systems for companies that are expanding their production capacity. He needs to be able to make a variety of computations on three-phase power systems with unbalanced loads so as to establish bounds on line-voltage fluctuations as additional electrical equipment is put into service. The results of these computations can be used to show his client whether additional transmission line capacity will be required. Your customer has prepared the mathematical algorithms that will make the necessary computations. He wishes to hire you to design and write the program that will implement the algorithms.

PROJECT PLAN

Outline a plan for the project in your lab notebook. Based on your discussion with your customer you decide on the use of Pascal as a programming language, and the use of an IBM-compatible personal computer as the machine on which the program will be implemented. The plan should include sections defining the project, giving the project objectives and constraints, and developing an overall strategy and plan of action.

PROJECT DEFINITION. My project is to design, write, test, and verify a program that uses an IBM-compatible personal computer to perform three-phase power system analysis.

PROJECT OBJECTIVES
- Balanced three-phase input with user-specified line-to-line voltages
- Line impedances specified by their real and imaginary parts
- Load impedances considered as delta-connected
- Load impedances specified by kilowatts and kilovars or by kilowatts and leading/ lagging power factor
- Line-to-line load voltages and regulation are to be calculated
- All input and output data to be displayed

PROJECT CONSTRAINTS
- Menu-driven program format
- Convenient user interface
- On-screen ''help'' displays
- Input of data from keyboard or data file
- Output of data to screen and data file
- Internal editing capability for easy correction/changes of data
- Multi-case capability to permit the study of ''what-if'' alternatives
- Thoroughly commented program code for easy maintenance and modification
- Program code is to be implementation-independent Pascal so that it can be re-compiled on any available compiler
- Compiled and source code versions of the program are required
- The design is to be completed in four weeks

STRATEGY. To attain my objectives, I will use the specifications given in the Project Objectives and Project Constraints sections and design a flow chart of the program. The flow chart will show the paths followed by the various options and the blocks that specify the structure of the program. Next I will design and test the various individual items of the program structure. Once the individual items are completed, the overall program can be tested and modified if necessary.

PLAN OF ACTION
1. Design the overall flow chart of the program.
2. Specify the properties of each of the blocks in the flow chart.
3. Assign names for the variables used in the program.
4. Layout the menus and windows to be used for the user interaction.
5. Develop standards for the input and output data files.
6. Write code for each of the blocks as subprograms.
7. Design test programs to verify the operation of each of the blocks.
8. Test the blocks and modify as necessary.
9. Form the main program from the component subprograms.
10. Test the main program and verify its operation.
11. Demonstrate the program to the customer and solicit his suggestions for modifications.
12. Write the documentation.
13. Deliver the final program and documentation.

The schedule I must follow to complete the project in four weeks looks like the following:

| | Week | | | |
Tasks to Do	1	2	3	4
Design flowchart	*			
Specify blocks	**			
Assign variable names	**			
Layout menus	**			
Develop standards	**			
Write code for blocks		*****		
Test code for blocks		*****		
Form main program		*	**	
Test main program		*	**	
Demonstrate/modify			***	
Write documentation			***	
Unknown extra tasks				*****

PROJECT IMPLEMENTATION

The project implementation involves two major steps, the technical design of the program structure and the writing of the code. The technical design step is where you develop a complete paper design of the program showing structure, subcomponents, flow chart, and screen and data format designs. The writing step is where you generate and test the program code.

Technical Design

The technical design phase begins with the structuring of the program into component blocks. Each block is specified by its data-processing and user-interface functions. Thus, the data that is input, the processing that is performed, and the data that is output must be specified. Flow chart paths linking the blocks must be designated and variable names for the different data must be chosen.

Writing the Program

The writing phase is initiated by first writing the code to implement the specifications of each of the component blocks in subprogram form. Coincident with this, test programs for verifying the operation of the subprograms should be prepared. Finally, the main program that links the various subprograms should be written and tested. Comments should be included as part of all the code to explain the implementation of the algorithms and the particular program constructs that are being used.

DOCUMENTATION

Proposal

When you prepared the outline of the project plan in your laboratory notebook, you outlined the major parts of a project proposal. The purpose of the proposal is to communicate a definition of the project, its objectives, and the strategy for meeting those objectives. The proposal also details a plan of action with the schedule for completion. It also usually seeks support of some kind.

The proposal should be written after enough work has been done, so that you can write with some authority on the project. In the three-phase analysis project that we are considering here, since the mathematical algorithms are being provided by the customer, only a small amount of feasibility determination need actually be done before writing the proposal.

PROPOSAL
Three-Phase Analysis Program

Project definition:	The goal of the project is to design, write, and test the code for a three-phase analysis program that will determine line voltage fluctuations as varying electrical loads are placed on a three-phase power system.
Project objective:	At the end of four weeks, the program will be completely written and tested. It will meet these specifications:
	Balanced three-phase input with user-specified line-to-line voltages
	Line impedances specified by their real and imaginary parts
	Load impedances considered as delta-connected
	Load impedances specified by kilowatts and kilovars or by kilowatts and leading/lagging power factor
	Line-to-line load voltages and regulation are to be calculated
	All input and output data to be displayed
Strategy for achieving objectives:	Structured programming and top-down techniques will be applied in the development of the program. A block diagram and flow chart will be prepared, then source code for each of the blocks will be written and tested. A main program will be written to link the component blocks. After final testing, documentation for the program will be prepared.
Plan of action:	Design the overall flow chart of the program.
	Specify the properties of each of the blocks in the flow chart.
	Assign names for the variables used in the program.
	Lay out the menus and windows to be used for the user interaction.
	Develop standards for the input and output data files.
	Write code for each of the blocks as subprograms.
	Design test programs to verify the operation of each of the blocks.
	Test the blocks and modify as necessary.
	Form the main program from the component subprograms.
	Test the main program and verify its operation.
	Demonstrate the program to the customer and solicit his suggestions for modifications.
	Write the documentation.
	Deliver the final program and documentation.
Reporting:	Weekly progress reports will be made. At the end of the project a completed and tested program will be presented.
Budget:	Programmer work-hours and computer usage charges will be billed at standard rates every two weeks.
Evaluation:	Verification of the way in which the project is progressing and the current status of the program will be made weekly. The final evaluation of the program will be made by the programmer and the customer.

Progress Reports

Since this is a relatively small project, the weekly progress reports will probably just consist of a phone call to the customer. If you were a design engineer for a large company, you would probably make a weekly written progress report to your technical manager. It might have the following form:

PROGRESS REPORT
Three-Phase Analysis Program—Week 1

Current Status:	The program design has been completed. There have been no delays. I am currently on schedule.
Work Completed:	The design of the program including the development of the block structure and the construction of the flowchart have been completed. Variable names have been selected and the layouts made for the different menus. Input and output data specifications have been completed.
Current Work:	I have started the generation of the code for the program.
Future Work:	During the second week of the project I plan to complete writing the code for the component blocks and testing them. By the end of the week I should be able to start writing and testing the main program.

Technical Manual

The project documentation for the three-phase analysis program will consist of a report describing the structure of the program and the function and specifications of the component blocks. A flow chart illustrating the program structure will be included. A list of the program variable names and their functions will be given. Examples of typical sets of input data and the resulting program output will be shown. Finally, a complete listing of the program source code will be given. Since the program is to be menu-driven, no user's manual would normally be required. The internal "help" information included with the program should be sufficient for assisting the user if additional information is required.

FURTHER READING

CHAPRA, STEVEN C., and RAYMOND P. CANALE. *Numerical Methods for Engineers with Personal Computer Applications.* New York: McGraw-Hill Book Co., 1985.

DORF, RICHARD C. *Modern Control Systems.* 4th ed., Reading, MA: Addison-Wesley Publishing Co., 1987.

FRANCO, SERGIO. *Design with Operational Amplifiers and Analog Integrated Circuits.* New York: McGraw-Hill Book Co., 1988.

HUELSMAN, L. P. *Engineering and Scientific Computations in Pascal.* New York: John Wiley and Sons, 1986.

HUELSMAN, L. P., and P. E. ALLEN. *Introduction to the Theory and Design of Active Filters.* New York: McGraw-Hill Book Co., 1980.

TUINENGA, P. *Spice.* Englewood Cliffs, NJ: Prentice Hall, 1988.

WAIT, JOHN V., LAWRENCE P. HUELSMAN and GRANINO A. KORN. *Introduction to Operational Amplifier Theory and Applications.* New York: McGraw-Hill Book Co., 1975.

7

ELECTRO-MAGNETICS MODULE

Stanley V. Marshall
University of Missouri at Rolla

INTRODUCTION

This electromagnetics module illustrates electromagnetic design by examining two specific projects: one related to radio waves, the other related to static magnetic fields. Each project is typical of design work that can be finished in a single semester, provided the student has had some prior time to select the project.

The first project, a radio direction finder, calls upon basic knowledge of wave propagation and the directional characteristics of certain forms of antennas. It also requires the knowledge of how to couple an antenna to a receiver to obtain the prescribed pattern. The project emphasizes the identifying of the application and planning the tasks such that everything can be completed in one semester (sixteen weeks). This design project may be particularly attractive to radio amateurs.

The second project, a vehicle detector, is more ambitious. It calls for knowledge of magnetic dipole fields of vehicles relative to the earth's magnetic field and the ability to apply this knowledge to a functioning system through various circuit techniques. The project lends itself to a team effort.

SUGGESTED PROJECT TOPICS

Most electromagnetics projects are of necessity combined with other special areas such as computers, circuits, controls, or power. In the following lists of suggested topics, consider the role that electromagnetics plays in each project, and the role played by other subsystems.

- Log-periodic antenna
- Yagi antenna
- Delay line
- Spiral antenna
- Attenuator
- Electronic compass
- Magnetic anomaly detector
- DC current monitor
- Presence detector
- Baluns
- Depth sounders
- Satellite antenna dish receiving system
- Microwave amplifier
- Portable 60-Hz field meter
- Communications system

EXAMPLE PROJECT:
RADIO DIRECTION FINDER

NEED IDENTIFICATION

The manager of a marina suggested to an engineering student friend of his that there might be a demand for an inexpensive portable radio direction finder. Such a device could not only be used aboard marine craft but could also be taken ashore to carry on hikes into unmarked areas. Assume that this direction finder would operate in the AM band only. The relative bearing of two known stations and the directions given by a pocket compass would be sufficient to pinpoint one's location. This engineering student, who also happened to be a ham radio operator, remembered reading in the *Radio Amateur's Handbook* about how in some areas a sport is made of hunting down hidden transmitters. The radio direction finder seemed like a worthwhile experiment in design. Assume that you are that engineering student.

The entire unit must be very light and battery-powered. Since the AM band is being suggested, an inexpensive receiver suitable for the project may be purchased at Radio Shack, Wal-Mart, or other retail outlet. You remember that loop antennas are associated with direction finders, but you also remember that AM receivers generally have a built-in "loop-stick" receiving antenna. Perhaps this antenna can be used for the direction-finder loop, provided certain modifications are made, modifications that you aren't able to completely identify as yet. You recall that you have rotated an AM receiver to determine the direction of the maximum signal. Thus, the receiver is already a direction finder of sorts.

Further conversations with the marina manager and with your ham friends convince you that a worthwhile direction finder would be accurate to within ±5 deg., that is, the direction finder will indicate a direction that is at most only 5 deg. to the left or 5 deg. to the right of the true direction of the transmitter. The direction finder must furthermore be able to resolve the 180-deg. ambiguity in the figure-eight pattern of a loop antenna. This means that a "sense" antenna is required. You decide to read up on this sense antenna to see how it works.

You find that ideally, the loop antenna responds only to the magnetic field of the wave and that maximum response is when the magnetic field vector "threads through" the loop, that is, is normal to the plane of the loop. Minimum response (a null) is when the magnetic field vector is parallel to the plane of the loop. If two stations are 180 deg. apart, the relative phase from the two stations is 180 deg. when referenced to a vertical antenna at the same location, and the induced voltage from each is 90 deg. out-of-phase with the voltage from the vertical antenna. It is possible to combine the output of the vertical (sense) antenna with that from the loop and remove the 180-deg. ambiguity. That is an important part of the project and will be discussed later in the section under project implementation. You find that direction finding is certainly not a new topic, but dates back to the beginnings of radio. However, the art of direction-finding continues to occupy design groups to this day, for the problems of ionospheric effect on propagation render some forms of direction finding useless for certain frequencies. In this project, we will concentrate on ground-wave propagation in the broadcast AM band.

Because light weight and portability are of paramount importance, you will probably choose to use only the built-in speaker or earphones to determine when the antenna is pointed toward a null in the pattern.

PROJECT PLAN

Sketch a plan for the project in your lab notebook. Based on discussions with the marina manager and your friends, you have developed some preliminary specifications for the radio direction finder. It should operate from 550 kHz through 1650 kHz, should be easily carried, and should be accurate to within ± 5 deg. for relative bearings.

An off-the-shelf AM broadcast receiver should be satisfactory. Perhaps the existing loop stick antenna can be used for the direction-finder loop. The loop will have to be electrostatically shielded to ensure response to the magnetic field only, and the receiver may also have to be placed in a shielded box.

The sense antenna may be an AM automobile antenna, preferably one that is collapsible. It will be coupled to the receiver in such a way that the input from the sense antenna will be in-phase with that from the loop for one of the maxima, and out-of-phase for the other maxima. This makes it possible to remove the 180-deg. ambiguity. A switch will be provided to switch the sense antenna IN or OUT. Both the loop and the sense antenna will have to be mounted on some kind of base. It would be convenient to have the loop mounted on a turntable with degree markings for reading the relative bearing.

The project easily divides itself into at least five subprojects: selection of a suitable receiver; designing the loop antenna (or modifying the existing loop); designing coupling networks for coupling the now external loop and the sense antenna to the receiver first stage; designing a base (including possibly a turntable) for the antennas; and shielding both the loop and the receiver.

PROJECT DEFINITION.   My project is to design, build, and test a highly portable radio direction finder that operates in the AM broadcast band.

PROJECT OBJECTIVES
- Measure relative bearing from my location to an AM broadcast station to within ±5 deg.
- The 180-deg. ambiguity error is resolved through use of a sense antenna.

PROJECT CONSTRAINTS
- Total price of parts is not to exceed $50.00.
- Must be built and tested in one semester.

STRATEGY.   To attain the objectives stated, an inexpensive AM-band receiver will be purchased and the antenna modified. The loop-stick antenna will be removed, and an extension harness fabricated that will permit the antenna to be 2 or 3 feet removed from the receiver will be attached. The loop stick will be enclosed in a shield, but the shield must not form a closed loop or it will short out the time-varying magnetic field and be ineffective. The receiver will then be completely enclosed by a metal shield to prevent signal leakage into the receiver by a path other than through the antenna.

Using several broadcast-band stations as signal sources, tests of the antenna will determine how deep the nulls in the figure-eight pattern are. Following successful tests of the loop antenna, the design will proceed to design for the sense antenna and 90-deg. phase-shift network.

The preliminary tests outlined above will determine whether the design can be accomplished in a manner planned. Some experimentation with shielding is anticipated. The cable harness lead from the antenna shield should be grounded to the receiver shield.

PLAN OF ACTION
1. Purchase the receiver.
2. Review all literature available on direction finders.
3. Purchase shielding materials, connector, and wiring for antenna harness.
4. Construct shielded antenna and connect to wiring harness.
5. Test antenna for depth of null.
6. Construct shielded enclosure for receiver.
7. Test receiver and antenna together.
8. Construct suitable turntable (optional) or other mounting for antenna loop.
9. Construct 90-deg. phase-shift network for sense antenna.
10. Couple sense antenna to receiver with ON OFF switch.
11. Conduct tests of overall unit to verify proper coupling of sense antenna, both in magnitude and phase.

The schedule required to complete the project in one semester is as follows:

Tasks to do	Week 1 2 3 4 5 6 7 8 9 10 11 12 13 14 15 16
Purchase receiver	**
Review literature	****
Purchase materials	*****
Modify and shield antenna	**********
Shield receiver	****
Test receiver and antenna	** **
Construct sense antenna	***
Couple sense antenna to receiver	***
Conduct tests of system	****
Write report	*******************************

PROJECT IMPLEMENTATION

Under the Project Plan—Strategy, the preliminary tests have determined that the project is feasible. Implementing the final design will be applying the results of the preliminary tests to a prototype unit. The prototype constitutes the final design. Changes can be made, but they must be documented for incorporation into subsequent prototype or production units. A block diagram of the system is shown in Figure 7.1, and the concept is illustrated in Figure 7.2. A loop-stick antenna, taken from a $5.00 pocket AM receiver, is shown in Figure 7.3. Circuit connection details are not available, and would be difficult to trace for an actual unit, but if the wires are clearly tagged before disconnecting the loop antenna from the receiver, the extension harness can be reconnected to the correct wires. A connector will be provided to connect the extension to the receiver.

Prototype Construction

For this example project, the prototype construction will be based on a Panasonic R-1007 AM pocket radio. The loop-stick antenna is as pictured in Figure 7.3. The first order of business is to disconnect the antenna (after carefully labeling the wires) and to proceed to install a connector and wiring extension cable to enable the antenna to be connected to the receiver from 2 or 3 feet away. One must be sure the radio is operating as it was before the extension was added before proceeding.

The loop antenna must be shielded electrostatically. This is accomplished by placing the loop in a channel as is illustrated in Figure 7.4. The receiver and the antenna extension cable must be totally shielded. The shields should be tied to a common point.

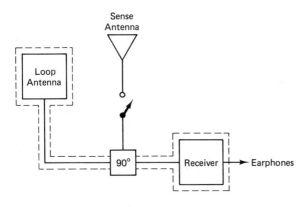

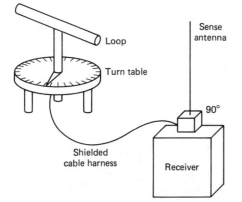

Figure 7.1 Block diagram of radio direction finder.

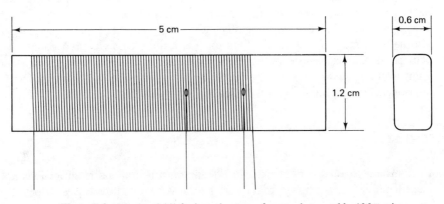

Figure 7.2 The concept of the system.

Figure 7.3 "Loop-stick" ferrite rod antenna from pocket portable AM receiver.

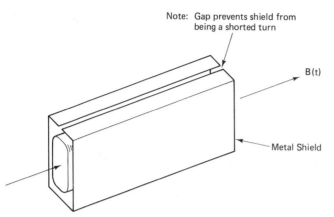

Note: Gap prevents shield from
being a shorted turn

B(t)

Metal Shield

Figure 7.4 Shielded loop-stick antenna.

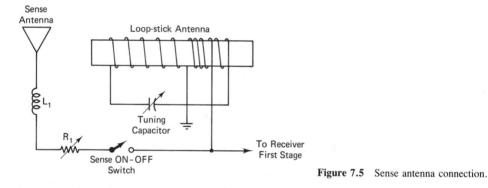

Sense
Antenna

Loop-stick Antenna

L_1

Tuning
Capacitor

R_1

Sense ON–OFF
Switch

To Receiver
First Stage

Figure 7.5 Sense antenna connection.

It will be necessary to consult the references for an understanding of what the sense antenna does. Basically, it feeds an input to the receiver that is 180 deg. out-of-phase with the signal from the loop for one orientation of the loop, but feeds a signal that is in-phase with the loop when the loop is rotated 180 deg. The sense antenna signal must be shifted in-phase by 90 deg. to accomplish this, and the amplitude of the sense signal must also be the same as that from the loop for best results. One way to accomplish the 90-deg. phase shift is to insert a ferrite toroidal inductor in series with the sense-antenna input to the receiver. A variable resistor in series with the sense antenna will be the adjustment for amplitude. This is indicated in Figure 7.5.

DOCUMENTATION

Documentation consists of keeping records of construction and modifications needed to make a radio direction finder from an ordinary AM-band radio receiver. Block diagrams, wiring diagrams, and construction details must be recorded, so that you or someone else could build the same unit a year or more from now from your documentation.

The Final Report or Technical Manual is begun almost as soon as the project commences. If the writing parallels the construction, it will take only a week or two to put it in final form when the project is completed.

EXAMPLE PROJECT: VEHICLE DETECTOR

NEED IDENTIFICATION

There is a need for a device that will activate an alarm or alert system whenever a vehicle, from a motorbike to a large truck, comes to within a radius of 20 feet of the entrance to a storage or garage area. The system must be reliable and capable of continuous operation. The system must be able to self-adjust to the continued presence of a vehicle—that is, it should respond only to the presence of a new vehicle. After having responded to the new vehicle, it readjusts to the new ambient conditions and is ready to respond to the next new vehicle.

There are many technological approaches to this problem, including those that utilize radio-wave interference, sound, seismic disturbance, infrared sensing, and sonar detection. But a particularly attractive approach utilizes magnetism—it detects the magnetic field of a vehicle. Magnetic anomaly detectors, as they are still referred to in submarine detection, have been used for decades for exploration for oil and mineral deposits.

In the northern hemisphere, vehicles become magnetized from the vertical component of the earth's magnetic field so that the top of the vehicle becomes a south magnetic pole. In the southern hemisphere, the top of the vehicle becomes the north magnetic pole.

Preliminary studies would indicate that possibly either a Hall effect probe or a fluxgate sensor may be used, but the fluxgate is more sensitive. The project will begin with the assumption that a fluxgate sensor is to be used, but for completeness, the project director might wish to assign a person to study the Hall probe application.

PROJECT PLAN

Sketch a plan for your project in your lab notebook. Based on preliminary considerations, you have decided to use a fluxgate sensor, and there is some available information from the literature that indicates that a vehicle should be easily detected from a distance of 20 feet.

The least understood part of this project will probably be the sensor itself. Infinetics, Inc., of Wilmington, DE, is one source of toroidal cores that are specifically made for use as fluxgate sensors. Since not every engineering school will have a toroidal core winder in its equipment inventory, the construction of the sensor will involve some tedious hand-winding. But other than the sensor and driver transformer, the circuitry can be constructed from standard readily-available components.

It is suggested that the project be divided into at least three subprojects: sensor construction and driver circuitry, detection and DC amplification, and power electronics for operation of alarms, etc. A suitable power supply, $+15$ V, -15 V, and $+5$ V will be required, but it is assumed that this would not be part of the design project. Once a working unit has been constructed, it would be desirable to obtain empirical data as to the magnetic field strength expected from various vehicles. A measurements program is indicated that would perhaps parallel refinement of the circuitry.

PROJECT DEFINITION.   My project is to design, build, and test a vehicle detection system that utilizes the magnetic field from the magnetized vehicle as the sensor input. The system must adapt to new ambient conditions after some adjustable period of time from the entrance of an intruder.

PROJECT OBJECTIVES
- The device must detect the presence of a vehicle and activate an alarm when a vehicle comes to within 20 feet of the protected area.

PROJECT CONSTRAINTS
- Total cost of parts is not to exceed $75.00.
- Device must be built and tested in one semester.

STRATEGY.   To attain the objectives stated, the first order of business is to review the literature and decide on circuitry. Obtain all the information possible on the magnetic moments of various vehicles. This may be proprietary information and not available in some cases. Make calculations of the effective radius of the protected area using various assumptions concerning the vehicle fields. Decide on how to handle the earth's relatively huge DC magnetic field. Compensate coils or magnets may be used.

After the preliminary considerations mentioned above, the specific assignments should be made. A project of this magnitude should involve at least one person for each major area, that is, at least three people.

PLAN OF ACTION
1. Review the literature.
2. Develop the block diagram of the system.
3. Design the circuitry.
4. Purchase the sensor and other parts.
5. Construct the driver portion of the circuitry.
6. Wind the sensor and test the sensor-driver combination.
7. Construct the detector and amplifiers.
8. Test the system through the last amplifier stage.
9. Design the nulling feature that readjusts for a new ambient field. This may be simply an integrator, or it may consist of some timing circuit.
10. Construct the power electronics. A triac may be used, for example, to actuate the alarm system.

11. Conduct measurements of vehicles.

12. Conduct tests of the overall system.

Tasks to do	Week 1 2 3 4 5 6 7 8 9 10 11 12 13 14 15 16
Review the literature	********
Develop block diagram	*****
Design circuitry	*******
Purchase parts	****
Construct driver and sensor circuitry	****
Construct sensor electronics	****
Test sensor and electronics	*****
Power electronics construction	*******
Complete system tests	**************
Vehicle measurements	********
Final Report	******************************

PROJECT IMPLEMENTATION

The complete block diagram is shown in Figure 7.6. The parts have been ordered and the detailed design begins. If this is a three- or four-person project, this is the time to make assignments for various parts of the total system. For the one assigned to the sensor and driver, the first order of priority is to wind the sensor and driver transformer. Figures 7.7 through 7.9 show the circuitry and winding details. It is important that the exact same number of turns are on each half of the sensor. For the transformer T1, the exact number of turns is not important, as the collector and emitter windings will be perfectly symmetrical because of the technique of connecting the wires. Also, the drive to the sensor will be symmetrical. Switching of the transistors in the driver occurs when at the end of each half-period, the sensor core saturates. Presence of an ambient magnetic field causes the sensor output to have an even harmonic content.

The compensate coil is a solenoidal coil surrounding the sensor, the purpose of which is to balance out any ambient field, including that of the earth. Additional compensation for the earth's field may be accomplished by using magnets. In the circuit described here, the output of an integrator is used to balance out the field after a new intruder has been on the scene for some determined length of time. This circuitry is shown in Figure 7.10 along with the detector/amplifier portion of the circuitry. Other circuitry may be suggested.

The detecting scheme shown in Figure 7.10 is a differential peak detector. The pulses from the sensor output will be predominantly positive for one direction of the magnetic field, and predominantly negative for the other direction of the field. Some sophisticated fluxgate circuits use second harmonic detection instead of peak detection, but peak detection is simpler.

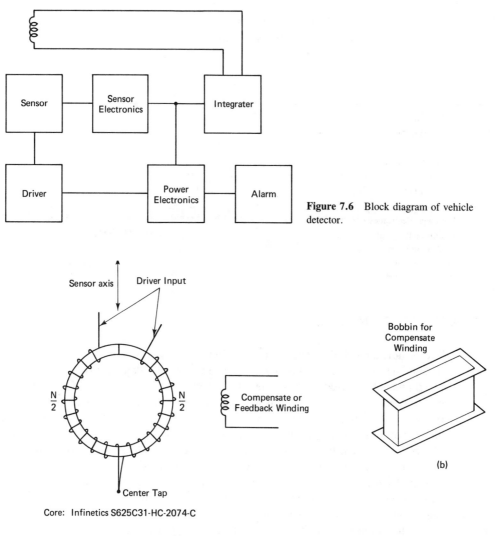

Figure 7.6 Block diagram of vehicle detector.

Figure 7.7 The fluxgate sensor.

The power electronics are shown in Figure 7.11. The DC output of the sensor electronics drives the photo-coupler, which in turn triggers the triac, which can be used to operate any 120 VAC device. An additional stage of amplification before the triac driver may or may not be needed.

The circuit described is a circuit that works, but you see obvious improvements as you proceed through the design. Some time can be given to pursuing other designs, but you must keep to the schedule if the project is to be finished on time. Document what appear to be design improvements in your final report.

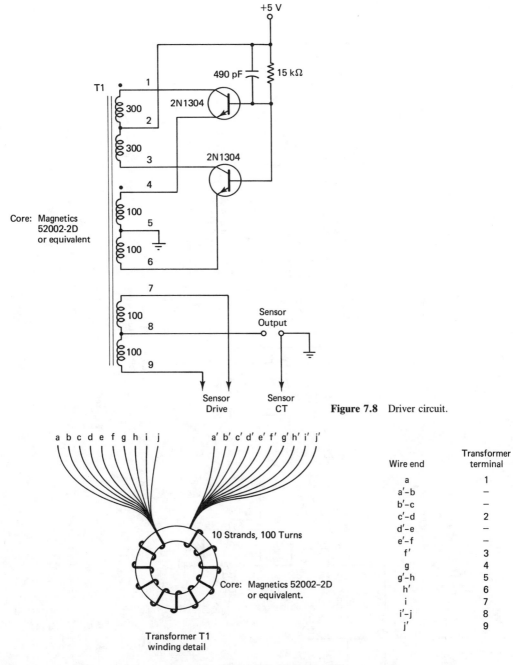

Figure 7.8 Driver circuit.

Wire end	Transformer terminal
a	1
a′–b	–
b′–c	–
c′–d	2
d′–e	–
e′–f	–
f′	3
g	4
g′–h	5
h′	6
i	7
i′–j	8
j′	9

Figure 7.9 Transformer T1.

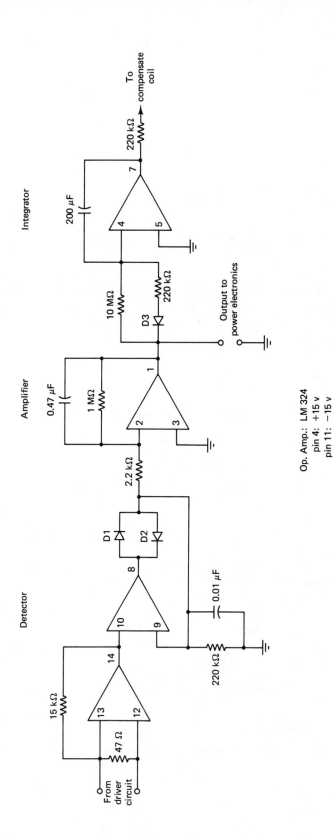

Figure 7.10 Sensor electronics.

Op. Amp.: LM 324
pin 4: +15 v
pin 11: −15 v

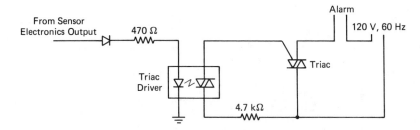

Figure 7.11   Power electronics.

Prototype Construction

The sensor driver, detector, amplifier, and integrator can easily be put on a small protoboard. For convenience, the transformer T1 may be mounted on a small board that can be plugged in to the protoboard. Because of the 60-Hz field that can interfere with the detector operation, the power electronics should be located on a separate chassis or protoboard.

   The packaging of the sensor is the most difficult part of the project. A good deal of thought should be given to this part. The cable to the sensor should be long enough to permit the sensor to be located in a convenient spot without placing the electronics too far from an electrical outlet, and of course the electronics should be in a shelter.

DOCUMENTATION

Documentation consists of recording the schematics of all circuits and the identities of all components (remembering to include part numbers). Keep in mind that someone else should be able to reconstruct the system using your documentation.

   The Final Report or Technical Manual should be begun as early as possible in the project. While the project progresses, this document will be a continuously changing rough draft. The final copy can then be completed within a few days after the completion of the project.

FURTHER READING

The ARRL Antenna Book. Newington, CT: American Radio Relay League, 1988. Chap. 14.

The ARRL 1985 Handbook. Newington, CT: American Radio Relay League, 1985. Chap. 39.

TERMAN, F.E. *Radio Engineer's Handbook*. New York: McGraw-Hill, 1943.

BOND, DONALD S. *Radio Direction Finders*. New York: McGraw-Hill, 1944.

MARSHALL, S.V. "Design and Application for a Portable Gamma-Level Magnetometer." *Proceedings of the NEC 1969*. pp. 236-241.

MARSHALL, S.V. "Vehicle Detection Using a Magnetic Field Sensor." *IEEE Trans. on Vehicular Technology*, Vol. VT-27, No. 2, May 1978, pp. 65-68.

8

FEEDBACK CONTROL MODULE

Charles L. Phillips
Auburn University

INTRODUCTION

The purpose of this feedback control module is to illustrate digital control system design by listing several projects, and by describing two specific projects in detail. Each project is typical of design work that an undergraduate student can finish in a single semester. However, some obvious extensions are suggested for a two-semester design project. In addition, the general area is well-suited to a group of students performing a coordinated design project.

Because each student differs in experience, background, and so forth, some students may not be able to complete a particular project in the allotted time. The projects then should be partitioned into modules, such that a report can be written if the project is terminated after a given module. The report should be written such that another student can begin the project at that point and continue it, without having to reproduce completely the work already accomplished.

The first project, a digital controller for a temperature control system, is a software project that requires knowledge of specific computer interface hardware and software. The project emphasizes the practical aspects of digital control and goes well beyond the usual academic problems encountered in class work.

The second project, a temperature control system, is an analog hardware design. This project requires the choice of an electric heating device, the design of all of the hardware for the actuator that is to control the heater output, and the design of the sensor system for measuring the temperature. The actuator is to be controlled by either a D/A output or a special-purpose interface. The sensor output is to be applied to an A/D input. Depending on the approach used and the hardware already available, this project may be more suitable for a team assignment.

SUGGESTED PROJECT TOPICS

Many feedback control projects can be performed in conjunction with a personal computer. The IBM PC and compatible computers will be the personal computer types discussed in this module, because of both the wide availability of these computers and the large body of literature available on interfacing these computers. However, any personal computer can be used that has:

1. Expansion slots to the computer bus
2. Adequate technical documentation
3. Higher-level language support

The expansion slots are required for the relative ease of connecting hardware to the computer bus. Adequate technical documentation is required so that the hardware and software needed for the connection and control of external hardware can be designed.

Without the availability of high-level languages, such as C, FORTRAN, PASCAL, or BASIC, assembly-language programming is required. When this is the case, the projects degenerate into assembly-language debugging work, and most of the suggested projects requiring extensive software development cannot be completed in the allotted time. However, some of the projects may require that some routines be written in assembly language and linked to the high-level language programs.

In the following lists of projects, the numbers in brackets refer to the list of references at the end of this section. The suggested topics are:

1. *A buffer-board design for the IBM PC.* A buffer board that connects the project hardware to the IBM PC internal bus is required. The buffer board is required to drive external hardware. Also, with this buffer board, any inadvertent incorrect connections to the computer will damage only chips on the buffer board, and not computer chips. The chips on this board should be mounted in sockets for easy replacement. Diagnostic software should be included so that a user can verify the proper operation of the board [1-5].

2. *Data-acquisition and control hardware.* This hardware forms the interface from the computer via the buffer board to the systems external to the computer. The board should contain as a minimum:
   a. A 12-bit analog-to-digital (A/D) converter
   b. A 12-bit D/A converter
   c. A multiplexer that allows at least two analog inputs into the A/D converter

   d. A digital input-output port, such as an Intel 8255A programmable peripheral interface

   e. A timer, such as an Intel 8253 Programmable Interval Timer

   f. Associated control hardware for operation

This project must be coordinated with Project 1 [1-5].

3. *Software to control the data-acquisition and control board.* This project generally requires assembly-language programming, and must be coordinated with Project 2. In addition, the programming must be compatible with the remaining software projects. For example, if FORTRAN is used in the projects below, the software for this project should be written as subroutines that can be linked directly to a FORTRAN program. Diagnostic software should be included such that a user can verify the proper operation of the interface [1-5].

4. *Software for phase-lead, phase-lag, and proportional-integral-derivative (PID) digital controllers.* The IBM PC is to be programmed in a high-level language such that the user can choose between the digital controllers for a closed-loop physical system. The physical system is to be connected to the computer through the A/D and the D/A hardware developed in Projects 1, 2, and 3 [6-8].

5. *Software for modern control design.* This software, written in a high-level language, implements modern controllers for a design based on pole-placement or steady-state linear quadratic (LQ) optimal control. For cases in which all states cannot be measured, a current observer and a reduced-order observer is to be included in the controller software. [7,8].

6. Design and construction of a position control system. This project requires that a complete position control system be designed and constructed, except for the controller. The components required are a DC motor, a power amplifier to drive the motor from the D/A converter of Project 2, and position and velocity sensors for the motor. The sensors must be designed to interface with the A/D converter of Project 2 [6,9,10].

7. *Classical design of a digital position-control system.* This project requires a physical position control system, such as the Feedback, Inc., MS150 or ES130, or the control system constructed in Project 6. The transfer function of the plant can be determined with the software of Projects 12 or 13, or by some other system identification technique. The controller is to be implemented with the software of Project 4. For example, this design can be considered to be a joint control system for the arm of a robot, and the control system specifications are then based on the requirements of the robot [6-8].

8. *Modern design of a digital control system.* Repeat Project 7, except that the design is pole-placement or LQ optimal. An interesting aspect of this project is the specification of the matrices of the cost function in the LQ design to yield a satisfactory robot-arm response. Model the plant as second-order, and realize the controller as full-state feedback, reduced-order observer, and full-order observer. The control-observer is to be implemented with the software of Project 5 [7-8].

9. *Design and construction of a temperature control system.* This project requires that a complete temperature control system be designed and constructed, except for the

controller. The components required are a source of heat controlled by either a DC voltage (D/A output) or a programmable peripheral interface; a medium to be heated; a power amplifier to drive the heat source from the interface of Project 2; and a temperature sensor. The sensor must be designed to interface with the A/D converter of Project 2 [6,9,10].

10. *Classical design of a digital temperature control system.* This project requires a physical temperature control system, such as the Feedback, Inc., Process Trainer PT326, or the control system constructed in Project 9. The transfer function of the plant can be determined with the software of Projects 12 or 13, or by some other system identification technique. The controller is to be implemented with the software of Project 4 [6-8].

11. *Modern design of a digital temperature control system.* Repeat Project 10, except that the design is pole-placement or LQ optimal. An interesting aspect of this project is the specification of the matrices of the cost function in the LQ design to yield a satisfactory transient response. Model the plant as second-order, and realize the controller first as a reduced-order observer and then as a full-order observer. The control-observer is to be implemented with the software of Project 5 [7,8].

12. *Software for least-squares system identification.* This software, written in a high-level language, will calculate a transfer function for a physical system, based on input-output measurements of the system using the hardware of Projects 1 and 2 [7-8].

13. *System identification using the Fast Fourier transform (FFT).* This software, written in a high-level language, will calculate a transfer function for a physical system, based on input-output measurements of the system using the hardware of Projects 1 and 2. The system frequency response is calculated first by the FFT, and a curve-fitting algorithm is then used to fit a transfer function to the frequency response. The resulting device (hardware and software) is a simplified implementation of the Hewlett-Packard HP3562A Dynamic Signal Analyzer [11,12].

14. *PID digital controller for a temperature control system.* This project involves designing a digital PID controller with many of the properties and capabilities of a commercially available digital controller [6,7].

15. *Hardware for analog controllers.* This project is similar to Project 4, except that the controllers are to be analog rather than digital. The analog controllers are to be based on operational amplifiers, and are to allow different analog transfer functions to be realized [6,13,14].

16. *An analog transfer-function simulator.* An analog circuit, based on operational amplifiers, is to be constructed. This circuit is to simulate first-, second-, and third-order transfer functions. This circuit is actually a much-simplified analog computer, and is useful in verifying the proper operation in real time of many of the projects given above [6,13,14].

17. *A programmable controller.* A PC-based logic programmable controller is to be constructed. This controller will open and close relay contacts based on logic expressions that are functions of time and/or digital inputs [21].

EXAMPLE PROJECT:
PID DIGITAL CONTROLLER FOR A TEMPERATURE CONTROL SYSTEM

In this project, assume that you are a design engineer at a controls company. It has been decided that the company will produce a temperature controller based on the IBM PC. The final product will be a software package that utilizes existing hardware interfaces, with software drivers, between the control system and the computer. In addition, a technical manual will be written to accompany the package.

This project is to be broken down into a number of steps. Then, if the entire project cannot be completed, it may be terminated at a convenient point, with the software that has been written completely debugged and a completed software manual.

NEED IDENTIFICATION

Because of the general availability of IBM PC-compatible computers, your company has decided that a market exists for a temperature controller based on these computers. Engineers at companies that currently use analog controllers for temperature control may then easily test digital controllers in the loop; thus they can determine the advantages of replacing the analog controllers with digital controllers. Of course, this digital controller may also be utilized in systems other than temperature control systems.

One advantage of a digital controller based on the IBM PC is that the controller is more versatile than a commercially available controller. For example, the main software of the controller will be furnished in both executable form and in a higher-level language. Hence the engineers at a company that purchases these controllers can modify the software if it is desirable to do so. The controller can then be given the characteristics of various commercial microprocessor-based controllers, and the engineer can decide which controller suits his purposes best.

Another advantage is that the PC-based controller can be converted to a data-acquisition system by slight modifications or additions to the software. Also, while the software of this controller will be programmed to realize a PID controller, other controllers, such as those required for modern control, can easily be programmed in the high-level language.

PROJECT PLAN

Sketch a plan for the project in your lab notebook. You decide, from talks with potential customers and from your own experience, that the controller input should be an A/D converter and the controller output should be a D/A converter. Usually a commercial digital controller will allow a number of different types of inputs and outputs, but we limit these in this case to have a project of reasonable length. An extension of this project would be the design and implementation of hardware and software for other types of inputs and outputs.

PROJECT DEFINITION.   My project is to design and verify the software required to implement a PID digital controller for the IBM PC, using existing interfaces.

PROJECT OBJECTIVES

- Write the software to implement a digital PID controller.
- Make the software easy to use (user friendly).
- Set the gains and the sample period of the controller to default values.
- Change the gains and the sample period using an ''up'' key for increasing a parameter and a ''down'' key for decreasing it, that is, use a simplified keyboard.
- Use the software drivers for existing interface hardware.
- Include a display of the temperature.
- Include an audible alarm for out-of-range temperatures.
- Include a manual start-up feature.
- Include diagnostic software to verify the proper operation of the controller

PROJECT CONSTRAINTS

- Write the software in a high-level language.
- Include sufficient documentation such that a controls engineer can easily understand and modify the software.
- Make the audible alarm the computer speaker.
- Control all operations using only three keys of the keyboard.

STRATEGY.   To attain my objectives, I will study and understand the existing hardware and hardware drivers. I will write and test a PID controller and will link my software to the existing hardware drivers to utilize the existing hardware interfaces. I will write the software in subroutines (procedures) and will thoroughly test each subroutine before beginning the next one. Next, I will write the software for controlling the user interface and the alarm, and will program a model of a temperature control system. After designing a controller for the system and thoroughly testing the controller software, I will write the documentation for the temperature controller.

PLAN OF ACTION

1. Understand the existing hardware and software.
2. Write a simple program in FORTRAN to test linking to the existing software and to test the existing hardware.
3. Develop a complete flowchart of the required software, as I understand it at this point. Keep the flowchart current as the project progresses.
4. Write a simple program to implement a PID controller, and run a time response of the controller, with the controller input applied to the A/D, and the controller output taken from the D/A.

5. Add comments to the software, taking care to make them complete, so that others would be able to understand and use the software if the project were terminated at this point. Include comments in any modules added to the software after this point.

6. Add the menu key, the up key, and the down key. Only these three keys will be used to control the operation.

7. Add the temperature display, the alarm, and the software prompts to ask for the alarm limits.

8. Add the manual start-up, and make it compatible with menu key, the up key, and the down key.

9. Add the diagnostic software for testing of proper operation.

10. Write the documentation.

The schedule that I must follow to complete the project initially appears as shown. (The student is to modify and complete this schedule.) If the original schedule is found to be unrealistic, modify your schedule as often as required, noting the unforeseen problems.

Tasks to Do	Week 1	2	3	4	5	. . .
1	****	****	****			
2	*	****	****			
3			***			
4			**	****	****	. . .
5				****	****	. . .

PROJECT IMPLEMENTATION

Before you get to this point, you should have completed the need analysis and synthesized a potential design. Once you have a reasonable design concept, draw it showing a hardware diagram as in Figure 8.1, and showing a software flowchart of the major modules, as shown in Figure 8.2. Flowcharts of each of the major modules are then constructed as shown in Figure 8.3. Figure 8.3 is shown as an example, and is not necessarily complete.

Next you begin the implementation of the design. The project implementation involves three major steps: understanding the existing interface, designing the flowchart, and implementing this flowchart. Do not expect your first flowchart design to be the final design; the final form of the flowchart will evolve as you learn more about the project. Thoroughly test each software module as you write it. However, do not be surprised if a "thoroughly debugged" module is later found to have errors.

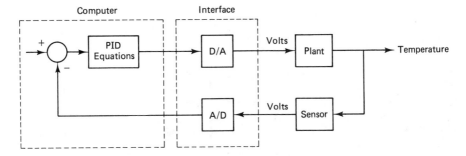

Figure 8.1   Hardware diagram for a temperature control system.

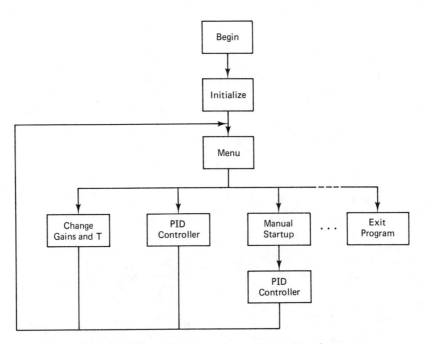

Figure 8.2   Flowchart of the major modules for the software.

Technical Design

The purpose of this design is the implementation of a digital PID controller in a computer as shown in Figure 8.1. First the operation of a digital PID controller must be understood. The output of an analog PID controller is expressed as

$$m(t) = K_p e(t) + K_I \int e(t)dt + K_D \frac{de(t)}{dt}$$

where $e(t)$ is the controller input, $m(t)$ is the controller output, and K_P, K_I, and K_D are controller gains determined by the control system design. In a digital PID controller, the

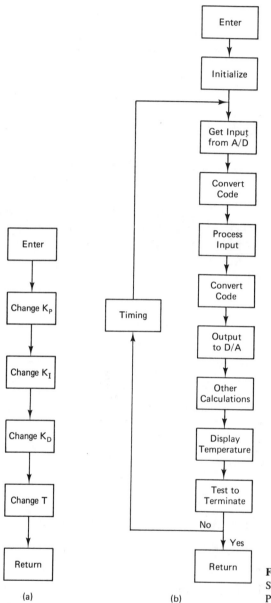

Figure 8.3 Examples of the modules. Shown are (a) change gains and T, and (b) PID controller.

integration, differentiation, multiplication, and addition are performed numerically every T seconds, where T is the sample period. To implement the PID algorithm, a numerical integration algorithm and a numerical differentiation algorithm must be chosen.

All operations are controlled from a menu, and the menu is stepped through by striking a specified key on the computer keyboard. A message is displayed each time that this key is struck; the message indicates which option of the menu is active.

The beginning of a possible flowchart for this project is given in Figure 8.2. The flow chart should be partitioned into modules, such that each module can be implemented directly. Next these modules are partitioned into subroutines (procedures) as shown in Figure 8.3. For example, in Figure 8.3a, the user is given the current value of each parameter and the option of changing that parameter. The user indicates his or her choice by striking a specified key that the parameter is to be left unchanged and the next parameter displayed, or by striking a different specified key that the parameter is to be incremented up (increased), or by striking a third key that the parameter is to be decremented down (decreased). This procedure is used in some commercial controllers to limit the number of keys required on the controllers.

A possible implementation of the PID algorithm, which must be solved in real time, is give in Figure 8.3b. The timing block is required since the algorithm must be solved in real time every T seconds, and is discussed below.

Tradeoffs.   As in most designs, a number a tradeoffs and choices must be made. Many of these will not be evident until implementation has begun. Some of the choices for this project are:

1. *Integer arithmetic or real arithmetic.* The PID algorithm can be programmed in either integer (fixed-point) or real (floating-point) arithmetic. Some advantages of integer arithmetic are:
   (a) Faster execution
   (b) Usually required for controllers implemented with an 8-bit microprocessor (used by most commercial controllers)
   Some disadvantages are:
   (a) Not as accurate as floating point
   (b) More likely to have overflow in the calculations
2. *Numerical algorithms.* Higher-order algorithms for integration and differentiation will give more accuracy, but take more time to execute.
3. *Bumpless transfer.* In the switch from manual control to automatic control in the start-up, you must decide whether additional programming should be included so that no large signals are generated at the controller output during switching—such large signals would "bump" the plant.

Timing.   Timing in a digital controller is of critical importance. The controller algorithm must be executed in real time every T seconds, where T is the sample period of the digital control system. Timing can be implemented using either the operating-system clock or the timer chip on the interface board (if one is available), or else no-operation code can be utilized to delay until the next sample instant.

The PC's system clock outputs a tick every one $1/18.2$ seconds. If this clock is used, an algorithm that counts the ticks can implement the sampling of the A/D converter. The sample period must then be restricted to be an integer multiple of $1/18.2$ seconds. Hence the smallest sample period available is approximately 55 milliseconds, or a sampling frequency of 18.2 Hz. This constraint may not be realistic for a temperature controller.

A second method of implementing the timing is to use the timer on the interface board, if one is available. This method is probably the best, since it allows more flexibility. However, a divide-by-N chip for reducing the system clock frequency may be needed to obtain a reasonable range of sample periods.

If a no-operation algorithm is used, the execution time of all components in the real-time algorithms must be determined. Of course, this execution time must be less than the sample period T. For example, suppose that $T = 0.1$ second, and the execution time of the PID controller module in Figure 8.3b is 23 milliseconds with the timing block ignored. The timing block must then delay $(100 - 23) = 77$ milliseconds in no-operation execution for the module to operate in real time.

Another problem to consider is the possibility that the operating system automatically performs operations that will interrupt your algorithm and make the timing inaccurate. Are there interrupts that must be disabled during real-time operations? Many such questions as these will appear during the design and implementation of your project, and decisions must be made when they occur.

DOCUMENTATION

Proposal

When you first started the sketch of the project plan in your lab notebook, you outlined the major parts of the project proposal. The purpose of the proposal is to communicate a definition of the project, its objectives, and the strategy for meeting those objectives. The proposal also details a plan of action with the schedule for completion. In all likelihood, it also seeks to convince someone that the project is worth pursuing. The following small proposal to your company does all of this.

PROPOSAL
PID Digital Controller

Project definition:	The goal of this project is to design and construct the software of a PID digital controller for a temperature control system, based on existing interfaces.
Project objectives:	Software will be written for a PID digital controller. The software will be controlled by a simplified keyboard. The software will include an audible alarm for out-of-range temperatures. The software will display the current temperature The software will allow manual start-up for the control system. A technical manual will be written to accompany the software.
Strategy:	The project will be broken down into smaller tasks, and the software will be partitioned into modules. Each software module will be logical and can be completely debugged before the next module is started. Using this procedure, the project can be interrupted and restarted at a later date with little lost effort.

Plan of action:	The tasks are:
	Understand and test the existing interface.
	Partition the software.
	Write the PID software and link it to the interface software.
	Add the menu control and the simplified keyboard routines.
	Add the display and the alarms.
	Add the manual start-up
	Write the technical manual.
Reporting:	Weekly reports will be made. At the end of the project, working software and a technical manual will be presented.
Budget:	The funding required will be computer CPU time, estimated to be 100 hours at $5.00 per hour, or $500.00.
Evaluation:	Verification of how well the software meets the design specifications subject to the constraints will be made weekly and at the end of the design project. The final evaluation will be conducted by the design engineer.

The proposal should be written after enough work has been done so that you can write with some authority on the project. In this project, you may need to understand the interface and program a much-simplified PID algorithm to convince yourself that you sufficiently understand the project and can complete it. For many large government and industrial prosposals, a prototype software might be written and tested *before* the proposal is written.

Progress Reports

Normally, an oral or written progress report would be given to your engineering manager or project team members; a weekly report is typical. Customer progress reports are less frequent and their form and scope vary widely depending on the customer and the contract. For government contracts, monthly written reports and quarterly oral reports are not unusual.

If you were making a small written report to your technical manager, the progress report might take the following form:

PROJECT REPORT

Digital Controller Project—Week 4

Current status:	The interface hardware has been tested with a FORTRAN control program. The flowchart of the software for this project has also been completed.
Work completed:	During this week the flowchart of the software for this project was completed and a simple program for a PID controller was begun.
Current work:	The development of the simple PID controller is continuing and is scheduled to be completed over the next week or two.
Future work:	During the fifth week I plan to run a software time response of the PID controller. If time allows, I will run a time response using the hardware interfaces.

Technical Manual

The technical manual should be in the form of a user's manual that gives complete instructions on the use of the hardware and software. In writing this manual, remember that the user will not have exactly your background, and that instructions that seem unnecessary to you might be of great benefit to a user. Your experience in using technical manuals should have convinced you that a few extra words can save the user much time.

The technical manual is also to include a flowchart of the program, definitions of modules, definitions of variable names, and a complete listing of all software. The manual should be sufficiently complete, such that someone could reproduce your work and extend it, based on this manual. Recall that one of the purposes of this project is to produce a digital controller that can be expanded by the purchaser of the controller.

In addition, you are to include a very short final report of two parts. The first part is a time chart showing the actual hours each week that you devoted to the project. The purpose of this time chart is to enable you to correlate hours worked and work accomplished.

The second part of the final report is a critique of your work habits. In this critique, give the work habits that you think are good, and those that need to be changed. If you were just beginning the project, which work habits would you keep, and which would you change? As a final step, complete the two sentences:

My best work habit is . . . .
My worst work habit is . . . .

This final report is for your benefit, and will not influence the project grade.
For your technical manual, a possible outline is:

1. Introduction—a description of the project.
2. Background—a short discussion of the theory.
3. Hardware—a description of the hardware.
4. Software—a description of the software.
5. An example run—an complete example of the application of the digital controller, describing each step of the application.
6. Appendix—a listing of the software, with flow charts, descriptions, and so on.

EXAMPLE PROJECT:
A TEMPERATURE CONTROL SYSTEM

In this project, assume that you are a design engineer at a controls company. Your company has been contacted by a manufacturer who has need for a certain type of control system, and you have been assigned the task of designing and constructing a prototype. The final product will be a temperature control system that utilizes an existing digital controller based on the IBM PC. This digital controller was designed, constructed, and tested in an earlier project. Your task is the design, construction, and testing of the temperature control system external to the digital controller. In addition, a technical manual will be written to accompany the prototype.

This project is to be broken down into a number of tasks. Then, if the entire project cannot be completed in the allotted time, it may be terminated at a convenient point, with the hardware that has been constructed completely tested and a technical manual completed for that hardware. Depending on the approach used and the hardware already available, this project may be more suitable for a team assignment.

NEED IDENTIFICATION

A manufacturer has approached your company concerning the design and construction of several identical temperature control systems to be used on the manufacturer's assembly lines. The temperature control system is to furnish a small air stream at an accurately controlled temperature. The temperature of the air stream is to follow a specified temperature profile for a 5-minute interval. This profile is then to be repeated after a 5-minute pause, with this pattern repeated continually during the work day.

The manufactured product to be heated by the temperature control system is very small, and will assume the temperature of the air stream almost instantaneously. The volume of the air stream is approximately that of a hair dryer, and the temperature required is also about that of a hair dryer. However, the temperature must be accurately controlled over a profile. If the temperature of a hair dryer could be accurately controlled and varied, the hair dryer would be adequate.

PROJECT PLAN

Sketch a plan for the project in your lab notebook. You decide, through talks with the manufacturer, that a device along the lines of a hair dryer is acceptable, but the temperature must be adequately controlled. The flow of air is to be maintained constant and the temperature of the heating element is to be accurately controlled. A temperature transducer is to be placed at a convenient point downstream from the heater. The sensor output is to be a voltage that is compatible with a A/D input of 0 to 10 V.

The heater power, which is to be from an AC source of 120 V, is to be controlled electronically, probably using a triac. The control of the triac is to be sufficiently accurate to give the temperature control required. The triac is to be controlled directly from the digital controller, which may require that the IBM PC interface and controller software be modified. An alternative design would be the off-on control of the heater; that is, the heater is either off or full voltage is applied. However, with this design, accurate control of the temperature may not be possible.

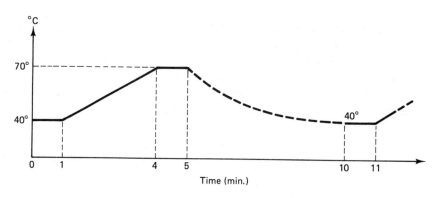

Figure 8.4 Required temperature profile.

PROJECT DEFINITION.   My project is to design, construct, and test a temperature control system that meets certain specifications.

PROJECT OBJECTIVES

- A temperature control system is to be constructed that has the approximate air-flow output of a hair dryer.
- The air-flow output is to have the temperature profile shown in Figure 8.4, with an accuracy of ±1°C.
- A sensor is to be inserted at a convenient point downstream from the heater.
- The heater energy is to be from a 120 VAC power source.
- The digital controller for this system is to be an existing controller. Modification of the controller output interface and its driver may be necessary.
- Both the desired temperature and the output temperature are to be displayed.

PROJECT CONSTRAINTS

- The total cost is to be less than $100 for parts.
- The project must be partitioned into tasks such that, if the total project cannot be completed in the allotted time, the work can be stopped at a convenient point, and a technical manual for the completed tasks can be written. This manual must be sufficiently descriptive that another engineer can continue the project without having to repeat all the work.
- The final device must be safe, such that no one can be burned by the heater, and such that the heater cannot overheat. The blower must be operating any time the heater is activated.

STRATEGY.   To attain my objectives, I will use a blower and a heating element similar to those of a hair dryer. As a first step I will design, construct, and test the triac control circuitry. This control circuitry will be designed to interface with the digital controller.

  Next I will choose the transducer (probably a silicon thermistor) and design, test, and calibrate the sensor circuits. Then I will add the sensor to the heater system and test the complete system. I will then write the technical manual.

  If time constraints allow, I will connect a PI (proportional-integral) digital controller to the system and design the controller by trial and error. Next I will run a time response of the plant (triac input to sensor output). I will use system-identification techniques to obtain a transfer function. Using this transfer function, I will design and test a controller to meet the control-system design specifications.

PLAN OF ACTION

1. Obtain a blower, heater, and cylindrical tube to form the heating system.
2. Obtain a triac electronic switch, study the operation of the device, and test it.
3. Decide on the method of control for the triac, and design and test the control circuits.
4. Choose a temperature transducer that is accurate and linear in the proposed range of operation. Design any required circuits to give a sensor output voltage that is proportional to the temperature. Add sensor circuits such that the range of the A/D is best utilized.
5. Add any required circuits to the computer interface to control the triac by computer software.
6. Design a PI controller, by trial and error, which will maintain a constant temperature.
7. Obtain a transfer function for the plant.
8. Analytically design a digital controller that will meet the system specifications.
9. Test and evaluate the complete system.
10. Write the documentation.

The schedule that I must follow to complete the project initially appears as shown. (The student is to modify and complete this schedule.)

Tasks to Do	Week					
	1	2	3	4	5	...
1	****	**				
2	****	****	****			
3		**	****	****		
4				**	****	...
5						
.						
.						
.						

PROJECT IMPLEMENTATION

Before you get to this point, you should have completed the need analysis and then synthesized several potential design alternatives. (Refer to Chapter 2, Sections 2.2 and 2.3 for additional information.) Once you have a reasonable design concept selected, draw its block diagram as in Figure 8.5, and begin the project implementation. Each task of the project implementation involves two major steps: first the technical design and then the construction of a prototype model for that part of the system. The technical design is a complete paper design of each task; the construction phase of a task is the construction unit and the testing of it for proper operation.

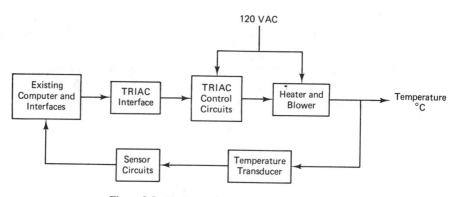

Figure 8.5   Hardware diagram for the control system.

Technical Design

The technical design phase begins with the block diagram of the desired system and finishes with the hardware and software description of the product. The design is on paper in sufficient detail to fully predict how well the product will meet the specifications. For this reason, all your hardware designs and computer programs must be well-documented.

As you draw each of the blocks in the system, you are in effect partitioning the system into functional modules. Each module has a purpose, and you should define each according to its operation, inputs, and outputs. For example, the purpose of the triac control circuits is to give accurate control of the firing of the triac. The triac circuit accepts a signal from the interface which is compatible with the circuit. The interface signal tells the triac when to fire, and in some cases, when to stop firing. Thus the electrical energy to the heater is controlled.

As in most designs, a number a tradeoffs and choices must be made. Many of these will not be evident until implementation has begun. One of the choices for this project is the method of controlling the triac. In using the triac to control the electrical energy into the heater, you are using pulse-width modulation.

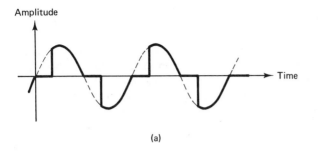

(a)

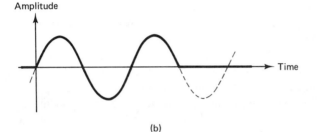

(b)

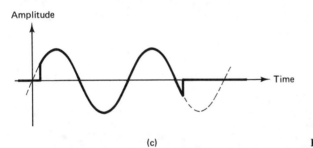

(c)

Figure 8.6 Methods of TRIAC control.

The AC voltage can be pulse-width modulated in a number of ways. Figure 8.6a illustrates detecting the zero cross-overs of the 120 VAC and controlling the width of each half-cycle applied to the heater. Figure 8.6b illustrates detecting the zero cross-overs and conducting an integer number of half-cycles in a specified total number of half-cycles. For example, the triac will conduct an integer number of half-cycles in every 30 half-cycles. This will give a resolution of 1/30, which may not be sufficiently accurate. Figure 8.6c illustrates the same procedure, but the zero cross-over is not detected. The control is Figure 8.6b is not as electrically noisy as the other two methods, since large currents are not switched.

Once you have all the tasks roughly sketched, then you can design the detailed circuits and hardware. The design at this point is completed to the final design, with all the components and their interconnections shown in detail. Actual parts should be selected and fully documented. The design should be in accordance with any design rules that have been set for the project. Any software design is also done in detail from the top-level functions down to the flowcharts and code.

Any time that you design the hardware and software for any of the tasks, be sure that the other tasks are considered in terms of being compatible. Although shown in Figure 8.5 as separate modules, remember that the various hardware and software designs must work together when integrated into the final form.

Prototype Construction

The purpose of building a prototype is to demonstrate that your paper design is correct and to uncover the oversights that will hinder the product's performance. You can easily use your completed prototype in a number of different experiments to adjust the design and verify its performance.

In building the prototype, build it module by module. This holds whether you use wire-wrap, a prototype board, or solder for your actual construction. Hardware can be constructed and tested one module at a time, just as you might write a computer program one module at a time. The reasoning is this: if you build one small module and test it fully for proper operation, then you can use it as part of a larger subsequent module. If any problems develop with the larger module, then you know that the difficulty is probably in the circuit you just added. This modular approach to building and testing hardware is far easier than wiring the entire circuit and then trying to diagnose an elusive malfunction in the system.

DOCUMENTATION

Proposal

When you first started the sketch of the project plan in your lab notebook, you outlined the major parts of the project proposal. The purpose of the proposal is to communicate a definition of the project, its objectives, and the strategy for meeting those objectives. The proposal also details a plan of action with the schedule for completion. In all likelihood, it also seeks to convince someone that the project is worth pursuing. The following small proposal does all of this.

PROPOSAL
Temperature Control System

Project definition:	The goal of this project is to design and construct a temperature control system, using an existing digital controller.
Project objectives:	A temperature control system will be designed and constructed.
	The control system is based on an electrical heater controlled by a triac.
	The temperature of the output air stream will follow a specified temperature profile with an error with $\pm 1°C$.

Both the current commanded temperature and the current actual temperature will be displayed.

A prototype of the control system will be constructed.

A technical manual will be written to accompany the prototype.

Parts for the prototype will not cost more than $100.

Strategy: The project will be broken down into smaller tasks, such that each task is logical and the hardware can be completely tested before the next task is started. Using this procedure, the project can be interrupted and restarted at a later date with little lost effort.

Plan of action: The tasks are:

Select the electric heater and blower.

Select the triac to control the energy output of the heater.

Choose the method of pulse-width modulation for controlling the electrical energy into the heater, and design and test the required circuits.

Choose a temperature transducer based on the required temperature range and accuracy.

Add the required sensor circuits to the transducer.

Add the required displays.

Design a PID controller for the system.

Completely test the prototype.

Write the technical manual.

Reporting: Weekly reports will be made. At the end of the project, a prototype and a technical manual will be presented.

Budget: The initial funding requires $100 for parts.

Evaluation: Verification of how well the prototype meets the design specifications subject to the constraints will be made weekly and at the end of the design project. The final evaluation will be conducted by the design engineer and the customer.

The proposal should be written after enough work has been done so that you can write with some authority on the project. In this project, you may need to understand the operation of a triac and construct and test a simple control circuit for the triac. You may also want to test a temperature transducer with sensor circuits. These tasks may then convince you that you sufficiently understand the project, and can complete it. For many large government and industrial proposals, a prototype might be built and tested before the proposal is written.

Progress Reports

Normally, an oral or written progress report would be given to your engineering manager or project team members; a weekly report is typical. Customer progress reports are less frequent and their form and scope vary widely depending on the customer and the contract. For government contracts, monthly written reports and quarterly oral reports are not unusual.

If you were making a small written report to your technical manager, the progress report might take the form of the following:

PROGRESS REPORT
Temperature Control System Project—Week 4

Current status:	The triac control circuits have been completed and tested.
Work completed:	During this week the design and implementation of the triac control circuits were completed and tested.
Current work:	Some modifications of the existing computer output interface and software will be started this week, and is scheduled to be completed over the next week or two.
Future work:	During the fifth week I plan to initiate the design of a computer output interface to the triac control circuits. If time allows, I will write a driver for this interface.

Technical Manual

The technical manual should be in the form of a user's manual that gives complete instructions on the use of the hardware and software. In writing this manual, remember that the user will not have exactly your background, and that instructions that seem unnecessary to you might be of great benefit to a user. Your experience in using technical manuals should have convinced you that a few extra words can save the user considerable time.

In addition, you are to include a very short final report of two parts. The first part is a time chart showing the actual hours each week that you devoted to the project. The purpose of this time chart is to enable you to correlate hours worked and work accomplished.

The second part of the final report is a critique of your work habits. In this critique, give the work habits that you think are good, and those that need to be changed. If you were just beginning the project, which work habits would you keep, and which ones would you change? As a final step, complete the two sentences:

My best work habit is . . . .
My worst work habit is . . . .

This final report is for your benefit, and will not influence the project grade.
For your technical manual, a possible outline is:

1. Introduction—a description of the project.
2. Background—a short discussion of the theory.
3. Hardware—a description of the hardware.
4. Software—a description of any software.
5. An Example Run—a complete run of the system, with all steps explained.
6. Appendix—supporting information, such as a listing of any software, with flowcharts, description, and so on.

FURTHER READING

1. *IBM Personal Computer Technical Reference*. Boca Raton, FL: International Business Machines Corp., 1983.

2. TOMPKINS, W.J., and J.G. WEBSTER. *Interfacing Sensors to the IBM PC*. Englewood Cliffs, NJ: Prentice Hall, 1988.

3. LEVENTHAL, L.A. *Microcomputer Experimentation with the IBM PC*. New York: Holt, Rinehart and Winston, 1988.

4. LIU, Y.C. and G.A. GIBSON. *Microcomputer Systems: The 8086/8088 Family*. Englewood Cliffs, NJ: Prentice Hall, 1986.

5. *The TTL Data Book*. Dallas, TX: Texas Instruments, Inc., 1976.

6. PHILLIPS, C.L. and R.D. HARBOR. *Feedback Control Systems*. Englewood Cliffs, NJ: Prentice Hall, 1988.

7. PHILLIPS, C.L. and H.T. NAGLE, JR. *Digital Control System Analysis and Design*. 2nd ed. Englewood Cliffs, NJ: Prentice Hall, 1990.

8. FRANKLIN, G.F. and J.D. POWELL. *Digital Control of Dynamic System*. 2nd ed. Reading, MA: Addison-Wesley, 1989.

9. HORDESKI, M.F. *Design of Microprocessor Sensor & Control Systems*. Reston, VA: Reston Publishing. 1985.

10. DORF, R.C. *Modern Control Systems*. 5th ed. Reading, MA: Addison-Wesley, 1989.

11. BURRUS, C.S. and T.W. PARKS. *DFT/FFT and Convolution Algorithms*. New York: John Wiley and Sons, 1985.

12. *Hewlett-Packard Journal*. Hewlett-Packard Co., Palo Alto, CA, January, 1987.

13. MILLMAN, J. and A. GRABEL. *Microelectronics*. 2nd ed. New York: McGraw-Hill, 1987.

14. BERLIN, H.M. *Design of OP-AMP Circuits*. Indianapolis, IN: Howard W. Sams & Co., 1977.

15. GRAUPE, D. *Identification of Systems*. Malabar, FL: R.E. Krieger Publishing Co., 1972.

16. SHEINGOLD, D.H. *Transducer Interface Handbook*. Norwood, MA: Analog Devices, 1980.

17. *Analog-Digital Conversion Handbook*. Englewood Cliffs, NJ: Prentice Hall, 1986.

18. *iAPX 86/88, 186/188 User's Manual*. Santa Clara, CA: Intel Corp., 1985.

19. *1984 Databook*. Vols. 1 & 2. Norwood, MA: Analog Devices, 1984.

20. *Microsoft Fortran User's Guide*. Redmond, WA: Microsoft Corp., 1987.

21. VAN DE VEGTE, J. *Feedback Control Systems*. 2nd ed. Englewood Cliffs, NJ: Prentice Hall, 1990.

9

COMMUNICATIONS MODULE

Martin S. Roden
California State University at Los Angeles

INTRODUCTION

Electrical engineering is a very broad field. Communications is one of the largest and most comprehensive disciplines within electrical engineering. Even within communications is a broad array of sub-disciplines. These include major divisions between analog and digital, divisions based upon application, and divisions based upon the frequency range and/or communication medium being used. It is therefore virtually impossible to present what would be a truly representative design example—we can only scratch the surface.

In communication design there is also an important distinction between system design and hardware design. Indeed, it is possible to design a complex communications system in block diagram form with the expectation that the blocks can be filled in with off-the-shelf items; that is, for example, the diagram can contain a block labeled "oscillator," with the understanding that the specific oscillator design falls within the realm of "electronics." Alternatively, one can carry the design through to an actual circuit diagram containing integrated circuits and components. In the latter case, it becomes obvious that the communications engineer must have a working knowledge of the principles of electronic circuit design.

The purpose of this communications module is to illustrate communications design by examining two specific projects. One of the two projects deals with *hardware* design, the other with *system* design. The hardware design will be that of a remote controller. This device can be either analog or digital and can provide a number of useful features.

The system design will be that of an emergency communication system that is capable of transmitting codes, voice, and facsimile.

SUGGESTED PROJECT TOPICS

The following list of topics spans the broad area of communications.

- Light controller operating through power lines in home
- Basic lightwave communicator that allows transmission of coded signals by flashing a flashlight
- Walkie-talkie
- Wireless microphone (FM broadcast band)
- Voice scrambler
- Voice encryptor
- Remote telephone receiver
- A/D converter and FSK modulator
- Delta modulator
- Spread-spectrum modulator
- Voice digitizer
- Voice analyzer
- Simple facsimile system
- FSK PCM receiver

EXAMPLE PROJECT:
REMOTE CONTROL DEVICE

The purpose of this project is to present a basic design incorporating many of the concepts of communications as they apply to communications designs.

The assignment is to design the communications portion of a home remote controller. The design must be capable of transmitting over a particular distance with a low probability that the receiver will be triggered by unauthorized signals. It is assumed that you need only provide the communication link. You need not worry about switches controlling the individual devices.

NEED IDENTIFICATION

Although remote controllers are available in stores, you want the satisfaction of designing and building your own device. You wish to test the concepts you have learned in class. Furthermore, you want to provide a form of coding that would make it difficult for an unauthorized person to activate your devices. You wish the design to have expansion capability so that you can add control of other devices, such as a gate, lights within your house, security system, stereo, door lock, robot, and a recording device that will announce your arrival to those inside your house. (Think of the possibilities for thwarting a burglary in progress.) In addition to all of the above, the design must be both safe and economical.

Nobody is supplying the specifications, so your first job is to develop them. The questions you must answer in order to set specifications are the following:

a. Over what distance must your transmitter be capable of sending a signal?
b. How many different devices must your device be ultimately capable of controlling?
c. What is the maximum budget for this project (time and dollars)?
d. What is the highest acceptable probability for false triggering?
e. How many different people must use this device? Are there any security implications?

After you answer these questions, you are ready to approach the second level of design, this being the hardware specification. Questions to be answered during this phase include

a. What are the relevant FCC regulations and how do they affect your design?
b. What is the power source for your transmitter?
c. What kind of circuitry should be used?
d. How should the circuit be constructed (e.g., printed circuit, wirewrap)?
e. How should the design be packaged?
f. Am I forgetting a much simpler solution?

STRATEGY

You should get into the habit of starting every design by spending time in the library. The first thing to look for is someone who has already solved your problem or has solved a related problem where modifications are possible. In the case of a remote controller, I would research the popular electronic magazines such as *Radio Electronics*. Try looking at the abstracts. For a simple (hobby-type) project, you might start looking at the *Reader's Guide to Periodical Literature*. If you cannot find someone who has already written about a project identical or similar to yours, you must then conduct a wider search. For example, you could begin by researching FCC rules in order to set the basic transmitter constraints.

We will divide our overall design into six major categories as follows:

1. Set Specifications
2. Conduct Overall System Design

3. Conduct Detailed Design
4. Prototype and Test
5. Final Construction
6. Documentation

Set Specifications

Let us begin by answering the questions raised in the "Need Identification" section.

a. *Over what distance must your transmitter be capable of sending a signal?*
The device we are designing is a remote controller. We envision using it to control both non-moving devices, such as lights, and moving devices, such as doors or gates. Considerations of safety require that we either be within view of the devices being controlled or design sophisticated safety devices (e.g., to stop moving a door if it encounters an obstacle). The simplest approach would be to design for short transmission distances, not exceeding about 50 feet, with the understanding that the operator will exercise caution in controlling moving devices that he or she cannot see.

b. *How many different devices must your controller ultimately be capable of controlling?*
This is generally difficult to decide. It is easy to count the number of devices that you wish to control at present, but predicting the future requires a good imagination. Fortunately, most design approaches can easily be expanded, so we shall start with a requirement for 10 separate control functions.

c. *What is the maximum budget for this project (time and dollars)?*
If you are designing the project for your own use, you should be able to answer these questions. If you are designing for someone else, they should be able to supply the necessary information. Let us assume that you have given yourself up to 2 months to finish the project, and that your total budget is $150.

d. *What is the highest acceptable probability for false triggering?*
This depends upon the nature of devices you are controlling. If, for example, you are controlling a lamp, an occasional "false alarm" may not be critical. If, on the other hand, you are controlling a remote siren burglar alarm, the false alarm rate must be considerably lower. When public safety is involved, the false alarm rate must be extremely close to zero. Let us assume that your applications permit up to one false alarm per week.

e. *How many different people must use this device and are there any security implications?*
The number of people using the device has an effect upon several aspects of the design. For example, is there to be one controller in an accessible location, or must each user carry an individual controller? Are there some devices that should only be controlled by a limited set of users? We will choose the simplest situation: you are the only user and security is not a problem.

Conduct Overall System Design

We are now ready to perform the overall hardware decisions. Earlier, we outlined questions whose answers would help in this phase of the design. Let us begin by attempting to answer them.

a. *What are the relevant FCC regulations and how do they affect your design?*
There are several ways to research FCC regulations. Many libraries contain government publications, and by looking into these publications you will be going straight to the source. But since government regulations make for complicated reading, an easier way to research is to look in the library for books that *describe* the FCC regulations. In the case of radio transmissions, an often useful source of information is the American Radio Relay League (ARRL). The premier publication of the ARRL is the *ARRL Handbook* (formerly the *Radio Engineer's Handbook*), which began publication in 1923 and is updated annually. This comprehensive publication is geared toward the radio amateur. The ARRL also publishes the *FCC Rule Book*.

FCC rule 97.3 states that *radio control operation* is one-way radio communication for remotely controlling objects or apparatus other than amateur radio stations. Rule 97.3 goes on to define local control, remote control, automatic control, and control link. Restrictions are given, both in terms of frequency and power. Certain frequencies may be used if unmodulated carriers are not sent (i.e., the transmitter is not left on between transmissions). Even parts of the citizens band are allocated for use by remote-control hobbyists.

One can carefully read the FCC regulations and arrive at candidate frequency ranges for our project. We would then have to design the transmitter to assure power levels below the FCC maximum requirements.

However, if we restrict transmission to approximate line-of-sight transmission, we have two attractive alternatives to radio transmission, neither of which require conformity to any FCC rules. One alternative is to use pressure waves (sound), the other light waves (e.g., ultraviolet). Ultrasonic transmission uses less power than does ultraviolet, but it has limited bandwidth (thus requiring slow control of fewer items) and is more susceptible to interference and crosstalk. However, because we anticipate operation in a controlled environment, speed and capacity specifications are not demanding, and because power is critical to us (we want to use a battery-operated portable transmitter), we shall choose ultrasonic transmission. There is a little bit of hindsight in this decision, since it assumes an awareness of available circuitry and detectors. The inexperienced designer would probably have to make this decision further along in the process.

b. *What is the power source for the transmitter?*
Because we do not wish to have a fixed transmitter, nor do we wish to tie the transmitter to line power through an extension cord (a safety consideration), we

need a portable source of power. In most cases, this means batteries, although you should not overlook solar energy for outdoor projects.

c. *What kind of circuitry should be used?*
This is dictated by the specifications (such as speed of operation, complexity, etc.) and by the candidate power source. Because we do not want to have to replace batteries very often, we should probably use a low-power form of circuitry, such as CMOS. It is probably best to use digital circuitry for maximum flexibility. For example, if security becomes an issue, digital circuitry allows for such exotic techniques as encryption. Digital circuitry is also less susceptible to false alarms from additive noise. If only a single device had to be controlled, we would probably consider analog circuitry.

d. *How should the circuit be constructed?*
This depends upon how many devices we are constructing. If you are to be the only user, and appearance doesn't really matter, you might opt for constructing the entire circuit on a breadboard. However, these boards are not intended for long-term application, and the wires have a tendency to come loose. You might therefore choose wirewrap. But if you were going to make more than several of the devices, wanted each of them to be fairly compact, and had access to appropriate fabrication facilities, printed circuits would be the best approach.

e. *How should the design be packaged?*
Again, this depends upon who is going to use your invention. People will often judge the quality of your work by the packaging. If others are going to use this device, it is probably best to purchase enclosures and to label controls properly. Indeed, regardless of aesthetics, it is critical that other users be able to understand the proper use of your invention.

f. *Am I forgetting a much simpler solution?*
This is a critical question. We seem to be leaning in the direction of an ultrasonic digital controller custom-designed and implemented on a printed-circuit board. Are we overlooking any other obvious solutions? For instance, does your room have a switched socket into which the device can be plugged? Then you could control it from the light switch on the wall. Should we be thinking of redesigning an off-the-shelf item? For example, an excellent garage door opener can be constructed using a child's walkie-talkie as the basic communication device. How about a flashlight aimed at a photocell? Can something this simple fit the specifications? Do not overlook the obvious! This cannot be emphasized enough. History is full of instances in which complex solutions were implemented (sometimes known as *Rube Goldberg* inventions) where much simpler ones were possible. Take the time to give this issue some serious thought.

In fact, in our particular case, the "breakthrough'" is the realization that the variable-control capability we are trying to achieve is similar to remote control of a television receiver. In the TV application, you wish the capability of selecting channels, varying volume (including mute), turning the set off and on, and a variety of other functions. We could either attempt to purchase surplus TV remote controllers (and modify as appropriate), or search deeper for the mechanism used in the manufacture of television controllers.

Conduct Detailed Design

We have now made a number of critical preliminary decisions based upon the specifications of our project. It is now time for the detailed design. We can start with an overall block diagram of the system, as shown in Figure 9.1. The *human interface* might be a keyboard, or if we wanted to get very fancy, it could be a voice-recognition system. The *coder* formats the various controls into distinguishable signals. The *transmitter* contains the modulator that takes the output of the coder and modifies it to a form that will transmit through the channel. The *receiver* intercepts the transmitted sequence, demodulates and reproduces the coded signal. The *decoder* decodes this signal to ensure that the proper device is receiving the control signal. The *controller* might be a relay that is activated by the decoder. This broad block diagram omits additional levels of sophistication such as encryption and user identification.

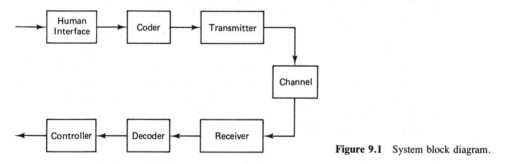

Figure 9.1   System block diagram.

It is at this point that we should take the time to research the literature to find articles describing remote control applications. In fact, a number of articles have appeared in *Radio Electronics*. One such article is

"A Versatile Remote Controller," *Radio Electronics,* Vol. 56, Part I: October 1985, pp. 65-8; Part II: November 1985, pp. 64-6.

Reading the article makes you aware of a set of CMOS IC chips from Motorola, the MC14457 and MC14458, which seem ideally suited to our applications. These are remote-control transmitter and receiver ICs developed for use in remote control of television. As such, they have the capability of controlling as many as 272 functions: 256 channel selections, 12 analog control functions, and 4 toggle control functions.

The next step is to research the Motorola data books to find details of the operation of this pair of chips. Alternatively, you could contact Motorola and request data sheets. The approach you use depends upon how much time you have left to complete the project. In fact, details appear both in the *Motorola CMOS Integrated Circuit Data Book* and in the *Motorola CMOS/NMOS Special Functions Data Book* (Motorola, Austin, TX).

The coded input to the MC14457 chip consists of five rows and four columns. The output is in the form of an FSK signal using frequencies of 38.46 kHz and 41.67 kHz for binary zero and one. These two frequencies are derived by starting with a 500-kHz clock signal and dividing by 13 and 12, respectively.

The actual chip operation and data sequences are rather complex, and permit a two-mode operation consisting of commands and data. This is well-suited to television control. Since our initial application requires a maximum of 10 controlling outputs, we can considerably simplify the design by assuming that only one data digit is required.

A careful examination of the chip specifications indicates that we need to design a transmitter and a receiver.

Design of transmitter. The Motorola MC14457 contains almost all of the necessary functions. It is illustrated in Figure 9.2. R1 through R5 specify the five rows in the input message set, and C1 through C4 specify the four columns. The inputs are active in the low state (ground). The DATA output can be used to drive a display indicating which instruction is being given. We will not use this feature. The output and inverted output will be used to drive our transducer. These outputs can be connected directly to ceramic transducers or to light-emitting diodes (LEDs).

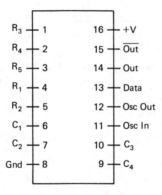

Figure 9.2 MC14457 transmitter chip.

The only external circuitry are the components necessary to set the internal oscillator frequency, the power source, the input device switches (i.e., keyboard), and the transmitting transducer. The external connections are shown in Figure 9.3.

The keyboard, or array of switches, serves the purpose of grounding one input row pin and one input column pin of the MC14457 transmitter. The chip has internal pull-up resistors. The NPN transistor provides a current path to ground. We are using only two of the column inputs, because we have decided to provide for only 10 control devices. If more devices are to be controlled, we would need a matrix-type keyboard. This would raise the price and complicate the operation considerably.

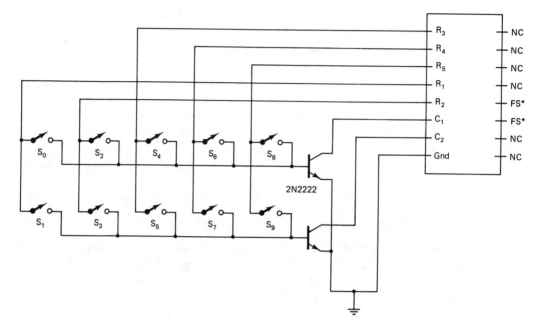

Figure 9.3 Input circuitry to transmitter.

The frequency-setting circuitry should tune the internal oscillator to 500 kHz. A ceramic resonator or crystal control circuit can be used; it is less expensive than a crystal, and the level of accuracy is sufficient for this application. A sample circuit suggested by the chip application sheets is shown in Figure 9.4. This is basically a phase-shift oscillator. You should refer to an electronics textbook for details of design of phase-shift oscillators.

Typical component values are

$$C_1 = 100 \text{ pF}$$
$$C_2 = 1000 \text{ pF}$$
$$R_1 = 10 \text{ M}\Omega$$
$$R_2 = 680 \text{ }\Omega$$

The internal chip construction is such that if none of the input keys are depressed, power is not applied to this oscillator portion of the circuit, thus conserving battery energy.

Design of receiver.   The MC14458 receiving chip is illustrated in Figure 9.5. The M1, M2, M4, M8, L1, L2, L4, L8 form the BCD code for a two-digit decimal number, M standing for most significant bit and L standing for least significant bit. These constitute the data signal, and since we are only using the 4-bit command word, we will not be connecting circuitry to these pins.

Pin 3 is labeled *POR* for "power on reset," and is tied to ground through a capacitor. This resets all internal chip systems to zero when the power is turned on. The incoming signal is fed into Pin 2. However, the signal at the output of ultrasonic transducer is not large enough to form the input to this chip. We must use an extremely high-gain, high-input impedance amplifier with output clipped to 0 V and to 5 V. A typical amplifier configuration (suggested by the data sheets) is shown in Figure 9.6.

Pin 1 of the MC14458 is the oscillator input. The same frequency oscillator must be used in both the transmitter and receiver. The receiver external circuitry must contain an active device, unlike the situation at the transmitter. A typical external connection is shown in Figure 9.7, where we again use a phase-shift oscillator. Note that an inverting amplifier has been added to the circuit of Figure 9.4. We could use an MC4069UB for this application. Finally, the 4-bit output of the MC14458 should be fed to a BCD-to-decimal converter (such as the MC4028B), thus giving 10 output lines. Each line is activated when the corresponding switch is depressed at the transmitter.

The detailed design is now complete. Before building and testing a prototype, we should see if our design can be implemented within the cost specification. In fact, the retail cost of our design is under $100, which is well within the design specification.

We became aware of the Motorola chip set through the article in *Radio Electronics*. Remote control is popular enough that others have entered the field. You might, for example, wish to refer to the Texas Instruments application report entitled, *Infrared Remote Control With TI Products* (TI Semiconductor Group, Dallas, TX). Texas Instruments has a family of chips (SN76832, SN76881, SN76882, SN76891) that suits our application.

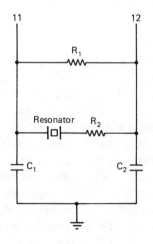

Figure 9.4 Frequency-setting circuitry.

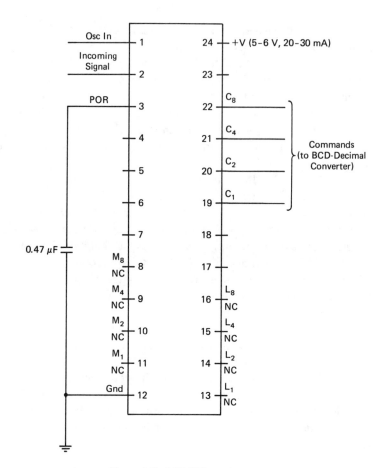

Figure 9.5 MC14458 receiver chip.

Prototype and Test

Now that we have completed the detailed design, it is necessary to build and test the prototype to see if it meets the specifications. Unfortunately, typical computer-aided circuit analysis programs (e.g., SPICE, MICRO-CAP II) do not contain models of these Motorola chips. A computer simulation of the entire system is therefore not practical, and we must resort to a hardware prototype. You may wish to simulate the phase-shift oscillator to see if you chose appropriate values for the resistors and capacitors. You may also wish to simulate the high-gain, high-input impedance amplifier.

The hardware prototype allows us to check the concept, and also to test the system against specifications such as range and false triggering. There is usually not very much ultrasonic energy within the confines of a home, so the probability of false triggering to external noises is extremely low. However, you should experiment with common household objects and devices that generate ultrasonic sound. For example, try jangling a set of

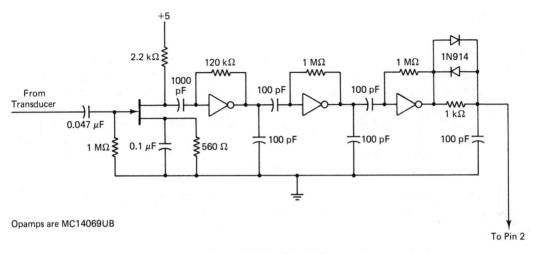

Opamps are MC14069UB

To Pin 2

Figure 9.6   Signal amplifier.

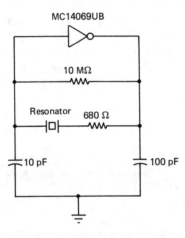

Figure 9.7   Frequency-setting circuit for receiver.

keys. Of course, the actual coding taking place in sending a 4-bit binary code will decrease the probability of randomly triggering any particular device, even when the receiver believes it is receiving a signal.

Final Construction

The circuit is not complex, since most of the operations are performed by the Motorola integrated circuits. It is probably reasonable to implement this using wirewrap techniques, although if you anticipate constructing more than several of these devices, you should consider printed circuits.

Documentation

If this is intended for your use only, minimal documentation is required. You certainly need accurate circuit diagrams, part number listing (a netlist is useful for wirewrap or printed circuits), and vendors (names, addresses, catalog part numbers, prices). While the design is fresh in your mind, you are advised to write operating instructions and a brief theory of operation. The operating instructions and theory of operation will become critical if you need to troubleshoot your system, or if you wish to expand to more than 10 devices in the future.

EXAMPLE PROJECT:
EMERGENCY COMMUNICATION SYSTEM

The purpose of this module is to present an overall system design incorporating off-the-shelf hardware.

The assignment is to propose a backup communication system for your university campus. The system must be capable of transmitting voice and/or facsimile (FAX) to an appropriate law enforcement agency. The product of this design is a proposal in a form suitable for submission to the university president. The proposal must give specifics of a proposed system. It must also contain convincing arguments for the campus to choose that approach.

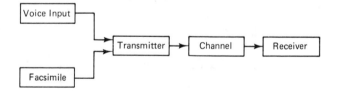

Figure 9.8   Block diagram of emergency communication system.

NEEDS IDENTIFICATION

This project will not involve any hardware design. The student must research the various available systems, compare them with respect to a number of evaluative criteria, and then make a recommendation.

The first task is to develop a list of specifications. This may involve library research in the areas of public safety, or it may involve interviewing key administrators and health and safety officers on the campus. The questions that must be answered in the specification phase of the project include:

    a. *What types of emergencies are we trying to prepare for?*

    b. *What is the likelihood that these types of emergencies will adversely affect the public communication system?*

    c. *What is the distance between your campus and the appropriate law enforcement agency?*

    d. *Will the law enforcement agency cooperate with the campus if doing so requires installing equipment and/or a special antenna at its facility?*

    e. *What is the likelihood that the emergency will adversely affect power supplies and equipment access?*

    f. *What is the number and nature of signals that must be transmitted? In the case of voice, is only one person to be speaking at a time, or must multiplex capability be provided? In the case of facsimile, what type of documents will be transmitted and what is an acceptable transmission speed?*

    g. *Where should the equipment be located?*

    h. *How long would the campus be likely to wait for total deployment of this system?*

    i. *How much is the campus willing to pay for the system?*

STRATEGY

You should start every design project by spending time in the library. The first thing to look for is documentation by someone who has already solved your problem, or who has solved a related problem where modifications are possible. You should look through the abstracts for relevant articles. This is no simple task. You might start with topic headings such as "emergency" or "disaster," or even the broader topic of "communications." You might begin your search by zeroing in on publications aimed at the health and safety professions. If you locate one recent article, it will often contain references that will lead you to other articles. Do not overlook government publications. These are a great resource. Various levels of government have a continuing strong interest in emergency preparation, and communications plays no small part in the planning process.

Following the library search, you should interview a variety of people on your campus to develop answers to the questions posed above. Then contact your local public communications company (i.e., telephone company) and call companies in related fields for advice. This process is often enlightening to students. You will be amazed at the willingness of people to talk. Engineers (in non-security positions) generally love to discuss their work. If you call a company, identify yourself as a student doing a project and ask to talk to an engineer, you will often find that the engineer is willing to spend a great deal of time with you, either on the phone or in person. Companies might see this as an outlet for the pride they have in their work. Be sure to express your appreciation and appear suitably impressed with the person's knowledge of the subject. Here is where all of your people-skills, as developed in most university general-education programs, come into play.

Set Specifications

Let us begin by attempting to answer the questions raised in the "Needs Identification."

    a. *What types of emergencies are we trying to prepare for?*
        We can classify emergencies into two broad categories—those related to environment and those related to people. Among the environmental emergencies are flood, earthquake, explosion, and fire. Among the emergencies related to people could be riots, hostage situations, and health emergencies. Most areas of the country have excellent emergency communication systems in the form of "911" dialing. As long as an emergency does not affect this form of communication, it is reasonable to rely upon public communication systems to summon help. We can therefore restrict our attention to those types of emergencies that might render the "911" system inoperable. These include major floods and earthquakes. Additionally, explosion or fire could affect such communications if these disasters occur in proximity to the campus switching system.

    b. *What is the likelihood that these types of emergencies will adversely affect the public communications system?*
        If we restrict ourselves to major floods, earthquakes, explosions and fires, we can readily research the likelihood of these affecting the public communication system. Major floods affect only certain parts of the country, and they could damage above-ground telephone wires. Major earthquakes could be expected to snap some elevated phone lines and perhaps sever buried cable running across an active fault. Explosions and fires have more local effects upon the public communication system. Indeed, such an occurrence in a telephone switching office can have a major impact upon the communication system. More serious problems in widespread natural disasters are the overloading of public circuits and the telephone company policy of focusing attention on certain categories of users in an emergency. It is quite likely, for example, that in a major earthquake one could call "911" and receive no answer (or a busy signal).

    c. *What is the distance between your campus and the appropriate law enforcement agency?*
        Only research will answer this question for your particular situation. Obviously, it could be less than a mile or many miles. Take a look at a detailed street map to locate the nearest police/sheriff station. Then visit that station to view facilities and talk to people. Finally, measure the line-of-sight distance on the map.

    d. *Will the law enforcement agency cooperate?*
        It is hard to determine the degree of cooperation needed until you propose a particular system. Some proposals will require virtually no additional effort on the part of the law enforcement personnel. Others will require dedication of time and space to install and monitor a system.

    e. *What is the likelihood that the emergency will adversely affect power supplies and equipment access?*

The type of emergencies that would render the public telephone circuits unusable are very likely to affect public power distribution systems. Clearly a backup power source is needed for an emergency communication system. Access to the system is also a serious consideration. It would not be very useful to set up an emergency communication system in a building that is inaccessible during the emergency situation.

f. *What is the number and nature of signals that must be transmitted?*

Our original system requirements indicated the need for voice and facsimile. Our interview of key campus administrators would probably lead to a specification for a limited set of users. We might, for example, wish the campus police, the health center, and the president's office to have access to our voice communication system. We would have to make a design decision on whether these authorized parties would have to move to a central location in order to use the system. If this is not the case, we would have to provide local communication from several points on campus to the emergency communication center. For purposes of this project, we will assume that all users will transmit from a single center. In fact, key personnel could be supplied with simple walkie-talkies, which would require only one person to gain access to the major system transmitter.

We have been told that the system must be capable of transmitting facsimile. Presumably, the person who told us had a good reason for this. We can surmise that we might be transmitting annotated campus maps (with serious damage locations marked), or floor plans of buildings with the location of injured people indicated thereon. This issue would require additional research. For example, if we anticipate the need to transmit many such diagrams in a short period of time, we might wish to make prearrangements with the law enforcement agency to exchange unmarked copies of campus plans. The transmitted information would then simply have to indicate locations on the copies of plans that both parties already have. For purposes of our design, we will assume that a limited number of drawings (perhaps five or less) would have to be transmitted, and transmission times on the order of 1 minute per page are acceptable.

g. *Where should the equipment be located?*

There are two issues that must be addressed. First, the location must be relatively immune from the anticipated disaster. If the concern is earthquakes, a reinforced one-story structure is preferable to a multistory structure with associated architecture that might block access. If fire is the disaster against which we are preparing, a fire-resistant location is mandatory. If the campus area is prone to floods, a high elevation point on campus is desirable.

The location must also be chosen such that it provides access to the various users. Once we identify potential users, the best location might be either the most central to all users or the location nearest one person who is expected to be the prime user of the system.

h. *How long would the campus be likely to wait for total deployment of the system?*

Interest in disaster planning typically peaks right after every disaster, and disappears within one year. However, pressure is building to learn from the mistakes of the past and plan for the future. The amount of time you have for this project depends upon where the idea initiated. If the campus is committed to a system, and has asked you for a recommendation, you will typically be required to complete your report in the time frame of 4 to 6 months. If you are the party initiating the idea, and then trying to sell it to the campus, you can take additional time.

i. *How much is the campus willing to pay for the system?*
This is difficult to determine until you make your proposal. It depends upon the attitude of administration, faculty, staff and students, upon the level of protection your system can provide, and upon the potential losses to the campus if a system is not installed. A typical campus might consider a $250,000 system to be appropriate, while another campus might consider this to be unacceptably expensive. We shall assume that it should not be difficult to convince the average campus to adopt the plan if it costs less than $50,000 (provided we do a good selling job).

SPECIFIC ISSUES

Because we are using off-the-shelf items, the specific issues can be divided into three decision categories:

- The transmission medium
- The modulation techniques
- The specific equipment

We have presented these in the order that you must make decisions. However, because the issues are interrelated, you might have to go through several iterations to arrive at a candidate system.

Let's address the issues individually.

Transmission Medium

The various candidate systems are listed below:

- Point-to-point leased telephone lines
- RF, including amateur radio and citizens band
- Microwave
- Dedicated coaxial cable
- Dedicated fiber-optic cable
- Satellite

We now examine the advantages and disadvantages of each medium. While you must perform this comparison in the design process, you must also be prepared to justify your choice in your final report to the campus. Therefore, the specific comparisons are critical, and you should give a great deal of attention to this phase of the design.

Point-to-point leased telephone lines.

Advantages:

- Your telephone company will provide technical assistance during the design and configuration.
- The fixed plant already exists, so the design and construction time is virtually instantaneous.
- Standard telephones can be used for the voice communication; standard commercial facsimile machines can be used for facsimile.
- Even though public switched networks may become overloaded due to multiple use in an emergency, a dedicated leased line is yours to use 24 hours per day.

Disadvantages:

- There is a monthly charge associated with leasing the line.
- If the leased line uses wires strung from telephone poles, these wires might be damaged during an emergency.

RF.

Advantages:

- RF does not require cables, so it is less likely to be out of commission in an emergency.
- Voice transmitters and receivers are readily available.
- Citizens band has already allocated a channel for emergencies, and many law enforcement agencies monitor this channel.

Disadvantages:

- An FCC license might be required.
- In an emergency, many users may be competing for the same frequency range (channel).
- In certain types of natural disasters, the channel may become very noisy.
- Facsimile machines, while commercially available for use on telephone lines, require some interfacing for use with RF transmission. High-speed facsimile machines, which rely upon combinations of modulation often including phase

modulation, may not be appropriate to the form of modulation used in RF communication.

Microwave.

Advantages:

- Microwave does not require cables between transmitter and receiver, so it is less likely to be disabled in an emergency.
- Voice transmitters and receivers are readily available.

Disadvantages:

- Microwave antennas must be installed at the transmitter site and at the receiver site. This requires dedication of real estate and protection of exposed equipment from tampering. The antennas are likely to be damaged in certain types of emergencies.
- Transmission is line-of-sight. This limits range.
- Transmission is subject to fading and weather-related degradations.
- Facsimile machines require some interfacing for use with microwave transmission. High-speed facsimile machines, which rely upon combinations of modulation often including phase modulation, may not be appropriate to the form of modulation used in microwave communication.

Dedicated coaxial cable.

Advantages:

- Because this is a dedicated channel, there will be no competition for use during an emergency.

Disadvantages:

- This system is extremely expensive to install.
- It requires rights-of-way.
- If elevated, it is subject to damage in disasters.
- If buried, access is required for installation.

Dedicated fiber-optic cable.

Advantages:

- Because this is a dedicated channel, there will be no competition for use during an emergency.

- Fiber-optic channels are not as vulnerable to noise as coaxial cable.
- The wider bandwidth of these channels permits higher-speed communication.

Disadvantages:

- This system is extremely expensive to install.
- It requires rights-of-way.
- If elevated, it is subject to damage in disasters.
- If buried, access is required for installation.

Satellite.

Advantages:

- The channel is not likely to be adversely affected by a local emergency, since the satellite is physically isolated from the earth.
- Leasing of a dedicated channel will prevent competition for use in an emergency.

Disadvantages:

- Monthly fees are required to lease a satellite channel. There is no assurance that satellite transponders will be available for lease for indefinite periods of time in the future.
- An uplink and downlink are required both on campus and at the law enforcement agency. This requires antennas that are properly aimed and are not subject to damage in emergencies.
- Transmission provides little privacy, as anyone with a receiving antenna can monitor the message.

Narrowing the Choices

As we look at the advantages and disadvantages of each transmission medium, we can easily reduce the number of possibilities.

Point-to-point leased line would be an attractive choice if history showed that the actual lines remained in operation after disasters. However, literature search would show this not to be the case: localized damage occurs in fires, and some elevated lines are severed in earthquakes. Nevertheless, the majority of telephone problems occur because of competition among many users for available circuits. This is not a consideration with leased lines.

RF must be rejected outright because of licensing considerations and because of competition from a large number of users. Voice communication on citizens band is simple and inexpensive, but there must be a backup system available in case too many users try to use the emergency channel at the same time.

Microwave is not practical both because of the line-of-sight consideration and because erection of antennas requires cooperation from the law enforcement agency. The antennas are also vulnerable to physical damage.

Dedicated coaxial cable and dedicated fiber-optic cable are ruled out because of the difficulty of either erecting elevated cable or trenching for buried cable. Most college campuses are in established areas where such construction would be prohibitively difficult, if not impossible.

Transmission via satellite, although an exotic technique that would get the attention of college administrators, is not practical because of the questionable availability of channels for long-term lease, and the highly inefficient and expensive use of a dedicated channel (transponder). This would be the system of choice if extreme reliability were required and if cost were not a significant factor.

After we take all of these factors into account, we have decided to recommend a leased line primary system, but with a backup of a low-cost CB radio. If a disaster is sufficiently serious to knock out the leased phone line, and to tie up the CB emergency channel continuously, then it is probably so serious that the campus would have to operate on its own for 24 to 48 hours anyway. In such cases, access to a communication system would not provide any additional advantages.

Our discussions with the telephone company have given us lots of information regarding the leased line data service (note that you must tell the company you plan to use a facsimile in addition to voice). The monthly cost is a function of distance. As an example, a 5-mile distance leads to a monthly fee on the order of $60.

Modulation Technique and Hardware

Now that we have chosen the particular channel, the choice of modulation technique becomes simple. Had we selected microwave or amateur RF bands, we would have significant decisions to make, such as FM versus AM and digital versus analog. In fact, with the choice of leased telephone lines and CB radio, the decisions have almost been dictated to us.

Voice communication on the leased line is by standard telephone set. It is recommended that we purchase or lease the equipment from the same carrier from which we lease the line. In that case, if service is needed we do not encounter the difficulties associated with determining the source of the problem.

Voice communication on the CB radio is by amplitude modulation, and we will recommend purchase of a commercial CB radio transceiver from a local distributor. If the distance to the law enforcement station is small and there are no significant obstructions, an inexpensive portable set is appropriate. One can be purchased for about $100. They are so inexpensive that we will recommend the purchase of three sets. If the distance is great enough or there are obstructions, we need a fixed-base station with backup power supply. The cost will then approach $2000. This decision can be made by viewing specifications supplied by local dealers.

Because we will be using standard telephone-type circuits for the facsimile, any commercially available system can be purchased. Since you have probably not learned about facsimile in your classes, you must do some library research. You learn that systems are classified into four different groups. Groups 1 and 2 are analog, and resulting transmission speed would not be adequate to our application. Group 3 machines are digital, and capable of transmitting a full page in less than 1 minute. Data transfer rates range from 2400 to 9600 bps. Group 4 equipment can transmit both teletext and mixed-mode. These machines are considerably more expensive than the other types, and they are not needed for our application. We therefore settle upon a Group 3 machine. These machines have a resolution of 98 lines/inch, which is sufficient for our intended purposes. (Some machines can be placed into a mode with twice that resolution.)

At this point, you should research the available models and prices. You can visit stores to do this, or do a catalog search in your university library. A starting point could also be business magazines and the business section of newspapers, which have increasing numbers of ads for facsimile systems. The least expensive units are in the range of $1000, while machines in the $4000 range contain some potentially useful features. In fact, we have decided to recommend a Sanyo 7021 device for the campus unit. This facsimile can store 60 pages in memory. We will be recommending that this memory be used to store such things as campus maps and floor plans. The machine simply shares a plug with the voice set we will be using. In fact, many facsimile machines include a voice set, thus eliminating the need for the separate telephone set. The facsimile machine requires a separate power source, so we will be recommending an emergency backup generator.

Documentation

We are now ready to convince the university to adopt this proposal. It is important that you make a convincing case without getting buried in technical detail. At the same time, however, you must convince the president that you know what you are talking about.

A three-layer approach is suggested. The first layer is composed of a simple cover letter that proposes the system and estimates cost. This letter should refer to attachments—the remaining two layers.

The second layer consists of a technical discussion of the reasons for the selection. Many of the points raised in our discussion in this chapter should be stated clearly and specifically in this second layer.

The third layer consists of supporting detailed documentation. Literature from vendors, published reports of reliability, and anything else that shows you "did your homework" should be included.

Following is a sample of the cover letter.

Dear President,
    In an environmental emergency such as an earthquake or major fire, our campus could be cut off from the outside world for a period of 24 hours or longer. In such cases, protection of life and property will require that we have timely access to communication services to request assistance. For example, we may have to

summon ambulances or fire fighting equipment to the campus.
There have been many examples of cases in which a public facility
was unable to use the normal modes of communication to seek such
aid in an emergency.

The attached report recommends an emergency backup
communication system for the campus. The system is capable of
transmitting both voice and written information to the local
police station. I have met with the local police authorities,
and they have agreed to support this system.

Installation of the system can be accomplished in as little
as 30 days, and the required finances are extremely low. In
fact, the initial expense for equipment is only $6500, and the
monthly cost of leasing the channel from the telephone company is
under $70. The system includes backup power generation equipment,
and two forms of communication (telephone and citizens band
radio) for extra reliability.

I am sure you will agree that this is a very inexpensive
form of insurance against much greater potential losses for the
campus.

My report details the reasons for the selections and the
names and phone numbers of the contact people who will supply the
system.

As a student, I am vitally interested in the safety of the
campus. I hope you will seriously consider this proposal, and
assign the appropriate campus personnel to take it up forthwith.

I am, of course, available to discuss this or to do additional
studies or supervision of installation, if you so desire.
Sincerely,

(Signature)

Electrical Engineering major

FURTHER READING

KILLEN, HAROLD B. *Telecommunications and Data Communication System Design with Troubleshooting.* Englewood Cliffs, NJ: Prentice Hall, 1986.

MCMENAMIN, J. MICHAEL. *Linear Integrated Circuits.* Englewood Cliffs, NJ: Prentice Hall, 1985.

RODEN, MARTIN S. *Digital Communication Systems Design.* Englewood Cliffs, NJ: Prentice Hall, 1988.

Radio Electronics. Farmingdale, NY: Gernsback Publications.

SMITH, JACK. *Modern Communication Circuits.* New York: McGraw-Hill, 1986.

10 POWER MODULE

Muhammad H. Rashid
Indiana University-Purdue, Fort Wayne

INTRODUCTION

The purpose of this power module is to illustrate project design by two examples. One project is typical of design work which can be completed in one semester as an undergraduate engineering student and the other project is typical of two-semester design work.

The first project, which is a converter-fed DC motor drive, is implemented by analog electronics with discrete components and emphasizes the techniques involved in the implementation of certain desired functions. The project illustrates the various steps of project design, from identifying the customer needs to technical report writing.

The second project, which is an inverter design, also involves analog electronics with integrated circuit components. It illustrates how technical details and price estimation of a project can be completed for project proposal and feasibility studies.

SUGGESTED PROJECT TOPICS

Although the example projects are illustrated with analog electronics, the functions can be implemented with digital electronics. In fact, most of the modern power electronics equipment use digital control. To simplify the signal processing for power control, manufacturers have developed ICs especially designed for power conversion or control. The developments of fast switching power devices and microprocessors are widening the scope of power electronics for power processing and power control/conversion in industrial applications.

There are many projects that are related to power engineering and power electronics. The following list describes briefly some of them. The full specifications require: (a) input voltage, current, and frequency; (b) output voltage, current and frequency; and (c) the output power. These projects can be implemented by analog or digital electronics, and a closed-loop feedback control may be applied to meet the desired performance specifications.

1. *Single-phase phase-controlled rectifier.* A rectifier is required to supply a DC output voltage. It is required to vary the output voltage from 0 to a maximum value of $V_{DC(max)}$. Thyristors are to be used as controlling devices and the output voltage is varied by delaying firing angles of thyristors. The ripple factor of output voltage should be less than 10%. [1, 2]

2. *Single-phase pulse-width modulator (PWM) controlled rectifier.* It is required to vary the output voltage from a minimum value, $-V_{DC(max)}$ to a maximum value, $V_{DC(max)}$. The voltage control is obtained by pulse width modulation and the controlling devices are gate-turn-off (GTO) thyristors. The ripple factor of output voltage should be less than 10%. [1, 8]

3. *Single-phase sinusoidal PWM-controlled rectifier.* This project is similar to Project 2, except the output voltage is varied by sinusoidal PWM control. [1, 8]

4. *Three-phase phase controlled rectifier.* This project is similar to Project 1, except the input is a three-phase supply.

5. *Three-phase PWM controlled rectifier.* This project is similar to Project 2, except the input is a three-phase supply.

6. *Three-phase sinusoidal PWM controlled rectifier.* This project is similar to Project 3, except the input is a three-phase supply.

7. *Single-phase AC voltage controller.* The input voltage is $V_s = 120$ at 60 Hz. The output voltage is required to vary from 0 to V_s. The controlling devices are Triacs. [1, 9]

8. *Three-phase AC voltage controller.* This project is similar to Project 8, except the input is a three-phase supply.

9. *Single-phase AC static switches for bus transfer.* A static switch is required to turn on and turn off power to a resistive load. The input is 120 V at 60 Hz. Thyristors are to be used as controlling devices. [1, 2]

10. *Three-phase AC static switches for bus transfer.* This project is similar to Project 9, except the input is a three-phase supply.

11. *DC chopper for DC motor control.* A DC chopper is required to control the speed of DC motors. The output voltage should be variable from 0 to V_s. The controlling devices are power BJTs or MOSFETs. [1, 4]

12. *Four-quadrant power controller or battery electric vehicle.* The load motors have four-quadrant operation: forward, reverse, brake while going forward, and brake while going in reverse. The controlling devices could be power BJTs or MOS-FETs. [1, 3, 7]

13. *Power controller for battery-powered wheel chair.* This project is similar to Project 12, except the load specifications and demand will be different.

14. *Power controller for battery-powered bicycle.* This project is similar to Project 12, except the load specifications will be different.

15. *Programmable light/heater control.* An AC voltage controller is required to vary the output voltage from 0 to V_s. The controlling devices could be thyristors or triacs. [1, 5]

16. *Wattmeter for pulsating voltage and current waveforms.* The output voltage and current of power electronic equipment are non-sinusoidal. The true power must be measured from the instantaneous voltage and current. [1]

17. *Computer control of energy meters.* This project is similar to Project 16, except the power must be multiplied by time to measure the energy.

18. *DC switched-mode power supply.* It is required to have regulated DC output voltage from a nominal DC voltage. The output voltage regulation should be less than 5%. The controlling devices are power BJTs or MOSFETs. [1, 10]

19. *High-frequency link AC power supply.* The input is a DC supply of 24 V and the output is 120 V at 400 Hz. The first stage converts a DC voltage to a high frequency AC, and the output is stepped up through a transformer to an appropriate level. A high-frequency link power supply provides isolation between input and output, and it reduces the sizes of components. [1, 13]

20. *High-frequency link DC power supply.* This project is similar to Project 19, except the final inverter stage is not required.

21. *AC source for induction heating.* The input supply voltage of typically 120 V at 60 Hz is rectified to DC and a resonant inverter gives an AC voltage at a high frequency of typically 100 kHz. The controlling devices could be BJTs or MOSFETs. [1, 2]

22. *DC power supplies with resonant inverter.* DC input voltage is converted to AC by a resonant inverter, and the output is stepped up or down by a transformer. The high-frequency AC is then converted to DC voltage. [1, 10, 11, 13]

23. *Single-phase AC power supply from a DC source.* A single-phase inverter with PWM control is required, and the output voltage should be 120 V at 60 Hz. [1, 8, 11]

24. *Three-phase inverter.* This project is similar to Project 23, except the output is three-phase AC.

25. *Synchronous motor drive.* A three-phase inverter with variable voltage and frequency is required to control the speed of a synchronous motor. The inverter is

PWM type and the controlling devices are power MOSFETs or BJTs. The line currents of the motor are controlled so that the inverter gating signals are generated based on the current error signal. [1, 2, 5]

26. *Induction motor drive.* This is similar to Project 25, except the load is an induction motor, the input voltage of the motor is controlled, and the inverter gating signals are generated based on the voltage error. [1, 2, 5]

27. *Gate drive circuits for GTO thyristors.* GTOs are turned on by applying a small positive pulse of typically less than 10 V and turned off by a negative voltage of less than 20 V. The durations of gating pulses are less than 100 μs. The input source is 120 V at 60 Hz. [1, 8, 9]

28. *Crowbar protection.* In the case of faults, it may not be possible to protect the electronics equipment by fuses. A crowbar is commonly used to divert the fault current through a thyristor of higher current rating than the normal rating of the equipment. When the fault is detected, the crowbar circuit is initiated and a fuse associated with the crowbar burns out. [1]

29. *Static transformer tap changer.* The secondary of a transformer has a tap so that the output could be 60 V or 120 V. A static tap changer is required to supply a resistive load with 60 V or 120 V depending on the load demand. This change should be done while on-line. [1, 4]

EXAMPLE PROJECT:
AC-DC CONVERTER-FED DC MOTOR DRIVE

This project could originate from a customer's request, or it could be a new development project of a company, a part of another project, a requirement of senior engineering design project, or a laboratory development. At this stage, the specification is minimum. The title says simply that the load is a DC motor and the input is an AC source, and the motor is supplied through a converter. The project requires further details. Let us assume that this project is a requirement for a senior engineering design course and that it is suggested either by a student or by a professor.

NEED IDENTIFICATION

DC motors are commonly used in variable speed drives for many industrial applications—the textile, cement, aluminum, and machine tool industries in particular. Depending on load demand, the motor speed is required to vary continuously over the entire speed range. The input is normally an AC source and a power converter is employed to provide variable DC output voltage from a fixed AC source. For this project, the input is a voltage source of 120 V at 60 Hz, the maximum output power requirement is $P_L = 2$ kW, and the speed range is N $= -1000$ to 1000 rpm.

As a prototype unit, the motor should be capable of operating in forward or reverse direction under open-loop conditions. It should be noted that a practical drive would have the capability of four-quadrant operations and would be operated on closed-loop control with appropriate analog or digital or microprocessor-based controller. The controller, which could be a standard module for a variety of DC drives in a company, might be developed as an another project. Once a prototype unit is developed with open-loop conditions, the controller unit can easily be integrated to form the final product, which would meet the customer's demand.

PROJECT PLAN

In many industrial situations, a project consists of many technical functions, and several engineers work as a team. To expose the students to industrial situations, two or three students are required to work on a senior design project. The first thing is to identify the project classification, the project title, the engineers involved, the academic advisor, and the project duration. In industrial situations, the role of the advisor could be played by a consultant, an industrial representative if the project is supported by a company, or the manager in charge. Thus, our project could be headed as follows:

Project Code: Senior Engineering Design—EE 440 & EE 460
Project Title: AC-DC Converter-Fed DC Motor Drive
Team Members: M.H. Rashid, H.M. Rashid and F. Rashid
Academic Advisor: M.H. Rashid
Project Duration: One academic year

PROJECT DEFINITION.   It is required to design, build and test a power converter to vary the speed of a DC motor under open-loop condition.

PROJECT OBJECTIVES
- Select a suitable motor to handle 10 kW over the required speed range of 0 to 1000 rpm for a maximum voltage of 100 V.
- Select a suitable power converter to vary the motor voltage from 0 to 100 V.
- Complete design of power converter.
- Development and testing of a prototype unit.
- Prepare a technical report for the project.

PROJECT CONSTRAINTS
- Simple design
- Components cost should be less than $200
- Design must be completed during the first semester

- The prototype unit must be built and tested before the end of the second semester.
- The final technical report must be completed before the end of the second semester.
- The drive must operate in a maximum ambient temperature of 40°C.
- The ripple current of the motor is limited to 10% of DC value.

(Note that in real life situations, the constraints would include steady-state and dynamic response of the drive, four-quandrant drive capability, shut-down sequence, and starting sequence. Note also that the final cost of the project would include the production cost, company overhead, and profits. The typical cost estimation of a product with a basic cost of x is illustrated as follows:

Components cost	x
40% production cost	$0.4x$
50% company overhead	$0.5x$
30% profits	$0.3x$
Final cost	$2.2x$

In this example, the final cost of the product is 2.2 times the basic cost. It is the final cost that must be competitive. Just meeting the specifications is not adequate. The designer must strive to develop or innovate a product within the price constraint.)

STRATEGY

1. Search literature for all possible converter topologies and decide on one that is suitable.
2. Identify various functions by block diagrams and distribute the responsibilities to team members according to their respective specialty or expertise.
3. Develop a computer program to simulate and predict the control performance of the drive and to determine the control range of the converter, input power factor, and load current ripple.
4. Design functional blocks.
5. Build and test each functional block separately on a solderless breadboard. Modify each block if necessary until it works properly.
6. Combine all blocks with the motor as a load.
7. Build and test the prototype drive to confirm the theoretical predictions and to verify the design requirements.
8. Make a survey of good technical reports and obtain samples of each.

WORK PLAN SCHEDULE

Tasks to Do	1	2	3	4	5	6	7	8	9	10	11	12	13	14	15	16	17	18	19	20	21	22	23	24	25	26	27	28	29	30	31	32	33
Team Formation	*																																
Literature Search	*	*	*	*	*	*																											
Work Plan				*	*	*	*																										
Motor Selection				*	*	*																											
Design of Power Converter						*	*	*	*	*	*																						
Thyristor ratings						*	*																										
Converter performance								*	*																								
Protection										*	*																						
Design of Control Circuit						*	*	*	*	*	*																						
Develop block diagrams						*	*																										
Design electronic circuits								*	*																								
Design feedback circuit										*	*																						
Design of Isolation Circuits						*	*	*	*																								
Design of circuits						*	*																										
Design of pulse transformers								*	*																								
Design of Power Supplies										*	*																						
Components											*	*	*	*																			
Specify all components											*	*																					
Price and order components													*	*																			
Semester Report														*	*	*																	
Blocks Development and Testing																*	*	*	*	*	*	*	*	*	*	*	*	*	*	*	*	*	*
Power Converter																*	*	*	*	*	*	*	*	*	*	*	*	*	*	*	*	*	*
Control Circuit																*	*	*	*	*	*	*	*	*	*	*	*	*	*	*	*	*	*
Isolation Circuits																*	*	*	*	*	*	*	*	*	*	*	*	*	*	*	*	*	*
Power Supplies																*	*	*	*	*	*	*	*	*	*	*	*	*	*	*	*	*	*
Prototype Development																											*	*	*	*	*	*	*
Test and modifications																											*	*	*				
Take measurements																													*	*			
Interpret results																														*	*		
Prepare Final Report																										*	*	*	*	*	*	*	*
Presentation																																*	*

PROJECT IMPLEMENTATION

Once the project plan is defined, the next stage is the project implementation, which requires many steps, namely, literature search to evaluate several potential alternatives, identification of functional blocks, work plan, technical design, and prototyping.

Literature Search

The literature search is a very important part of any project. It is performed to find the available circuit topologies and to get some background ideas on the project. The reference materials could be books or other published materials, technical reports, monographs, or patents. The best source is Section B of *Science Abstracts* (on electrical engineering) that lists the summary of almost all published materials in electrical engineering under topics heading. The topics for manual (or computer-aided) search for this project could be "converters," "motor control," "converter-fed DC motors," "drives," "DC motors," and "microprocessor-controlled DC drives."

Functional Block Diagrams

The next step is to identify the functional block diagram as shown in Figure 10.1. Because the input is an AC voltage and the converter should be simple, a single-phase delay-angle controlled thyristor converter would be most suitable. To generate firing pulses for thyristors, a control circuit must be designed and tested. Linking the converter to the control circuit requires isolation because the control circuit cannot be exposed to the main power supply of the converter. The converter will be designed for a specified load condition, such as a DC motor. Circuit equations describing the operation of the drive should be derived and analyzed to determine the thyristor rating and the theoretical converter performance in terms of motor torque, motor average current, and motor ripple current as a function of thyristor firing angle.

The prototype development of the project can be divided into five parts:

1. Design and testing of AC-DC power converter. Selection of DC motor.
2. Design and testing of control electronic circuits to generate appropriate logic signals.
3. Design and testing of isolation circuit. The converter, which is operated from 120 VAC main supply, must be isolated from the control electronics circuits operating typically from a 10 VDC supply.
4. Design and testing of power supplies for control electronics and isolation circuit.
5. Computer program development and theoretical control characteristics.

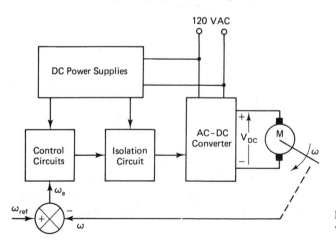

Figure 10.1 Block diagram for converter-fed dc motor drive.

TABLE 10.1 MILESTONE LOG OF AC-DC CONVERTER-FED DC DRIVE

Task	Milestone	Scheduled Completion (Weeks from start)	Date
1	Team Formation	1	9/7
2	Literature Search	5	10/7
3	Work Plan	7	10/21
4	Motor Selection	9	11/7
5	Design of Power Converter	12	11/28
	Thyristor ratings	10	11/14
	Converter performance	11	11/21
	Protection	12	11/28
6	Design of Control Circuit	12	11/28
	Develop block diagrams	10	11/14
	Design electronic circuits	11	11/21
	Design feedback circuit	12	11/28
7	Design of Isolation Circuits	11	11/21
	Design of circuits	10	11/14
	Design of pulse transformers	11	11/21
8	Design of Power Supplies	12	11/28
9	Components	14	12/14
	Specify all components	13	12/7
	Price and order components	14	12/14
10	Semester Report	15	12/21
11	Blocks Development and Testing	26	2/28
	Power Converter	26	2/28
	Control Circuit	26	2/28
	Isolation Circuits	26	2/28
	Power Supplies	26	2/28
12	Prototype Development	29	3/28
	Test and modifications	31	3/14
	Take measurements	32	3/21
	Interpret results	33	3/28
13	Prepare Final Report	37	4/28
14	Oral Presentation	38	5/7

Work Plan

At this stage, the functional blocks are identified and the function of each block is specified. It is possible to draw a work plan and work schedule of the project. The milestone log of the project is shown in Table 10.1.

Technical Design

The technical design is the most important part of any project. The success of any project depends on meeting the specifications or desired objectives. It is very important to maintain records for the circuit designs, calculations, computer results, and other details in a log or lab book. The logbook will serve as the basis of further modifications, technical reports, or documentation. In many industrial applications, standards are set by professional societies. If you are not sure about the desirable specifications for meeting industrial standards, you can refer to standards. In many areas, the IEEE has established certain standards and procedures. Once the functional blocks are identified, the next step is to specify the detailed design of each block to meet the desired objectives and constraints. When designing each block, answering the following questions is usually very helpful:

1. What does the block do to meet the functional requirements?
2. How well must the block perform to meet the performance requirements or specifications? Must the unit block work within a certain accuracy and temperature range? Must it operate from a specified input voltage? Must it output a specified voltage?
3. What system interactions are required to meet the overall performance of the drive? For example, does the drive need feedback for speed control, current feedback for torque control? Does it have input and output impedance requirements? Does it need to inhibit all pulses under fault conditions? Does it need initiating start-up and shut-down sequences, and precautions against overheating and excessive speed?
4. What operator interaction is required to meet the operational facilities? Can the unit have manual speed control, manual start and stop, or manual reset?
5. What hardware interface is required? In case of digital control and microprocessor-based control of drives, the compatibility of bus bar, interface, or logic gates should be considered.

Power converter.   The power converter must perform the following functions:

Functional requirements	Converts from fixed AC to variable DC
Performance requirements	Input of 120 VAC, output from 108 VDC to -108 VDC, ambient temperature of 40°C.
System interactions	Operates from AC main supply; the output must be capable of handling the voltage, current, and power demand of the motor, $V_{DC} = 100$ V, $P_L = 2$ kW, $I_{DC} = 2000/100 = 20$ A, under worst-case conditions.
Operator interaction	Thyristors and fuses must be assembled in such a way that they are easily accessible for replacement. The input line must be isolated by a circuit breaker or manual switch.
Hardware interface	Converter-generated harmonic in the line should be less than 10% of the dominant harmonic.

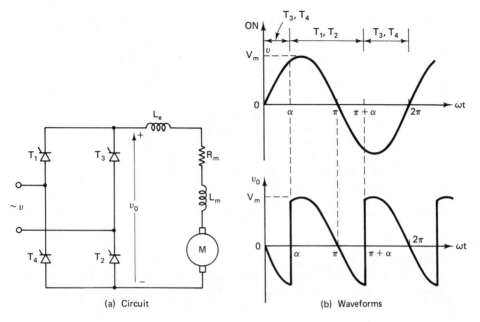

Figure 10.2 AC-DC thyristor converter.

For the sake of simplicity, a single-phase thyristor converter, as shown in Figure 10.2a, is selected, and it should provide the required output voltage control. When thyristors T_1 and T_2 are fired, the input voltage appears across the output, and current flows to the motor via T_1 and T_2. When thyristors T_3 and T_4 are fired, thyristors T_1 and T_2 are turned off. The current is then transferred from T_1 and T_2 to T_3 and T_4, respectively. The inverse of the input voltage appears across the load. The waveform for the output voltage is shown in Figure 10.2b. If α is the delay angle, the average output voltage[1] is found from

$$V_{DC} = \frac{2 V_m}{\pi} \cos \alpha = (2 \times 169.7/\pi) \cos \alpha = 108 \cos \alpha$$

Therefore, by varying α from 0 to π, the average output voltage can be varied from 108 V to -108 V. Also,

- The average load current is $I_{DC} = 20$ A
- The RMS ripple current is $I_r = 0.1 \times 20 = 2$ A
- The RMS value of load current is I_o $[20^2 + 2^2]^{1/2} = 20.1$ A
- The average thyristor current is $I_A = 20/2 = 10$ A
- The RMS of thyristor current is $I_R = 20.1/\sqrt{2} = 14.21$ A
- The peak thyristor current is $I_p = 20 + \sqrt{2} = 21.14$ A

[1]Equation 4-17 in Reference 1.

TABLE 10.2   ELECTRICAL AND THERMAL CHARACTERISTICS OF 25R1A60

$I_{T(RMS)}$	Maximum on-state rms current	40 A
$I_{T(AV)}$	Maximum on-state average current	25 A
I_{TSM}	Maximum peak on-repetitive current	350 A
V_{RRM}	Maximum voltage rating	600 V
dv/dt	Critical value of dv/dt	100 V/μs
I_{GT}	Maximum required DC gate current to trigger	90 mA
V_{GT}	Maximum required DC gate voltage to trigger	3 V
P_G	Maximum peak gate power	8 W
R_{JC}	Junction to case thermal resistance	0.75 °C/W
R_{GS}	Case to sink thermal resistance	0.25 °C/W
i^2t	Maximum i^2t for fusing 8.33 ms	560 A²s
T_J	Maximum junction temperature	125 °C

International Rectifier thyristor type 25R1A60, which has a voltage rating of 600 V, and an average current rating of 25 A, would meet the requirements. Table 10.2 shows the summary of thyristor characteristics.

Heatsink.   Due to current flow through thyristors, there will be power dissipation in the thyristors. The junction temperature, which would rise, must be kept within the maximum limit of $T_J = 125$°C. The device is normally mounted on a heatsink. For an average current of 10 A, the power dissipation would be $P_D = 25$ W (from the characteristic curves of the device). The thermal equivalent circuit of the thyristors is shown in Figure 10.3, where $R_{JC} = 0.75$°C/watt, $R_{CS} = 0.75$°C/watt, $T_J = 125$°C, and $T_A = 40$°C.

The required thermal resistance of the heatsink, R_{SA}, is given by

$$P_D (R_{JC} + R_{CS} + R_{SA}) = T_J - T_A$$

or

$$R_{SA} = \frac{T_J - T_A}{P_D} - R_{JC} - R_{CS}$$

$$= (125 - 40)/25 - 0.75 - 0.25 = 2.4°C/watts$$

Fusing.   Thyristors must be protected under fault conditions by fuses. The i^2t of fuses must be greater than that of thyristors. International Rectifier Corporation power semiconductor fuse of type SF13X30, which has an RMS rating of 30 A at 130 V, should protect the thyristors. It should be noted that the fuse for a power semiconductor device could be more expensive than the thyristor it is protecting.

dv/dt protection.   A thyristor must be protected by snubber network as shown in Figure 10.4 to limit the dv/dt to 100 V/μs. The maximum voltage is $V_m = 169.7$ V. Thus, from Reference 1, equation 14-10,

$$\frac{dv}{dt} = \frac{0.632 \ V_m}{R_s C_s} = \frac{0.632 \times 169.7}{R_s C_s} = 100 \ \text{A/}\mu\text{s or } R_s C_s = 1.072 \ \mu\text{s}$$

Let us assume that the peak discharging current of the snubber capacitor is to be limited to 2 × average load current, that is, the discharging current is $I_d = V_m/R_s = 169.7/R_S = 2 \times 10 = 20$ A, or $R_S = 169.7/20 = 8.5 \ \Omega$. Choosing $R_S = 10 \ \Omega$ yields $C_s = 1.072/10 = 0.107 \ \mu\text{F}$. Let us choose $C_s = 0.1 \ \mu\text{F}$. Therefore the snubber values are $R_s = 10 \ \Omega$ and $C_s = 0.1 \ \mu\text{F}$.

Input filter.   An input filter is normally required to limit the harmonic injection to the supply. A simple LC-filter and its equivalent circuit for harmonics are shown in Figure 10.5. From Reference 1, equation 4-25, the RMS value of dominant harmonic is obtained by letting $n = 3$:

$$I_3 = 2 \ \sqrt{2} \ I_{DC}/3\pi = 2\sqrt{2} \times 20/3\pi = 6 \ \text{A}$$

$$I_s = \frac{-j/(n\omega C)}{jn\omega L \ - \ j/(n\omega C)} I_3 = \frac{1}{1 \ - \ (n\omega)^2 \ LC} I_3$$

For $n = 3$, $\omega = 377$ rad/s and $I_s = 0.1 \ I_3 = 0.1 \times 6 = 0.6$ A, the filter frequency is found to be $1/\sqrt{LC} = 3751.1$ rad/s. Letting $C = 200 \ \mu\text{F}$ gives $L = 0.355$ mH.

Motor selection.   The desired motor should have $P_L = 2$ kW, $V_s = 100$ V, $I_m = 2000/100 = 20$ A. Suppose that the motor, which is a separately excited type, has an armature inductance of $L_m = 25$ mH. The maximum average output voltage $V_{DC} = 2V_m/\pi = 2 \times 169.7/\pi = 108$ V, $I_{DC} = 20$ A.

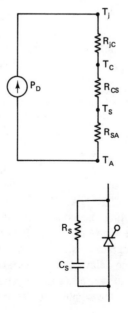

Figure 10.3   Thermal equivalent circuit of thyristor.

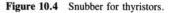

Figure 10.4   Snubber for thyristors.

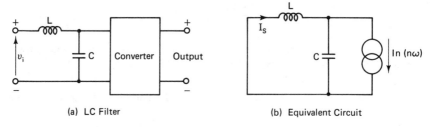

Figure 10.5 Input LC-filter.

Also, from Reference 1, equation 2-63, the RMS value of dominant harmonic voltage at a delay angle of $\alpha = 0$ is $V_R = 4V_m/(\sqrt{2} \times 3\pi) = 50.93$ V. Limiting the RMS value of the load current to 5% of average value and for a supply frequency of 60 Hz, the RMS load current is $I_R = 50.93/(2 \times 2\pi \times 60 L) = 0.05 \times 20 = 1.0$ or $L = 67.64$ mH. The additional inductance required is $L_e = 67.64 - 25 = 32.64$ mH.

Control circuit.   The control circuit must perform the following functions:

Functional requirement	Generates thyristor gating signals, which are delayed from the zero crossing of input sinusoidal voltage.
Performance requirements	Input of 120 VAC at 60 Hz, output pulse of 5 to 10 VDC with variable delay, and delay angle from 0 to π.
System interactions	Detector for shut down sequence and misfiring protection circuit. Feedback signal, which is proportional to motor speed, would control the delay angle.
Operator interaction	Speed control capability by manual override.
Hardware interface	Must be isolated from the 120 V main supply; output voltage should be a pulse of 5 V to 10 V with width of approximately 100 μs; capability of supplying at least 100 mA.

The first step in implementing the control circuit is to identify the functional block diagram as shown in Figure 10.6. The block for the zero crossing detector receives the input sinusoidal voltage and gives a square-wave output. The positive-going edges represent 0 deg. and 360 deg. The delay block provides a shift by an angle α, depending on the feedback signal; its output is used to fire thyristors T_1 and T_2. If the output of delay block is shifted by 180 deg., the signal can also be used to fire thyristors T_3 and T_4.

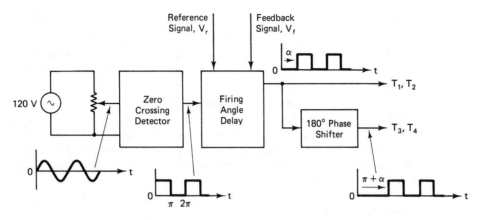

Figure 10.6 Initial block diagram for control circuit.

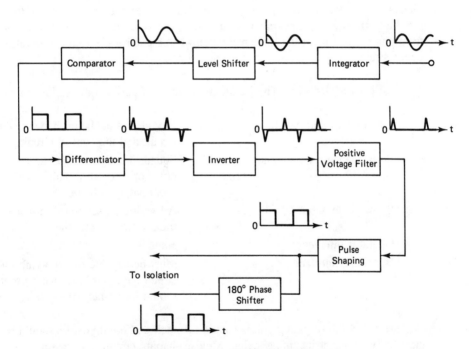

Figure 10.7 Block diagram for control circuit.

Although the scheme in Figure 10.6 generates the required gating signals, there is an alternative arrangement, shown in Figure 10.7, which would be easier to implement. The line voltage is stepped down to 12 V, and is then integrated to generate a cosine signal. The cosine signal is then passed through a level shifter. This shifted cosine signal, which acts as the reference signal, is compared with a speed feedback signal, V_f. The output of the comparator is a square wave whose negative edge is the firing instant of thyristors T_1 and T_2. If there is a short circuit, the shut-down sequence can be accomplished with a NAND gate. The signal from the shut-down detector is normally logic 0. If a short-circuit condition is detected, the shut-down signal would be logic 1, and the output of the NAND gate would be zero, thereby blocking all pulses to the power converter.

Misfiring protection can be incorporated by using a triggering circuit, which sends out a positive pulse at the first zero crossing and stops on the next zero crossing. If the output of the triggering circuit is sent to an AND gate, the thyristor pulse would only get through during the positive half-cycle, which is the firing region of thyristor T_1 and T_2. The emitter-follower after the AND gate is normally connected to serve as a high impedance load to the AND gate.

The gating signals for thyristors T_3 and T_4 can be generated by phase-shifting the output signal of the AND gate by 180 deg.

The circuit diagram of control electronics is shown in Figure 10.8. The opamps and diodes are assumed ideal. Figure 10.8 is not a unique arrangement. Most of the functions can be performed by integrated circuits for power conversion. However, the various techniques involved in the implementation of this control electronics circuit have been demonstrated.

Isolation circuit.   The isolation circuit must perform the following functions:

Functional requirement	Provides an isolation between the power circuit and the control circuit.
Performance requirements	Square input wave of 5 to 10 V; output pulse of 5 to 10 V with a width of approximately 100 µs.
System interactions	All gating pulses must be isolated electrically from each other.
Operator interaction	None
Hardware interface	Must be capable of supplying the required gating voltage and current. There should be no negative gate signal.

Because the width of gating pulses should be small and the thyristors should be fired at the positive edge of incoming signal, a pulse-shaping circuit is necessary. The input is differentiated to generate pulses of small duration at the positive and negative edges. The output of the differentiator is then passed through a transistor switch that will pass only the positive signal, which is passed to thyristor gates through pulse transformers.

To block any negative pulse from the stored magnetic energy, rectifiers are used before the gate terminals for thyristors T_1 and T_2. Similarly, the gating signals for thyristors T_3 and T_4 are generated.

The isolation circuit for firing pulses of T_1 and T_2 are shown in Figure 10.9. The positive signal corresponding to the positive edge turns on switching transistor Q_1. If Q_1

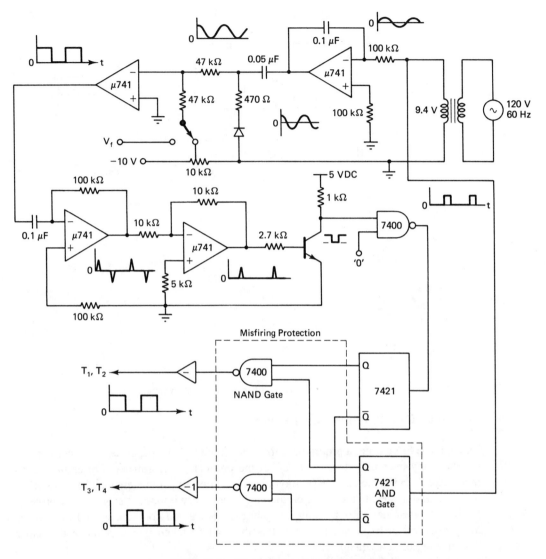

Figure 10.8   Circuit diagram for control circuit.

saturates, voltage V_{CC} is applied across the transformer primary and induces a voltage pulse at the secondary terminals, which is applied to the thyristors. When the drive pulse to the transistor base is negative or zero, the transistor turns off and the current caused by the collapsing magnetic field in the transformer flows through diode D_1. Diode D_2 passes only the positive pulses to thyristor gates. Diode D_3 prevents any negative signal appearing across the gate and cathode terminals. Resistor R_g limits the gate drive current. Resistor R_2 increases the dv/dt capability, and C_g removes high-frequency components. Similarly, the gating signals for thyristors T_3 and T_4 are generated.

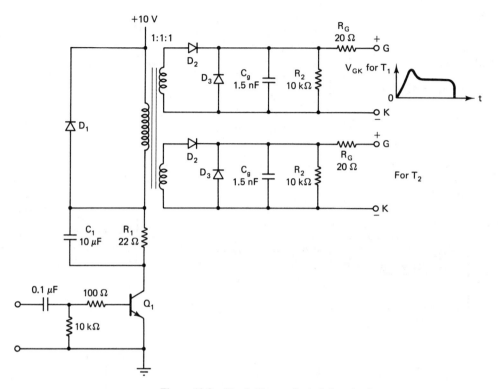

Figure 10.9   Circuit diagram for isolation circuit.

Prototype Development and Testing

The purpose of building a prototype is to demonstrate that the paper design is correct and to reveal any oversights that might affect the product's performance. Different experiments can be performed on the prototype unit, and design parameters may be adjusted to meet the design specifications. A prototype unit is a very important stage of any project. It gives the designer an opportunity to gain experience and confidence, and to learn of many practical difficulties and parameters that can be taken into account in the paper design stage of subsequent projects.

When building a prototype, it is advisable to build it module by module. The modules should be built, tested, and perfected one at a time, rather than building and testing the whole prototype. Building module-by-module enables the designer to spot problems easily: if any problem arises with the larger unit, then it is obviously in the circuit that has just been added. This modular approach to building and testing is much easier than wiring the entire circuit and trying to diagnose the causes of malfunction in the system.

The breadboarding of a module consists of choosing the actual values of circuit elements, finding the best location on the breadboard, placing the elements on the breadboard, and wiring them. The thyristors are mounted on heatsinks; thermal grease should be applied between thyristors and sinks to provide a better heat transfer path. Note that the heatsinks are at the anode or cathode potential of the devices: since this is the case, any contact of the heatsinks by the operator is a dangerous situation. Vinyl grommets could be inserted into the mounting slots of the heatsinks to provide electrical isolation. Anti-arcing glue may be painted over the heatsink face that is closest to the thermal case of the devices.

Next, each block of the controller should be built and tested on a breadboard. This module can be tested by using a sinusoidal input voltage from a signal generator, with an external voltage source to run the logic chips. Once the controller is working satisfactorily, the circuit can be transferred to a permanent printed-circuit board model.

Without capacitor C_1, the pulse duration may not be long enough for the thyristors to latch on. The charging of capacitor C_1 prolongs the duration of the output pulse. A lab pulse generator may be used to simulate the incoming pulses and to test the isolation module.

The control and isolation circuits require an isolated DC power supply, which consists of a step-down transformer and two full-wave bridge rectifiers with filter capacitors. The transformer, which is rated at 120 V and has multiple windings, is used to create an isolated power supply. The transformer has three secondaries, two of which are connected to two bridge rectifiers, the third secondary being used as a reference signal for the control circuit. The integrated-circuit regulator provides the required power-supply voltage of 10 V. The parts and price list for the converter and the associated control circuits is shown in Table 10.3.

DOCUMENTATION

The documentation for a project could be in various forms, namely progress reports, technical report, users manual, technical manual, and proposal.

Progress Reports

The progress reports might be required on a weekly or monthly or semester basis. The reports could be given by oral presentation or over the telephone or by making a brief written report to the technical manager or professor (or engineer) in change. The written report might take the form shown in the digital module on Temperature Control or the following form as:

ENGR 440 & 460 WEEKLY PROGRESS REPORT
AC-DC Converter-Fed DC Motor Drive

Prepared by: M.H. Rashid	Date: June 25, 1988
Accomplishments for week	The design in terms of block diagrams of control circuit and isolation circuit have been completed.
Plans for coming week	To translate the blocks to circuit implementations for the control and isolation circuits.
Problem areas	To locate the catalogs from various manufacturers, to choose component types, and to place a purchase order.

TABLE 10.3 PARTS AND PRICE LIST

Parts	Quantity	Price
25R1A60	4	$ 44.50
0.1-μF, 600-V capacitors	4	$ 3.24
10-Ω (0.5-W) resistors	4	$ 2.00
Fuse holders	2	$ 4.00
3-pole/single-throw switch	1	$ 10.00
Semiconductor mounting grease	1	$ 1.30
Vinyl grommets	1 (pkg)	$ 1.00
Anti-arcing glue (glyptol)	1 (btl)	$ 2.00
Transformer	1	$ 8.90
Bridge rectifier	2	$ 4.80
1700-μF 175-V filter capacitor	1	$ 10.00
500-μF 75-V filter capacitor	2	$ 10.00
1-kΩ (2-W) potentiometers	2	$ 2.00
450-Ω (2-W) resistors	2	$ 2.00
1.75-A circuit breaker	1	$ 3.00
800-μF 100-V filter capacitor	1	$ 6.50
25-Ω (25 W) rheostat for testing	2	$ 4.00
500-Ω rheostat	1	$ 3.00
10-kΩ (0.5-W) resistors	4	$ 1.00
10-Ω (0.5-W) resistors	6	$ 1.50
3-kΩ (0.5-W) resistors	1	$ 0.25
Pulse transformers	2	$ 20.00
1N4005 low signal diodes	10	$ 5.40
2N3904 switching transistors	2	$ 3.52
1.5-nF filter capacitors	4	$ 1.40
10-μF electrolytic	2	$ 1.60
μA741 opamps	4	$ 3.80
TCG1236AP switching transistor	1	$ 0.75
N74121 digital IC	2	$ 1.00
N7400 digital IC	1	$ 0.50
470-Ω (0.5-W) resistors	6	$ 1.50
Miscellaneous resistors	10	$ 2.50
Miscellaneous capacitors	5	$ 5.50
N302 aluminum heatsinks	4	$ 20.80
	Total	$193.26

Technical Report

A technical report is a formal report that is submitted to an authority—usually a company or government agency—that has sponsored the project. The technical report is aimed at technical readers. It should give details of theoretical background, work done, possible areas for further research, discussions, conclusions, and directions for future work. One

possible format for a technical report for the project under consideration is given in
outline below.

AC-DC Converter-Fed DC Motor Drive

Table of Contents

List of Figures
Abstract
Summary
1. Introduction
2. Drive System Design

    2.1 Motor Selection
    2.2 Design of Power Converter
    2.3 Design of Control Circuit
    2.4 Design of Isolation Circuit

3. Converter Development and Assembly

    3.1 Power Converter
    2.2 Control Circuit
    2.3 Isolation Circuit
    3.4 Low-Voltage Power Supply

4. Testing

    4.1 Power Converter
    4.2 Control Circuit
    4.3 Isolation Circuit

5. Design Modifications

    5.1 Power Converter
    5.2 Control Circuit
    5.3 Isolation Circuit

6. Results and Discussions

    6.1 Power Converter Output
    6.2 Motor Speed Response on Open-Loop Control
    6.3 Motor Speed Response on Closed-Loop Control

7. Conclusions
References
Appendix   A: Device Data Sheets
              B: Heatsink Data Sheets

EXAMPLE PROJECT:
SINGLE-PHASE INVERTER

This project originated from a company's desire to supply single-phase inverters to customers. The design/development engineer is required to provide the technical details of the project so that the sales department can prepare a formal quotation for supplying the inverters. The requirements of the project say simply that the input shall be a DC source and the output shall be an AC source, normally 120 V. At this stage it is not required to develop a prototype inverter, which is to be built and tested only if a contract is signed.

NEED IDENTIFICATION

DC-to-AC converters, which are known as inverters, are commonly used in industrial applications, namely, in AC motor drives, AC power supplies, DC power supplies with electrical isolation, and uninterruptible power supplies (UPS's). The DC input voltage of the inverter could be obtained from an AC-DC converter, from a battery, or from solar cells. For this project the input voltage is 48 VDC and the output is 120 V at 400 Hz. The maximum output-power requirement is 1 kW at 120 V and unity power factor.

The inverter could be designed as a standard unit to operate from 12-v, 24-v, or 48-VDC supply and to output 120 V at 400 Hz. The inverter could also be used as a

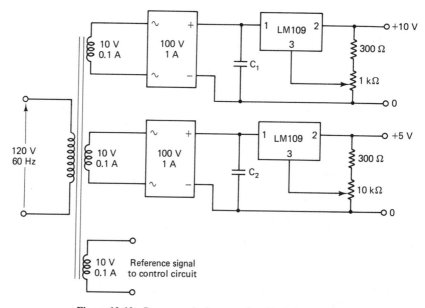

Figure 10.10 Power supply for control and isolation circuits.

module to form a three-phase supply by connecting three single-phase inverters. It should be noted that a practical inverter should have closed-loop control with appropriate analog, digital, or microprocessor-based controller. The controller, which could be a standard module for a range of inverters in a company, might be developed as another project. Once a prototype unit is developed with open-loop condition, the controller unit can easily be integrated to form the final product to meet the customer's need.

PROJECT PLAN

The project classification, the project title, the engineers involved, the academic advisor, and the project duration must be decided upon and the decisions recorded.

Project Code: Solar Energy Conversion
Project Title: Single-Phase Inverter
Team members: M.H. Rashid, and H.M. Rashid
Academic Advisor: M.H. Rashid
Project Duration: 16 weeks

PROJECT DEFINITION.   It is required to analyze and design an inverter to supply a single-phase AC load. The cost is a very important criterion, because the resulting unit must be competitive in the marketplace.

PROJECT OBJECTIVES
- For a supply voltage of 48 VDC, the fundamental component of the output voltage should be 120 V. The RMS value of load current is $1000/120 = 8.33$ A.
- Switching capability of 200 V, $(1000/48 =)$ 20.83 A peak.
- Switching frequency should be high to reduce the size of magnetic elements and filters.
- Resistive or inductive load floated or grounded.
- Prepare a proposal for the project.

PROJECT CONSTRAINTS
- The resulting design should be simple.
- The cost of components must be low—less than $225.
- The input current of the DC source should be continuous.
- The design must be completed within 16 weeks.
- The proposal must be completed by the end of 15 weeks.
- The inverter must be able to operate up a maximum ambient temperature of 40°C.
- The total harmonic distortion (THD) of the output voltage must be limited to 10%.

STRATEGY

1. Search the literature and decide on an inverter topology.
2. Identify various functions by block diagrams and distribute the responsibilities to team members according to their respective specialty or expertise.
3. Develop a computer program to simulate and predict the performance of the inverter.
4. Design functional blocks.
5. Make a survey of good proposals and obtain samples of each.

PROJECT IMPLEMENTATION

Once the project plan is defined, the next step is the project implementation, which requires many steps, namely, literature search to evaluate several potential alternatives, identification of functional blocks, work plan, and technical design.

Literature Search

The literature search is a very important part of any project. It is performed to find any existing circuit topologies and to get some background ideas on the project. The topics for manual (or computer-aided) search for this project could be "inverters" and "AC-to-DC converters."

Functional Block Diagrams

The next step is to identify the functional block diagram as shown in Figure 10.11. Because the input is DC voltage and the converter should be simple, a single-phase transistor inverter should be most suitable. To generate drive pulses for the transistors, a control circuit must be designed and tested. Linking the inverter to control circuit requires isolation because the control circuit cannot be exposed to the power supply of the inverter. The inverter should be designed for the load conditions that result in a maximum current through the inverter. Circuit questions describing the operation of the inverter should be derived and analyzed to determine the harmonic contents of the output voltage and the current ratings of inverter transistors.

Work Plan

At this stage, the functional blocks are identified and the function of each block is specified. It is thus possible to draw a work plan or work schedule of the project. The milestone log of the project is shown in Table 10.4.

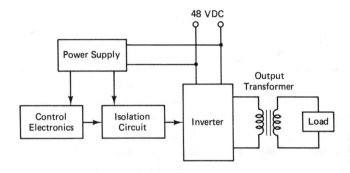

Figure 10.11 Block diagram for single-phase inverter.

Technical Design

Once the functional blocks are identified, the next step is to specify the design of each block to meet the desired objectives and constraints. In designing each block, the answer to the following questions are usually very helpful:

1. What does the block do to meet the functional requirements?
2. How well must the block perform to meet the performance requirements or specifications? Must the unit block work within certain accuracy, and within certain input

TABLE 10.4   MILESTONE LOG OF TRANSISTORIZED INVERTER

Task	Milestone	Scheduled Completion (Weeks from start)	Date
1	Team Formation	1	9/7
2	Literature Search	5	10/7
3	Work Plan	6	10/14
4	Design of Power Circuit	11	11/21
	Transistor ratings	9	11/7
	Inverter performance	9	11/7
	Protection	10	11/21
5	Design of Control Circuit	11	11/21
	Develop block diagrams	8	10/21
	Design electronic circuits	10	11/14
	Design feedback circuit	11	11/21
6	Design of Isolation Circuits	11	11/21
7	Design of Power Supplies	11	11/21
8	Components	12	11/28
	Specify all components	13	12/7
	Determine costs of all components	13	12/7
9	Formal Proposal	14	12/14
10	Presentation	14	12/14

and output voltage ranges? Must it operate from a specified input voltage? Must it output a specified voltage at a specified frequency?

3. What system interactions are required to meet the overall performance of the inverter? For example, does the inverter need voltage feedback for voltage control? Does it have input and output impedance requirements? Does it need to inhibit all pulses under fault conditions? Does it need initiating start-up and shut-down sequences, and precautions against overheating and excessive current?

4. What operator interaction is required to meet the operational needs? Should the unit have manual voltage control, manual start and stop, and manual reset?

5. What hardwire interface is required? In case of digital control and microprocessor-based control of the inverter, the compatibility of bus bar, interface, or logic gates should be considered.

Power circuit.   The power circuit must perform the following functions:

Functional requirement	Convert from fixed dc to fixed ac
Performance requirements	Input of 48 VDC, output of 120 V at 40 Hz, ambient temperature of 40°C.
System interactions	Operates from the DC supply. Output must be capable of handling the voltage, current, and power demand of the load, $I_{AC} = 1000/120$ A $= 8.33$ A, $V_{AC} = 120$ V, under worst-case conditions. The load could be resistive or inductive. The current drawn from the DC supply should be continuous.
Operator interaction	Transistors and fuses must be assembled so that they are easily accessible for replacement. The input line must be isolated by a circuit breaker or manual switch.
Hardware Interface	Dominant harmonic in the output voltage should be less than 5% of the fundamental component.

For continuous current from the DC supply, a single-phase inverter as shown in Figure 10.12a is selected. When transistors Q_1 and Q_2 are turned on, the output voltage is V_S. When transistors Q_3 and Q_4 are turned on, the output voltage becomes $-V_S$. The waveform for the output voltage is shown in Figure 10.12b. Thus,

- Output power is $P_o = 1$ kW
- The average supply current is $I_s = 1000/48 = 20.83$ A.
- The average transistor current is $I_A = 20.83/2 = 10.42$ A

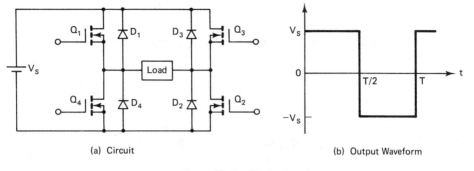

(a) Circuit   (b) Output Waveform

Figure 10.12   Single-phase inverter.

- The peak transistor current is $I_p = 20.83$ A
- The rms transistor current $I_R = 20.83 \times \sqrt{0.5} = 14.44$ A

International Rectifier IRF250 MOSFET, which has a voltage rating of 200 V, a continuous current of 30 A, and peak current 120 A, would meet the requirement. It should be noted that feedback diodes are built-in within the MOSFETs and there is no need of extra diodes. Table 10.5 shows the summary of transistor characteristics.

Heatsink.   Due to current flow, there will be power dissipation in the transistors. The junction temperature T_J, which would rise, must be kept below the maximum limit of $T_J = 155°C$. For an average current of 10.42 A, the power dissipation would be

TABLE 10.5   ELECTRICAL AND THERMAL CHARACTERISTICS OF IRF250

I_D	Continuous drain current at $T_c = 25°$	30 A
I_{DM}	Pulse drain current	120 A
V_{DS}	Maximum drain to source voltage	200 V
$R_{DS(on)}$	Maximum drain to source on-state resistance	0.085 Ω
dv/dt	Critical value of dv/dt	5 V/μs
V_{GS}	Maximum gate to source voltage	20 V
$V_{GS(th)}$	Gate threshold voltage	2 V
$t_{d(on)}$	Maximum turn on delay time	30 ns
t_r	Maximum rise time	150 ns
$t_{d(off)}$	Maximum turn off delay time	100 ns
t_f	Maximum fall time	120 ns
P_D	Maximum power dissipation	100 W
R_{JC}	Junction-to-case thermal resistance	0.83 °K/W
R_{CS}	Case-to-sink thermal resistance	0.12 °K/W
T_J	Maximum junction temperature	155 °C
I_S	Maximum continuous reverse diode current	30 A
I_{SM}	Maximum pulsed reverse diode current	120 A
V_{SD}	Maximum forward diode voltage	2 V

$P_D = R_{DS(on)} \times 10.42^2 = 9.4$ W, which is the on-state loss. The turn-on and turn-off losses of transistors, which are not included in 9.2 W, should be taken into account.

The required thermal resistance of the heatsink, R_{SA}, is given in Reference 1, Chapter 13, as

$$P_D (R_{JC} + R_{CS} + R_{SA}) = T_J - T_A$$

or

$$R_{SA} = \frac{T_J - T_A}{P_D} - R_{JC} - R_{CS}$$

For $P_o = 9.4$ W, $R_{JC} = 0.83°$K/W, $R_{CS} = 0.75°$K/W, $T_J = 155°$C, and $T_A = 40$ °C, R_{SA} = $(155 - 40)/9.4 - 0.83 - 0.12 = 11.28°$K/W.

Short-circuit protection.   It is not very easy to protect transistors by high-speed fuses under fault conditions, because the current-overload handling capability of MOSFETs is poor. The most common method is to protect by a crowbar, where a thyristor, which has the current-overload handling capability, is fired at the detection of a fault condition and the fuse F_1 is burned out. A crowbar circuit is shown in Figure 10.13, where T_1 is the crowbar thyristor and F_1 is the fuse.

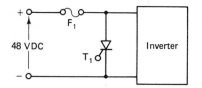

Figure 10.13   Crowbar protection.

di/dt and dv/dt protection.   A transistor must be protected by snubber networks to limit the rise times of current and voltages. For $t_r = 100$ ns, $I_P = 20.83$ A, V_s = 48 V, the equation[2] below gives the minimum value of di/dt limiting inductor as

$$L_s = V_s t_r / I_p = 48 \times 100 \times 10^{-9}/20.83 = 0.23 \ \mu H$$

For $t_f = 120$ ns, $I_p = 20.83$ A and $V_s = 48$ V, the value of snubber capacitance[3] can be found as follows:

$$C_s = I_P t_f / V_s = 20.83 \times 120 \times 10^{-9}/48 = 0.052 \ \mu F$$

The value of snubber resistance[4] is found by

$$R_s = 2 \sqrt{(L_s/C_s)} = 2 \times \sqrt{(0.23/0.052)} = 4.2 \ \Omega$$

[2]Reference 1, Equation 13-56.
[3]Reference 1, Equation 13-58
[4]Reference 1, Equation 13-59

Filters.   In practice, the input source would have a high impedance at the switching frequency, and an input filter should be connected to the input side to provide a low-impedance path for the switching current. The value of the input capacitance can be found approximately from

$$\frac{1}{2} C_i V_s^2 f_s = P_o$$

For $V_s = 48$ V, $P_o = 1$ kW and $f_s = 20$ kHz, $C_i = 40$ μF. For eliminating the high frequency, the load resistance with unity power factor is $V_L = 120$ V, $P_o = 1000$ W, $I_L = 1000/120 = 8.33$ A, and $R_L = 120/8.33 = 14.4$ Ω. Choosing the impedance of the output filter one-tenth of the load resistance, the approximate filter capacitance is found from

$$R_L = 10/n\omega C_e$$

For $n = 2$ and $\omega = 2\pi \times 20 \times 10^3$, $C_e = 2.76$ μF.

Control circuit.   The control circuit must perform the following functions:

Functional requirement	Generates transistor gate pulses, which are determined by pulse-width modulation of sinusoidal reference signal.
Performance requirement	Pulses of 5 V. The pulse width is dependent on the sinusoidal reference signal of 5 V peak. Fast turn-off and fast-rising gate pulses.
System interactions	Detector for shut-down sequence and misfiring-protection circuit. Feedback signal, which is proportional to output voltage, should vary the pulse width.
Operator interaction	Output-voltage control capability by manual override. There should be terminals for checking the proper functions of the control module.
Hardware interface	Must be isolated from the 48-VDC supply. During the first half-cycle of reference signal, the gate pulses for only transistors Q_1 and Q_2 will be released. During the second half-cycle of reference signal, the pulses for transistors Q_3 and Q_4 will be released.

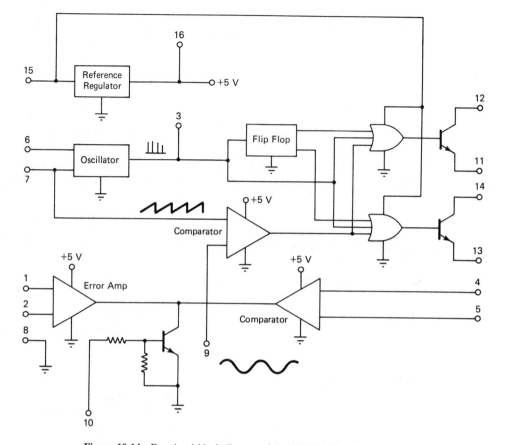

Figure 10.14 Functional block diagram of the SG1524. The pin numbers are used: 1-2 error amplifier inputs, 3 oscillator output, 4-5 control and regulation amplifier, 6-7 R_T C_T to generate the ramp signal for PWM comparator, 8 ground, 9 control and compensation imput, 10 shut-down input, 11-14 open collector output, 15 input supply, 16 reference-voltage output.

Most of the functions of the control circuit may be performed by an integrated circuit especially designed for PWM applications. With the developments of power-conversion techniques for power control, integrated circuits have been developed by various manufacturers to generate pulses for gating thyristors or transistors. The functional block diagram of the SG 1524, which can be employed for this project, is shown in Figure 10.14.

The error amplifier is a differential input transconductance amplifier with a DC gain of 80 dB. The gain can be reduced by feedback. The biasing voltage of the error amplifier is 5 V, and the common-mode voltage is restricted to 1.8 to 3.4 V. A voltage divider circuit can be used to drop to a level that is compatible with the amplifier input, as shown in Figure 10.15. Because a voltage amplifier has a very high output impedance of typically 5 MΩ, it can source or sink only 200 μA. Therefore, a programmed signal may be inserted at Pin 9 to override the error amplifier. Internal shut down and current-limiting circuits can be connected at Pin 9 to pull this point to ground thereby shutting off outputs.

The oscillator uses an external resistance R_T to establish a constant charging current into an external capacitance C_T. This constant charging current gives a linear ramp voltage, which provides an overall linear relationship between the error voltage and output pulse width. The frequency of the oscillator is set by the values of R_T and C_T as

$$f_s = \frac{1}{R_T C_T}$$

For switching frequency of $f_s = 20$ kHz and letting $R_T = 10$ kΩ, $C_T = 1/(10 \times 10^3 \times 20 \times 10^3) = 0.5 \times 10^{-8}$ F $= 5$ nF

The output of the oscillator at Pin 3 is a narrow clock pulse which occurs each time the capacitor C_T is discharged. This pulse can be used for performing several functions: (a) as a blanking pulse to both outputs to ensure that there is no possibility of having both outputs on simultaneously during transition, (b) as a trigger for an internal flip-flop that directs the PWM signal to alternate between outputs, and (c) as a convenient place for synchronizing an oscilloscope for system debugging and maintenance.

The output of the SG 1524 are two identical NPN transistors with collectors and emitters unconnected. The output circuit includes an anti-saturation network for fast response and current limiting set for a maximum output current of approximately 100 mA. The availability of both collectors and emitters enables driving NPN, PNP, or MOSFET external transistors, as shown in Figure 10.16. The matching outputs of the SG 1524 can be used for turning on transistors of push-pull converters. The oscillator sends a momentary blanking pulse to both outputs at the end of each period to provide a deadband, so that both outputs cannot be ON at the same time. The amount of deadband is determined by the width of the banking pulse appearing on Pin 3. The deadband can be controlled by (a) the timing capacitor C_T for a deadband of 0.2 to 1 μs, (b) by adding a small capacitor (of less than 1000 pF for reliable trigger pulses) from Pin 3 to ground, (c) by adding external circuits, such as a one-shot latch, a counter or a delay circuit for longer and controlled blanking pulses, or (d) by limiting the maximum pulse width by using a clamp to limit the output voltage from the error amplifier.

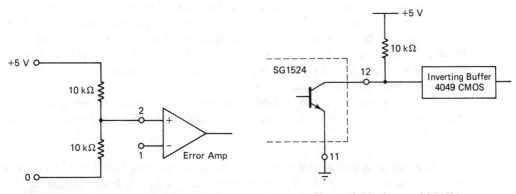

Figure 10.15 Voltage divider for error amplifier.

Figure 10.16 Output of SG1524.

The voltage reference of the SG 1524 is a complete linear regulator. It is designed to provide a constant output of 5 V, with input voltage variations from 8 to 40 V; the output current of the regulator could be up to 50 mA. It is used to generate a reference voltage as a regulated source for all the internal timing and controlling circuitry. The regulator can be bypassed by connecting Pins 15 and 16 together to the input voltage, in which condition the maximum input voltage is 6 V. The SG 1524 unit draws less than 10 mA, regardless of the input voltage. The complete pulse-width modulator (PWM) circuit, which is designed to generate appropriate pulses to the power switching unit, is shown in Figure 10.17.

Drive and isolation circuits.   The drive and isolation circuits must perform the following functions:

Functional requirement	Provides isolation between the inverter circuit and the PWM logic drive circuit, a high impedance to the PWM circuit, and transistor gate voltages with a low impedance.
Performance requirements	Square input wave of 5 to 10 V; output pulse of 5 to 10 V.
System interactions	Output pulses are isolated electrically from each other. However the pulses for transistors Q_2 and Q_4 can have a common point.
Operator interaction	None.
Hardware interface	Must draw a very low current from the PWM and supply sufficient current to the transistor.

An optocoupler offers a simple means of transmitting a signal that contains a DC component and can provide the required floating of the gate drive with respect to the ground. However, an optocoupler requires a separate and isolated power supply. Optically coupled gates are available with 50-ns delay times and 25-ns rise and fall times. MOS level transistors can be used at the output side. An isolation circuit is shown in Figure 10.18. The CMOS buffer drives, which give inverted output, are used to draw a low current from the PWM and the optocoupler.

Each output of the PWM will drive two optocouplers, thereby gating two power transistors of the inverter. Therefore, four optocouplers and eight buffers will be required.

Output power transformer.   The output transformer provides necessary voltage-matching between the output of the converter and the load voltage requirement. The transformer-coupled load can be considered an inductive load from the point of view of the power switching stage. For safety's sake, the design of the power switching unit should include an anti-parallel diode with the power MOSFETs; but because these diodes are built into power MOSFETs, there is no need for additional diodes. Ferrite cores are normally used for transformers. The selection of transformer core-material is made

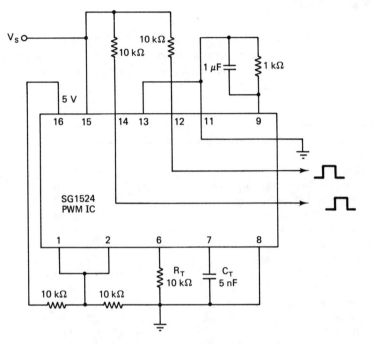

Figure 10.17   Complete PWM modulator circuit.

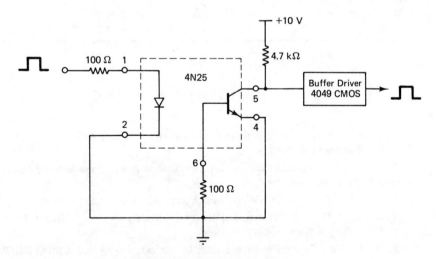

Figure 10.18   Drive and isolation circuits.

mainly on the basis of minimum core dissipation, volume, and cost for a given operating frequency.

DOCUMENTATION

The documentation for a project should be the form of proposal, which is illustrated in the project on the temperature monitor module. The parts and price list for the inverter and the associated drive circuits are shown in Table 10.6.

TABLE 10.6 PARTS AND PRICE LIST

Parts	Quantity	Price
IR250 MOSFETs	4	$ 60.00
Heatsinks	4	$ 22.40
Bridge rectifiers for logic power supplies	3	$ 5.70
Bridge rectifier for main supply	1	$ 4.45
Input power transformer	1	$ 22.50
Output power transformer	1	$ 25.00
Optocouplers	4	$ 6.00
Zener diodes for voltage protection	4	$ 5.00
CMOS buffer drives	8	$ 9.20
Voltage regulators	3	$ 4.50
Electrolytic capacitors for power supplies	4	$ 10.00
Resistors	10	$ 1.50
Capacitors	10	$ 5.00
Crowbar thyristor	1	$ 8.50
Current detection circuit	1	$ 12.50
Miscellaneous items		$ 10.00
	Total	$212.25

FURTHER READING

1. RASHID, M.H. *Power Electronics—Devices, Circuits and Applications*. Englewood Cliffs, NJ: Prentice Hall, 1988.

2. DEWAN, S.B., G.R. SLEMON, and A. STRAUGHEN. *Power Semiconductor Drives*. New York: John Wiley & Sons, 1984.

3. SEN, P.C. *Thyristor DC Drives*. New York: John Wiley & Sons, 1981.

4. DEWAN, S.B., G.R. SLEMON, and A. STRAUGHEN. *Power Semiconductor Drives*. New York: John Wiley & Sons, 1984.

5. BOSE, B.K. *Power Electronics and AC Drives*. Englewood Cliffs, NJ: Prentice Hall, 1986.

6. LINDSAY, J.F. and M.H. RASHID. *Electromechanics and Electrical Machinery.* Englewood Cliffs, NJ: Prentice Hall, 1986.

7. KUSKO, A. *Solid State DC Motor Drives.* Cambridge, MA: The MIT Press, 1969.

8. RICE, L.R. *SCR Designers Handbook.* Pittsburgh, PA: Westinghouse Electric Corp., 1970.

9. GRAFHAN, D.R., and F.B. GOLDEN. *General Electric SCR Manual, 6th ed.* Englewood Cliffs, NJ: Prentice Hall, 1982.

10. WOOD, P. *Switching Power Converters.* New York: Van Nostrand Reinhold, 1981.

11. McLYMAN, C.W.T. *Transformer and Inductor Design Handbook.* New York: Marcel, Dekker, 1988.

12. Institute of Electrical and Electronics Engineers. *IEEE Standards, Practices, and Requirements for Thyristor Converters for Motor Drives—IEEE std. 444-1973.* New York: IEEE, 1974.

13. PRESSMAN, ABRAHAM I. *Switching and Linear Power Supply—Power Converter Design.* Hasbrouck Heights, NJ: Hayden Book Co., 1977.

INDEX